1973

88172

HQ
769
.A355
1975

Akmakjian, Hiag

The natural way
to raise a
healthy child

The
NATURAL
Way To
Raise a
Healthy Child

The
NATURAL
Way To
Raise a
Healthy Child

HIAG AKMAKJIAN

PRAEGER PUBLISHERS • NEW YORK

PHOTO CREDITS

Elliott Erwitt: p. 1.

Sarah Kaufman Moon: p. 20.

© Anthony Wolff: pp. 30, 77, 88, 108, 142, 155, 176, 194, 214, 257.

Hiag Akmakjian: pp. 56, 69, 120, 237.

Burton Berinsky: p. 98.

Elaine Schuyten: p. 273.

Published in the United States of America in 1975
by Praeger Publishers, Inc.
111 Fourth Avenue, New York, N.Y. 10003

© 1975 by Hiag Akmakjian

Library of Congress Cataloging in Publication Data

Akmakjian, Hiag.
  The natural way to raise a healthy child.

  Bibliography: p.
  1. Children—Management. 2. Children—Care and
hygiene. I. Title.
HQ769.A355 1975   649'.1   74-15675
ISBN 0-275-50870-6

Printed in the United States of America

Lovingly dedicated
to my best teacher,
from whom I learned
the beauty of life's beginnings—

my son Nick

—to his "good enough" mother
—and to mine

Contents

Acknowledgments

The largest share of the credit for making this book possible belongs to the psychoanalytic theorists whose work has, over the past three or four decades, opened new territory at the frontier of knowledge: Anna Freud, Heinz Hartmann, Edith Jacobson, Margaret S. Mahler, René A. Spitz, and D. W. Winnicott. I take pleasure in acknowledging my great debt to them, especially because their names and their work in professional journals are cited only sparingly in the book, in order to avoid the forbidding feeling conveyed by pages crowded with footnotes. Although such citations have been held to a minimum, every attempt has been made to cite sources fairly.

I feel a deep sense of gratitude toward Dr. Margaret S. Mahler, who took the time to read Chapter 10, "The Beginnings of Psychological Separation," for her suggested corrections and refinements and her approval of the contents. My thanks go also to Dr. Fred Pine for his critical reading of the same material.

Before his death last year, Dr. René A. Spitz offered approval, for which I feel grateful, of all those portions of my book that present the results of his unique work in the study of infant development.

My indebtedness also extends to the many friends, colleagues, and acquaintances who helped in the development of the manuscript. First and foremost is Barbara Pollock Ruskin, who merits my profound gratitude for her painstaking editorial assistance, which went far beyond what I had expected or thought I needed. She caught an embarrassing number of purple patches, vague phrases, and indefinite antecedents, and with a sweeping impatience that was both exasperating and exhilarating queried or deleted them all. Her suggestions and comments helped to clarify, organize, and reshape the material. Whatever faults remain are of course mine.

I am especially grateful to my very good friend Michael R. Elia for his attentive critical reading of the manuscript in its earliest stage and for devoting valuable vacation time to this task. His editorial professionalism has come to serve as a model for me. Another good friend, Nina Klippel, offered me, out of her experience as a writer, an abundance of helpful suggestions on rhetoric and content, for which I am very thankful.

Because of the nature of our relationship, I owe an unrepayable debt to my patients, through whom I continue to deepen my understanding of human behavior. I thank all of them, past and present.

To my son Nick I owe a debt at least as large. It was by observing him in his early days and months that I learned, through the direct experience of parenting, much of what is in this book and discovered how pleasurable it is to share in childrearing. I appreciate his patience during my long involvement with "The Book" through its many revisions — in New York, on Fire Island, and on Cape Cod. Never once did he complain, just as he was never a complaining baby or child — for me convincing proof of the soundness of the psychoanalytic principles of childrearing espoused by this book.

A rereading of Dr. Spock's durable *Baby and Child Care* helped me not only in specifically pediatric matters but also in the treatment of the psychology of early childhood. Dr. D. W. Winnicott's *Mother and Child* provided new insights that also helped.

Although I have learned psychoanalytic developmental psychology (along with what used to be called "the psychology of the unconscious") from many teachers at several institutes and owe much to each of them, there are two who stand out. From Gertrude Blanck I acquired a thorough understanding of the theory and technique of "ego psychology," and from Susan Deri — and her far-ranging, indefatigable intellect — a vision of human-developmental possibilities based on Freudian meta-psychology.

My warm thanks go to the following for their criticism and assistance during the various stages of the writing: Penny Akmajian, Joyce Edward, Clem Elia, Judy K. Ippolito, Harriet Kramer, Joseph Marasco, Jeremy Ruskin, Nathene Ruskin, Louis Schneider, Patsy Turrini, and James H. Wallace. I would like also to thank Thomas J. Dembofsky, Kerry Demers, Gwen Jarvouhey, Betsy Kissam, Douglas H. Latimer, Paula Schwartz, Jim Wallace, and Karen Whitney, who offered helpful advice and whose interest acted as a spur.

For their typing assistance and comments, I would like to thank Irene Fekete, Barbara Glimm, Renate Kolar, Pamela Nye, Diane Parqueth, and Marilynne Wirsig, and a special thanks to my neighbor Carolyn Parqueth, who typed beautifully and quickly several versions of many of the chapters without once getting ensnared in the thickets of handwriting in all four margins. Apart from her typing help, Pamela Nye deserves citation for providing information on life in day-care centers derived from her work experience at the Leander Community Center.

The assistance and kindness of all incur a strong but pleasurable sense of obligation.

Introduction

WHY THIS BOOK?

The author of yet another book on childrearing must be prepared to justify its publication by stating how it differs from the others. So much has been written about infancy and childhood that parents might well wonder if anything remains to be said. Yet to those whose profession it is to study the first years of life, the popular literature on childrearing is, in some respects, thirty years behind the times. Although the psychological discoveries of the past three decades are extensive, even revolutionary, they are described only in professional journals, generally in a jargon that makes meaning all but unattainable.

This is an unfortunate state of affairs—but also one that cannot last. Young couples today tend to be more knowledgeable than even the most informed parents of the past. Their knowledge leads them to seek yet more information, to think in new ways about childrearing and human development and growth. Anna Freud, in a paper entitled "Answering Pediatricians' Questions," reports a discussion with Dr. Spock in which she commented: "I think all this advice to mothers is not really what is needed; the spreading of knowledge is what is necessary."

THE AIM OF THIS BOOK

The aim of this book is to provide parents with a conceptual tool to help them raise healthy, problem-free children by offering them psychological understanding of the behavior of babies and young children. Some parents don't know what happens inside their baby. They are not sure what feelings, if any, a baby has, and sometimes a baby's behavior is puzzling or exasperating to them. None of that is surprising: they have probably not been told about the psychological development of a baby or even that a baby has, in fact, a psychological life.

A grasp of the underlying principles of childrearing might enable parents to deal more effectively with the varieties of situations they will encounter in their children's early years without feeling a need to consult books and experts at the appearance of each new development. A thorough understanding of the ground from which problems spring could help them find spontaneous and creative solutions or, even better, to avoid them in the first place. A parent who understands the nature and causes of problems is in a position to deal with them as they arise.

Popular ignorance of the psychology of infancy is a curious phenomenon. It is as if a universal assumption has been made that babies are mostly *physical* beings who need to be cared for and loved until they grow up, at which point the problems start. Of course, love goes beyond physical upbringing, but the how and why of love are seldom spelled out. Nor is it made clear how much psychological development is implied in the words "cared for." Is "caring for" just seeing to it that a baby is fed, washed, clothed, worried over, and, later, educated?

It is the prerogative of every human being, adult and child, to be allowed to develop to his or her full potential. That is so much everyone's psychological right that we could call it a *natural* right. Parents can foster this development by understanding the mental and emotional processes of their child's early years.

I shall attempt to describe psychological development from birth to the age of five by explaining what babies are like, what they experience, and how they might be raised naturally to lead a fulfilling life. Perhaps feeding, toileting, and the other events of infancy and early childhood will be made easier for parents and children. More than that, if a few basic principles are understood and applied, there might not come a "time when problems start."

No relationship is more fundamental than the one between parent and child. The rearing we experience as children influences our lives forever. Every adult activity finds its taproot in the years of infancy and early childhood. Even political and social issues, which at first glance appear to be unconnected with childrearing, reflecting only those abstractions called government and society, have their emotional sources in the personalities of the individuals involved. The disastrous effect on our lives of the pathology of those with political authority over us is regrettably evident. Less clear is how those persons were molded in their formative years to cause them to act as they did—and why their victims, their constituents, were molded in *their* way to permit their victimization. Every psychoanalyst knows that the art of government begins at the breast. The treatment of a baby determines his or her subsequent treatment of all fellow human beings. Given so simple a principle, it is dismaying to think that the care and study of babies and children have not yet been made an integral part of everyone's formal education, especially when we consider how much psychological knowledge we already have in our grasp, asking only to be applied.

This book differs from most others on the subject in taking the view that, although each newborn, through genetic programing, faces the same developmental tasks to be gone through in a specific order, babies are endowed at birth with different constitutional givens. What is innate in each baby emerges, however, in a highly personal environment that either facilitates or interferes with psychological development. Parents feel that childrearing is a difficult time for them. It is. Children feel that childhood is a difficult time for them. It is. Parents and infants exert a reciprocal influence that shapes one another's development in a daily interaction. No person exists on his or her own. Everyone is a product of others, who are in turn products of others.

This book is not a medical handbook—books like Dr. Spock's *Baby and Child Care* supply that need—but an approach to the rearing of infants and young children based on the most up-to-date theory of psychoanalytic developmental psychology. Its underlying assumption is that there is a *natural* technique of childrearing that, when applied, leads to the best psychological outcome—a child who is alert and interested in life, who is characterized by self-fulfillment and conflict-free functioning, and who has no major psychological problems. And precisely because this childrearing is based on the natural needs and abilities of babies and children, it takes into account the equally natural needs and abilities of parents too. Nature is not prejudiced in favor of one or the other. It would be as mistaken to recommend, explicitly or implicitly, that parents arrange their lives strictly for their children's benefit as it would be to recommend that they arrange their children's lives strictly for their own benefit.

My purpose in writing this book is primarily preventive medicine. Dr. Karl Menninger says: "I've spent most of my life treating people and teaching young doctors to do so. But more and more I see the still greater importance of doing something preventive. Psychiatrists should eventually work themselves out of business by preventing illness or disorganization." As a psychoanalyst and psychotherapist, I have seen the immense amount of suffering caused by faulty childrearing resulting in part from a lack of information or understanding on the parents' part. Psychoanalysis and therapy help people come to grips with their problems and work them through in a lengthy and sometimes psychologically painful experience. Parents are in a much better position than psychoanalysts: they can prevent problems from starting.

But aside from attempting to further preventive medicine, I would like readers to learn how interesting babies are and thus to enjoy them more. Interested parents make better parents. What does a baby experience? What causes behavior? How does a baby grow psychologically? Why is it that development can't be speeded up? It is fascinating to observe babies as they gradually become aware of the world and learn about space, objects, color, people, animals, movement, gravity — the way we imagine creatures from outer space would do, requiring years to get the hang of life on earth. To understand babies is to enjoy them more — and to enjoy parenting more too.

THE NEW CHILDREARING

What makes it possible, now for the first time, to write a book of this kind is the research into infancy and early childhood done by psychoanalytic investigators of the second and third generations. The discoveries of these investigators offer us a more sophisticated comprehension of human psychology. Most books on childrearing emphasize the more obvious events of development as milestones of psychological growth —

teething, crawling, walking, speech, reading. But in the light of the work of Drs. D. W. Winnicott, Margaret S. Mahler, and the late René A. Spitz, to name three of the most influential analysts, the more subtle and revealing indicators of development are the way a baby learns to use the mother to satisfy his or her needs, the smiling response of the third month, the "no" response at sixteen months, and, from six to thirty-six months, the degree of the baby's success in psychologically (inwardly) separating from the mother.

We are fortunate today in having a body of knowledge based on extensive clinical experience. We know about babies and children from the direct observation of babies and children. Never have we stood on surer ground. Where past generations theorized about childrearing on the basis of scant behavioral experimentation (often on animals at that), we are in the more enviable position of being the inheritors of a half century of clinical study and observation of humans. Some of the research began with Freud—whose ideas, regrettably, still suffer misuse even though they continue to inform modern thought. Anna Freud's work, following in her father's tradition, is simultaneously a store of invaluable clinical material and an important transition to the more recent direction taken by psychoanalytic theory under the name of psychoanalytic developmental psychology, or "ego psychology."

In addition to the work of Sigmund and Anna Freud, this book leans heavily on the writings of Winnicott, Mahler, Spitz, Jacobson, and Hartmann. Rereading Winnicott's work while preparing the manuscript, I was struck anew by the profundity of his formulations. Such seminal contributions as "Ego Distortions in Terms of True and False Self" (1960) and "Communicating and Not Communicating Leading to a Study of Certain Opposites" (1963),* though technical, can be recommended to all readers whose curiosity is not satisfied by the more superficial. The concept "good-enough mother," which I have used in modified form throughout this book, was first introduced by Winnicott in "Transitional Objects and Transitional Phenomena" (1953).† And I learned much from Winnicott's *Mother and Child,* a series of radio talks to mothers originally broadcast by the BBC.

---

*Both in *The Maturational Processes and the Facilitating Environment,* New York, International Universities Press, 1965.
†*International Journal of Psychoanalysis,* 34 (1953): 89–97.

The work of Mahler and her colleagues* and that of Spitz (and his coworkers W. Godfrey Cobliner and Katherine M. Wolf) are also based on the direct observation of children — older babies and toddlers in the case of Mahler and her colleagues, newborns and infants in the case of Spitz. Both have considerably broadened our understanding of the psychology of the earliest years and have opened new paths of exploration.

Heinz Hartmann is not mentioned in the book, and the name of Edith Jacobson receives only a few brief mentions. But I have drawn in a general way from Hartmann's work, including his concept of the neutralization of drive energy. As for Jacobson's concept of self and object representations, so central to psychoanalytic theory, no explanation of the baby's psychological separation from mother, the problems of identity, and superego formation would be complete without it.

I would like to anticipate here the possible criticism that, with so many books written today about babies and childrearing, most of them offering conflicting advice, parents are at a loss to know which new "authority" they can trust. When it comes to behavioral science — in contrast, for example, with a "hard" science like physics — some even ask how analysts can know they are right, when behavior is so elusive.

The confusion is understandable. In a matter so important to society as the rearing of the young, it would be wise to bear in mind that a wrong view of childrearing, if widely adopted, would affect a whole generation — and more. But the difficulty might be resolved if we remind ourselves that though psychoanalysis, like medicine, is described as both a science and an art, and though in arriving at its formulations it may draw heavily on intuition (as do experimental chemistry and physics), its method is no less scientific than that of any so-called hard science. In fact, so far from being elusive, behavior is quite visible, whereas molecules are not — which deters no one from an unquestioning belief in molecules and their inferred behavior. The analysts whose writings form the underpinnings of this book are among the best and most careful workers in the field, and the conclusions they offer have been found repeatedly confirmed clinically. In fact, the reason our understanding of human behavior has been so slow to develop is that psychoanalysis moves deliberately precisely because of scien-

*Drs. Paula Elkisch, Manuel Furer, Bertram J. Gosliner, John McDevitt, Fred Pine, and Calvin P. Settlage.

tific method — and of course without it would not move at all. Spitz suggested that certain fundamental conclusions about human behavior can be accepted because of a "gratifying convergence of conclusions based on dissimilar research approaches which I have come to regard as one of the more convincing forms of verification of nonquantifiable psychological propositions."

Our present state of knowledge is far from perfect, but we nevertheless have at least one confirmation of the validity of psychoanalytically oriented childrearing principles: the knowledge does not need to alter to accommodate each generation's shifting cultural viewpoint. A valid psychological fact of behavior remains a valid psychological fact of behavior. There is a point beyond which the openmindedness of science justifiably becomes dogma: it can be categorically stated that under all expectable conditions two plus two never equals three. There is nothing in the formulations of Spitz, Winnicott, and Mahler that younger theorists find untenable. That some revision of their findings will occur there is no doubt, but that would only demonstrate the durability of the formulations: like the Constitution of the United States, they are revisable, not discardable. It is extremely doubtful that the revisions will be so extensive as to abandon past knowledge. They will more likely build on it in refinement — in response to new data, filling out knowledge ever more subtly. There is no system of human behavior to defend. There are only patterns of behavior, and those patterns have begun to be clearly understood.

We can say that for the first time in history we have begun to accumulate the precious knowledge of how to raise children as healthy and happy individuals. Just as emotional difficulties in parents are communicable to children, so are emotional health and wellbeing communicable. This book attempts to provide parents with guidelines for natural childrearing based on a clearer understanding of human psychology. As a society and as individuals we have a choice: apply our new knowledge or proceed as in the past, inconsistently and with bewilderment. "The fact that a problem will certainly take a long time to solve . . . is no justification for postponing the study," T. S. Eliot said. "Our difficulties of the moment must always be dealt with somehow, but our permanent difficulties are difficulties of every moment."

Our education is universally poor in one respect: we are taught dangerously little about our emotions, our bodies, our development, our selves. It is my hope that this book will, on a popular level, make its small contribution toward the overthrow of ignorance and indifference by new knowledge and concern.

NOTE TO THE READER

This book is addressed to mothers and fathers. The "you" throughout means either parent or both. Phrases like "you feed the baby" assume that — certainly in the United States but to a lesser extent elsewhere as well — the father feeds the baby some of the time. And even a father can "offer the nipple to the baby" — bottles have nipples.

Although I have attempted to exercise care in considering the feelings and needs of parents, not just those of the child, the responsibility for the optimal development of children, especially in the all-important parent-child relations of the first few years, rests with the parents. This, however, does not mean that parents should feel anxious and guilty about childrearing. This book tries to explain why.

The book, informed by psychoanalytic developmental psychology, makes statements that may at times sound dogmatic. But psychoanalysts know from the analysis of thousands of adults that specific experiences in infancy and early childhood have certain expectable outcomes in adulthood. The knowledge, so hard-won, is ours to use and not — as we have done for so long — to ignore. We know, for example, that to schedule-feed a newborn leads *invariably* to depression in adulthood. To stop thumbsucking forcibly leads *inevitably* to oral problems later in life. The book attempts to show the connections. In matters of such great importance as lifelong healthy psychological functioning it seems irresponsible to express oneself less than forthrightly. The tone of the book respects this spirit.

Human beings and especially the young are remarkably resilient. Parents should therefore feel reassured that even if they should make mistakes — or feel that they have already made mistakes — they can still modify their childrearing and expect a reasonably benign outcome. Genuine concern and love make up for many past errors. One wrong move, one selfish act, one instance of uncaring — these do not blight development. Most traumas result from an accumulation of acts — from parents' characteristic behavior over long periods.

The
NATURAL
Way To
Raise a
Healthy Child

I know the joy of fishes
In the river
Through my own joy, as I go walking
Along the same river.

—Chuang Tzu
ca. 369–286 B.C.

1

Anticipating Parenthood

The most important asset of a baby as he begins life is two emotionally healthy parents.

MARGARET A. RIBBLE

Life offers few satisfactions as deep as those of parenthood, including the subtle pleasure of being more involved in the world's affairs, as if through our children we become bound in some new way to the experience of living.

Becoming a parent is one of life's major events. Yet, although parenthood represents a new psychological level of functioning, that level is reached imperceptibly, so naturally does it issue from growth.

It takes a degree of personal development to lead a man and a woman to want the enduring emotional commitment of marriage. As another psychological step, the desire to have a child offers both partners a sense of still further personal development.

This is not to say that an expectant parent feels no misgivings or anxiety. Ordinarily parenthood comes at a time in life not so very long after the couple were themselves children. Now, knowing that they are about to be parents, both feel their adulthood more keenly, because from now on they are the ones who will be called on by a dependent being whenever the need should arise for strength and guidance.

It might be reassuring to prospective parents, anticipating this experience, to say at the outset that instinct is always there to help. We could agree with Dr. Karl Menninger:

1

"Children can be brought up by common sense. Most of them are. Most of us were." Although there *are*, as we shall see, guidelines to help us understand the psychological development of babies and children, the best advice to parents can be summarized succinctly: *enjoy your baby and try to feel easy in your relationship.*

THE "GOOD ENOUGH" PARENT

From conversations you have heard or books and articles you have read you might wonder at the amount of knowledge needed to be a good and loving parent. You might feel that if your childrearing is not psychologically supercorrect you are going to raise a child with emotional problems. You might even, in fact, feel guilt in advance that you are not going to parent in some "best possible way." Or you might feel that the only way to raise a normal child is for you to be the world's best parent—patient, wise, forbearing, self-sacrificing, and all-loving.

There is no need to have these doubts. Nature helps. As you feel your way along, you will surely make mistakes. Everyone does. You will be bewildered, frustrated, and even, in the difficult early months, almost tearfully helpless at times. These feelings are universal.

Merely to be "good enough" as a parent
means that you are doing an
extremely good job of childrearing.

You get no practice at being a parent, no trial period from which you can back away when the going gets rough and try again when you feel more up to it. Once you are a parent you remain a parent forever. As Jean Kerr puts it, "The thing about having a baby is, from then on, you *have* it."

You are plunged into parenthood, and no turning back. All you receive in the way of learning experience is on-the-job training. Sometimes you cannot rely even on the parenting you experienced as a child to press into use as a model. Perhaps you feel your upbringing was an experience you would rather not repeat. (Mother doesn't *always* know best. However, in defense of mothers, neither does anyone else.) But in a matter of only weeks you will be surprised at how much better you will be able to parent than you had thought, even without training or expert advice at each step of the way.

Some of those who turn out to be among the best parents were once afraid that having a child would be a nuisance and life a drag—and were pleasantly surprised.

You don't have to be perfect. If childbearing required perfect parents, none of us would be here. All you have to be is "good enough."

The phrase "good enough mother" was coined by a British psychoanalyst who is also a pediatrician, Dr. D. W. Winnicott. According to analysts, who adopted the phrase, in order to raise a psychologically healthy child, having no great emotional problems, all you have to be is "good enough." *Merely to be "good enough" as a parent means that you are doing an extremely good job of childrearing,* because a baby or child will go a long way toward meeting your help and guidance: growing and developing are things the baby *actively* does.

The concept "good enough" has undergone a substantial broadening of meaning since Dr. Winnicott first introduced it. "Good enough" parents are those who do things *fairly* well, who without making any really terrible mistakes are nevertheless far from perfect. They don't panic easily or feel a heavy load of guilt for whatever shortcomings they have or because they are not doing some exquisitely right thing. What is most important is that *they are attuned to the baby's needs and feel empathy.*

The importance—and beauty—of empathy cannot be overstressed. Empathy is what you feel when your child is playing among some large rocks in the park, scaling them with difficulty, and *you too* feel that they are the Rocky Mountains and exclaim, "How *high* you are!" Or when your child falls and scrapes a knee you don't say, "Oh come on, now, you're ok" but, "*Ow!* That must really hurt!"—your statement of empathy itself beginning to diminish the pain. To feel what children are feeling is the surest guide to their needs.

"Good enough" parents are easygoing rather than tense and anxious. They understand that development is a progressive unfolding of what is innate, like a flower opening its petals to sunlight. They are neither intrusive nor aloof. They allow behavior to happen, change, and develop, and they foster its growth. They sense that *normal development results largely from letting nature take its course, with help from the parents in the form of love, protection, and helping pointers.* In fact, all the pointers that we will discuss can be reduced to one fundamental guideline: *meet your child's emotional needs as they arise.*

"Good enough" parents understand that it is a function of parenting to clear away obstacles that the child can't surmount alone because he or she is not yet equipped to do so, to prevent the development of a feeling of inadequacy. Early obstacles are the commonest events — hunger, frustration. "Good enough" parenting means not pushing the development of the baby along lines intended only to satisfy the parents and fulfill their lives. They respect the baby's individuality and rights as a separate being. "Good enough" parents also recognize that children outgrow certain needs, that relations are perpetually evolving, as they are with all beings and things in life. No one remains quite the same from one day to the next. Everyone is in a state of becoming, shaping others and being shaped by them in an ongoing reciprocal influence. Parents gauge the baby's tolerance for frustration at any given developmental level. They regulate frustrations, letting the baby experience neither too few, which would be unreal, nor too many, which would be unbearable. For example, they neither pick up the baby each time at the very instant he or she cries nor let the crying go on desperately for ten minutes. They understand that it is not good to undergratify or to overgratify. Both are too much.

Growing and developing are things
the baby *actively* does.

According to the Talmud, "Wherever there is too much, something is lacking." Too much frustration makes a child anxious, tense, and unhappy. Too much gratification makes a child placid, passive — and unhappy. *Some* aloneness, *some* anxiety, and *some* frustration — *in small manageable amounts for any given age* — contribute to growth and spur development, but *only* if they don't exceed the baby's capacity at each step along the way. If these things happen at the right time and in the right degree, the baby's development is strengthened. (At the very beginning of life, however, and for the first several weeks, frustrations should be kept to a minimum.) "Good enough" parents thus set limits in order to avoid the extremes of experience, because extremes of experience make for hangups — "fixations."

An example of the reverse of a "good enough" parent is illustrated by the cartoon of a mother hen who looks with supreme irritation at the shell cracked open by her emerging newborn chick and says, "*Now* look what you've done!" Sad to say, there are parents like this.

Lest a storybook ideal creep into this description, "good enough" parents also get annoyed and even angry once in a while, don't deny their feelings (except those that would hurt or damage their baby), sometimes want to be let alone, get fed up with parenting, want to enjoy adult company, are concerned with *their own* needs too, and set aside part of their evenings as "adult time" once the baby has become a young child and understands the parent-child relationship.

ANXIETIES ABOUT BIRTH

To begin at the beginning, most parents-to-be feel considerable anxiety about the birth itself, especially if it is their first child they are expecting. The birth experience can be both exciting and frightening, particularly for the mother. A prospective first-time mother is never sure what will happen to her during the delivery. Without personal experience, she can easily be drawn into the myth of our culture that childbirth must *of necessity* be unbearable. But thresholds of pain vary with individuals and are influenced by many factors, physical and psychological — such as the state of the mother's health, the degree of her fatigue, the father's presence or absence during the delivery, and the parents' wish to have a child.

Women are often afraid that their bodies will be damaged in childbirth and parents that the baby will be deformed or stillborn. And although, with rare exceptions, neither fear proves to be justified, prebirth anxiety is often followed by the resurgence of an apprehension that husband and wife may have felt during pregnancy: will the baby be healthy and thrive, or will he or she have defects that will show up in the days or weeks after birth — mental retardation, a malfunctioning organ? Will they themselves be adequate to the demands of parenthood, demands that are now suddenly real for the first time?

It is natural to have fears while anticipating birth and for a time afterward, especially if it is a first baby. (According to pediatricians, second babies seem to provoke less anxiety, but curiously enough, third babies are apt to make expectant parents anxious again, almost as if a superstitious feeling asserts itself: will their luck hold up?) To have no fears is abnormal. But most fears of the unknown are exaggerated. In virtually all cases the birth is routine and there is a feeling of pleasure at having created life.

PREPARED, OR "NATURAL," CHILDBIRTH*

Birth is a natural process, not an illness. Many young women today want to remain conscious during the birthing and have the father participate in the delivery. Such a young mother wants to experience fully the pain and pleasure, all the apprehension and joy of having a human being actually emerge, wholly formed and alive, from inside her body, an event she has awaited for many long months. Many women speak of childbirth as among the happiest moments of their lives. A few say they even experience an orgasm during birth.

At the very beginning of life
and for the first several weeks,
frustrations should be kept to a minimum.

Some women have been so frightened by tales of childbirth that they approach it as a highly unpleasant chore they prefer not to face, letting others get the baby born for them. What is sad about this is that they renounce what Dr. Helene Deutsch calls "the ecstasy of the first contact with the child." Some women who have been anesthetized say that they feel almost unreal, depersonalized, as if their emotions were missing and they were not participating in the event but watching a film of it.

*Prepared childbirth was formerly called "natural childbirth," a phrase coined in 1933 by Dr. Grantly Dick-Read, but that term has in recent years given way to "prepared childbirth." It is also sometimes called participating childbirth, educated childbirth, or cooperative childbirth. Prepared childbirth is a method of giving birth without the use of drugs or anesthetics. The mother is "awake and aware."

Many mothers who practice the methods of prepared child-birth advocated by Dr. Fernand Lamaze find delivery easier, recovery faster, and the whole experience more exciting and pleasurable.* Preparedness training takes the mystery out of the natural process of birth. Many obstetricians today encour-age prepared childbirth, and some hospitals and community groups offer six-week preparedness courses for both prospec-tive parents. Preparedness training is more and more consid-ered an essential part of giving birth, because even if drugs are to be used for delivery, labor can sometimes be many hours long, and knowing what to expect can make the birth experi-ence easier.

There is increased interest among prospective fathers in participating in the birth.

In addition, there is increased interest among prospective fathers in participating in the birth. In prepared childbirth the father is invaluable as a labor coach. Having gone through training with the mother, he is not shut out of this basic experience in life but is present from the beginning of labor through the moment of delivery. Childbirth becomes the shared experience it naturally is. (Some hospitals still don't permit the father to be in the delivery room. Parents should check in advance with their hospital.)

ANESTHETICS AND ANALGESICS IN CHILDBIRTH

Typically in a hospital setting, a woman in labor is given drugs to deaden or eliminate pain, very often scopolamine or Demerol in combination with barbiturates and tranquilizers.

*Mothers who have not yet had their babies and would like to try prepared childbirth might find the following books helpful: Fernand Lamaze, *Painless Childbirth: The Lamaze Method,* Chicago, Regnery, 1970, Marjorie Karmel, *Thank You, Dr. Lamaze,* Philadelphia and New York, Lippincott, 1959, Irwin Chabon, *Awake and Aware,* New York, Dell, 1966, Elisabeth Bing, *Six Practical Lessons for an Easier Childbirth,* New York, Bantam, 1967, Elisa-beth Bing and Gerald S. Barad, *A Birth in the Family,* New York, Bantam, 1973, which is replete with pictures, including photos of the birth of a child. See also, Dick-Read, *Childbirth Without Fear.*

Barbiturates (for example, Seconal and Nembutal) and tranquilizers are analgesics, or painkillers. Tranquilizers (Librium, Valium, Equanil, and Miltown are commonly used) relax tension and deaden pain during the brief climactic period of the actual birth. Many mothers, however, get through this period without difficulty or drugs if they have been prepared for it and know how short its duration generally is. Barbiturates slow the breathing and reactions of mother *and* baby. The anesthetic scopolamine diminishes the mother's ability to push in labor, thus contributing in some cases to the long labors some experience. Scopolamine also accounts in part for the occasional use of forceps in hospital deliveries. The drug burdens the natural process. If scopolamine is given too soon, it can stop labor completely. If given too late, the child's respiration can be blocked, and he or she can die of asphyxia.

Scopolamine has other effects too. It can cause hallucinations, sometimes even paranoid reactions. Chemically, it is similar to LSD. It makes the mother restless, sometimes to the point of requiring restraint to keep her from involuntarily jumping from the bed, although she will never be aware of that, because scopolamine also produces amnesia. Some mothers drugged with scopolamine do not realize they have given birth for hours after they are out of the delivery room. They have to be told about it, or they look down and see by the change in their shape that the baby is gone. They have no recollection of the birth and sometimes no recollection of the next day or two. A period of time is missing from memory, and the experience of childbirth that they had been looking forward to for so long is a mental blank.

To give birth while in a drugged state also may have undesirable side effects. Virtually all obstetric medications — amnesics, analgesics, and anesthetics, including medication used in caudal, paracervical, and pudendal anesthesia* — pass through the placenta in minutes and enter the fetal blood, making it difficult for the baby to breathe because they reduce the oxygen flow to the brain and tissues. In consequence, the

---

*An amnesic dulls the senses and blots out memory — causes amnesia. Analgesics deaden pain, anesthetics eliminate it. An anesthetic that is caudal is one given at the tip of the spine. A paracervical anesthetic is an agent injected into either side of the cervix (neck of the womb). A pudendal anesthetic is injected into the vagina or the skin on either side of the vagina. For more information see W. Bowes *et al.*, "The Effects of Obstetric Medication on the Fetus and Infant," Vol. 35, No. 4, monograph, Society for Research in Child Development, University of Illinois, Chicago, University of Chicago Press, June 1970.

baby is born in a drowsy state — actually drugged — and his or her first experience in life is identical with that of an addict: forced passivity. The baby sleeps it off for several hours or even days. Thus at birth, the most helpless time in life, the baby is subjected to an unnatural handicap.

Despite this drawback, however, medication may be necessary for women whose threshold of pain is low. "Drugs and anesthesia *are* needed in obstetrics, but they do not need to be given just because women are afraid of childbirth. Also they do not need to be given in doses larger than necessary to do the job they are intended to do, nor should they replace teaching women about childbirth."*

In contrast, an undrugged baby, born naturally, can begin feeding from the mother's breasts as early as fifteen minutes after being born, putting to use all the practice in sucking gained in the uterus, where he or she may have thumbsucked from the fourth month on, and then falling asleep after that enormous first effort in the world — a much better start. And the mother who delivers without anesthetic recovers very quickly from childbirth, usually feeling exhilarated by the experience. Many mothers who go through preparedness training are able to leave the hospital two hours after delivery.

ROOMING IN

Some hospitals nowadays are enlightened enough to keep mother and infant together, placing the baby in a bassinet near the mother's bed. She feeds and cuddles the newborn at feeding time, and both baby and mother become acquainted with each other in a natural way. This arrangement is called "rooming in."

Rooming in provides emotional satisfaction to mother and infant and the opportunity for the mother to learn how to care for the baby while nursing assistance is available. It helps reduce the possibility of cross-infection in the nursery, which, though not frequent, does occur. Perhaps most important of all to the mother, rooming in prepares her for what is to come. She has two or three days to get used to being a mother (especially important to a mother with her first child) and is not plunged all at once into the hard work of parenting. Also, when the father comes to see mother and baby he is not treated like a

*Constance A. Bean, *Methods of Childbirth: A Complete Guide to Childbirth Classes and Maternity Care,* New York, Dolphin, 1974, p. 130.

visitor, nor is he compelled to view the baby from a distance and through glass, but can be with his family. In Scandinavia, the Netherlands, and other parts of the world, rooming in is standard, and prepared childbirth is widely practiced too.*

We might wonder, however, about the desirability of rooming in if the delivery is *not* a natural one. If a baby spends the first hours or days sleeping off the drugs the mother has taken during labor, does it matter where he or she is kept during that time?

Even if the baby is in a drugged condition, it *does* matter that mother and baby be roomed together, for two reasons. First, the mother derives emotional wellbeing and experiences a special feeling of closeness from seeing her newborn breathing and sleeping peacefully at her side. From birth there is no unnatural separation of mother and child. And second, with the filling up of her breasts she experiences a desire to hold and feed, and the moment the baby wakes up she and the baby will need no help or administrative permission to be brought together but instead will find each other naturally. Aside from the fact that it feels right to both to be within reach of each other, the mother can give the baby any needed attention. The infant is not left to lie in a roomful of newborns, staring at a stimulus-free environment of plastic and stainless steel, and has something more to reach out for than sterilized linen. Where mother and baby are kept together, in the most natural circumstances, the baby, guided by the sense of smell, turns to the mother and, even if he or she does not feed, feels a continuation of the great closeness experienced in the womb and is comforted by flesh and the human touch. The transition from womb to world is considerably eased, and the very first experience of life gives pleasure.

CHOOSING AN OBSTETRICIAN AND A PEDIATRICIAN

During pregnancy, parents might consult more than one pediatrician, if necessary, before choosing. Even though a pediatrician is not needed till after birth, all the events of pregnancy, childbirth, and the earliest months of childrearing go together. For example, if the mother plans to breastfeed, it would be necessary to choose an obstetrician who performs

*In social legislation and practice, Sweden is far ahead of most countries. For example, it gives pregnant women a six months' leave of absence from work *with* pay beginning with the last month of pregnancy.

deliveries without drugs. Breastfeeding can then begin minutes after birth. Similarly, birth and the experiences of the first few days of life are so crucial to getting the baby off to a good start in mental health that it is important to have a warm and friendly relation to the pediatrician.

A mother might think of the obstetrician, hospital nurses, and pediatrician as her professional assistants. The doctors and the hospital staff must inspire confidence, be compassionate and supportive, and accommodate the mother's need to enjoy physical and emotional closeness with her baby. The obstetrician must respect the mother's wishes in the kind of medical care and types of pain-relieving drugs to be used, if she desires any, and must be willing to explain how they are administered and to discuss all options honestly and fully with her. Neither a mother's choice of drugs nor her rejection of them should be a cause of ridicule or coercion. The obstetrician should show convincing concern for the mother's safety and dignity and should welcome the participation of the father.

A mother might determine for herself how she feels about these specialists and how they feel about her by asking them questions in the prenatal period. She might visit local hospitals and ask specifically how the staff treats the birth experience. Do they regard pregnant women as ill, wheelchairing them to their room? Do they deliver babies on a narrow table with stirrups for the mother's legs in a glaringly illuminated room from which the husband is barred, or is the delivery room a pleasant, softly lit room where husband and wife can both participate in the birth of their child? Do the nurses seem friendly, or are they merely efficient? If the prospective mother knows someone who has used the obstetrician's and the hospital's services, was she satisfied or did she find that they broke promises — for example, injecting Demerol at the crucial moment in spite of a prior agreement not to? Is a woman in labor routinely given an enema; and if so, can she ask to have that or any other hospital routine modified? If routines cannot be modified, do the staff explain why, and is their explanation fully satisfactory? And perhaps most important of all, what attitude toward parents or mothers is implied by the tone of voice they use? Are they condescending or glad to help?

If the mother does intend to breastfeed, the prospective parents should make certain as labor begins that the staff has been alerted that no drugs are to be used. Hospital routines are sometimes so entrenched that in the throes of the delivery a staff member can forget instructions given only hours earlier. Or the day nursing staff changes to the night shift. Besides, it is in critical moments like these that some hospital staffs unfortunately tend to treat fathers and mothers as children, telling them what is "best" for them in disregard of the prospective parents' right to personal preferences. Staffs sometimes seem to forget that it is the *woman's* childbirth and the *parents'* baby. In many hospitals, the mother who wants to breastfeed faces resistance by the medical and nursing staffs: a nursing mother is a considerable nuisance to hospital administration.

In Chapter 3, when we discuss how to feed the baby, we will see that bottlefeeding, if done properly, is psychologically just as beneficial as breastfeeding. But if the mother intends to breastfeed, parents must make sure that the hospital staff knows it so that she will not be given Stilbestrol, a drug that dries up her milk. This "dry up" shot is administered in the delivery room, when the mother is most apprehensive and therefore most vulnerable to suggestion, and it is often recommended, usually by a male doctor, in tones of authority ("Everyone uses formulas. No one breastfeeds any more") or ridicule ("You don't want to be a cow, do you?"). The purpose of these manipulative remarks — namely, to ease the work of the hospital staff — is not mentioned. (One nurse was heard to ask a young mother, "Are you going to breastfeed your baby or feed him normally?") For the sake of efficiency in hospital administration, some doctors and nurses tend to encourage bottlefeeding, which is widely recognized as nutritionally inferior for babies.*

The field of perinatal care is changing rapidly as a result of the protests of women and books like *Our Bodies, Ourselves* by the Boston Women's Health Book Collective† and Constance Bean's *Methods of Childbirth*.‡ Many hospitals now permit and some even encourage prepared childbirth and family-centered maternity care. Doctors and nurses are becoming more deeply aware of the mother's psychological needs and

*Mothers who receive dry-up shots and then change their mind might be interested to know that they *can* breastfeed if they nurse frequently — between the baby's meals at first in order not to frustrate or starve the baby.
†The Boston Women's Health Book Collective, *Our Bodies, Ourselves*, New York, Simon and Schuster, 1971.
‡Constance A. Bean, *Methods of Childbirth: A Complete Guide to Childbirth Classes and Maternity Care.* See also Frederick Leboyer, *Birth Without Violence*, New York, Knopf, 1975.

parents' rights. Some hospitals now have nurses whose sole responsibility is the care of babies, and some offer rooming in around the clock, not just during the day.

THE PARENTS' NEED FOR LOVE

Although the role of martyr is harmful to all concerned, it would be wise for mothers and fathers to anticipate the need for giving up some of their pleasures, in fact for more self-sacrifice than they may care for. They might resent the loss of their freedom, the open-ended responsibility, and the work of childrearing. But most adults feel they can handle the amount of self-sacrifice needed. Something in them tells them — and they gradually learn to accept it — that from now on they will have to do certain things according to their baby's needs to provide him or her with the foundations of trust and love in order to develop to full potential. They are no longer alone. They will be sharing their life with a third person.

Psychologically healthy childrearing
is most probable when parents
are happy to be together.

The father might be surprised to find that he has mixed feelings toward his wife and some jealousy toward the baby. He may not always be aware of the intensity of his jealousy, but the closeness between mother and baby in the early weeks might at times make him feel shut out, resentful in spite of himself. This will be all the more true if he loves possessively. And in those first weeks matters are not helped by his feeling sexually deprived ("because of the baby," he might feel). If there are other problems as well — financial or job problems, for example — his worries could easily increase his resentment. He might need to feel that he is a partner, not a spectator, and also that the mother is a partner as well as a mother and can be relied on to be emotionally supportive. They are a team.

Because the father might feel that the baby is receiving all the mother's love, the mother might try to show outward signs of caring. But in fact, beginning with the later stages of pregnancy and on through the first month or two following birth, the mother needs her husband's affection more than usual and needs to have it warmly expressed. She wants to feel attractive and desired and needs to hear him say how much he appreciates her. As her need is satisfied it helps her to feel closer to him — and that satisfies his need too. Each wants and appreciates reassurance that the changes in their lives have not altered their feelings for each other. Psychologically healthy childrearing is most probable when parents are happy to be together.

FATHERHOOD

Fatherhood begins at birth. That would seem too obvious to state, but the impression is so often fostered that birth and early infancy are purely a mother-baby interaction. Unconditional love is not the woman's province alone. In fact, many fathers — especially those who participate in prepared childbirth — feel a bond develop starting from the time the fetus kicks in the uterus. The father is very much a part of the baby's environment, and the baby soon grows to love him just as much as the mother.

The father's warmth and love, which will have a beneficial and long-lasting effect on the child's growth and development, are not emotions most fathers feel at some later time but appear from the start. "Good enough" fathers have no fear of expressing their love and affection to babies, nor do they feel less male if they help to raise and take care of a baby.

It is true, though, that in our society it is men who, for the most part, go somewhere else to work — disappear, from a baby's viewpoint, and reappear later in the day. In our current societal roles, therefore, the father cannot have the same early importance to the baby as the mother does. But whether or not society changes, the relations between father and baby will in any case change as the baby grows older and develops an increasing awareness of the person called "father." Meanwhile, in the baby's first months of life the father is at the very least another interesting person, another face and voice in the baby's environment to whom he or she forms a deep attachment.

CHANGES IN YOUR LIFE

It would be unwise to have a child without knowing that

caring for a baby is hard work, at moments even drudgery, and that some of the spontaneity and free-wheeling pleasures you have enjoyed before the baby's birth will from then on be quite circumscribed. For example, you will probably go to the movies less often from now on. You might stop seeing friends for weeks at a time. If you like living according to some loose personal schedule, you may feel that a rigid and intractable routine has been forced on you.

Having a child is not an activity that you add on to your marriage. It doesn't work that way. Having a child altogether transforms your marriage and with it your lifestyle. And it does so irrevocably. Although it would be quite foolish to minimize this fact, few couples are even half aware of it when they decide to have a child.

Where before you primarily had only your own life to be concerned about, now the life of another is a large part of your concern as well. Surprisingly, if at moments you should feel you are not mature enough to take on the responsibility, the responsibility itself compels you into a new and unsuspected maturity. Necessity induces growth. When your baby is born, your awareness of the baby's complete "incompetence" suddenly endows you with a degree of competence you never thought you had.

You feel a considerable loss of freedom, and of peace too. Your marriage alters in character. Conversations between husband and wife sometimes take place in short bursts cut off by the baby's urgent interruptions. Sometimes a conversation is continued off and on over three or four days, as circumstances permit, and sometimes not. Life becomes hectic. You begin to value what you formerly took for granted – a whole night's sleep, a quiet, uninterrupted meal, an occasional late morning.

AMBIVALENCE AND PLANNING

This loss of freedom might make you resentful and angry. A baby is helpless and dependent and demands much of your time and patience. In fact, for the first few months of parenthood you feel you no longer have a life of your own. And so you begin to feel ambivalent toward your baby. You love your baby but wish you could be free again. Besides, the change in your marital relationship is a profound one, and you recognize that your life has taken a course over which you now have only partial control. The possibility of feeling ambivalent is one of the most important reasons for having children only when you are ready and eager to do so.

But this ambivalence is universal. It does not mean you are a "bad parent," and it would be unavailing to feel guilty about it. It is a natural feeling to have.

ADAPTATION, NOT MARTYRDOM

As you begin to feel your way you soon discover that you are not so trapped as you thought. In the first few months of life, babies sleep more than they do anything else, which gives you time also to nap or to do other things you might want to do. When you crave adult conversation, you find that there is time, after all, for an occasional long phone session, a visit, or a meeting. You also find time for projects you have long thought about but have not been at home enough to carry through. In sum, things fit together. The newborn baby goes through long periods of sleep, as though still in the uterus, and this gives mother and father time to adapt to their new state.

In other societies a young mother can share the burden with the extended family: uncles, aunts, cousins, and grandparents. In our society the father generally participates in the raising of his baby primarily by helping out with household chores in the first few days and secondarily by helping to care for the baby — although other arrangements may of course be devised.

Laying the foundation for the baby's future life and wellbeing may call for temporary sacrifices. It does not, however, call for martyrdom. As George Bernard Shaw said, "If you begin by sacrificing yourself to those you love, you will end by hating those to whom you have sacrificed yourself."

Martyrs make poor parents.

Your baby does not need you to be a slave or martyr. On the other hand, a baby is not aware that there is more to life than his or her needs. It is up to you to arrange your affairs to accommodate the baby's needs as well as your own. Your baby can't do it — you can. Plan to have leisure, take the time to do the things you want to do, and remind yourself that nothing is better for a baby than having parents who enjoy life. Martyrs make poor parents.

THE REWARD

The reward for going through these difficult moments and putting up with small temporary sacrifices is a healthy and fulfilling life for your child. Although these first months and years may not always be easy for you, for the baby they lay the foundation for all that is to come. The experiences of the earliest months and years create nothing less than *the core of personality and mental health.* When it comes to psychological development, parents are the most important persons in the baby's life, now and ever. The aim of all that follows is to explain how this comes about.

There is a reward for you too. Consciously helping your child attain a healthy and fulfilling life, aside from being a fascinating experience, will make your life easier through the long years of growth by greatly reducing the possibility of emotional difficulties in your child.

ALL YOU NEED IS LOVE—
AND A LITTLE TIME TO ADAPT

Everything we have said so far might make childrearing sound complicated, and perhaps it would be without the essential ingredient of love. You love your baby in actuality more than you loved the idea of having a baby. And when the baby smiles at you and curls a fist around your finger and utters a delightfully meaningless gurgle, all your efforts seem rewarded. You can't help feeling that much of what you are occasionally aware of being deprived of is no longer worth having, at least for a while. You have something better, a pleasure that touches you deeply. You might even find yourself feeling sorry for those of your friends who have not had a baby yet, despite all the pleasures of their freedom, for which you yearn now and then.

It is also good to anticipate that you will *not* welcome your baby with a rush of joy but will need time to become accustomed to him or her. It is not common to fall in love with a stranger, and at birth that is what your baby is to you. No baby looks like what you had in mind, and every baby needs getting used to. What need getting used to even more are the baby's crying and fussy demands, feeding—a routine that requires time for its establishment—and, in the mother's case, her exceptional postbirth fatigue. Labor was hard, and nighttime feedings are exhausting.

It may take a few weeks to love your baby, just as it takes weeks or even months for a man and a woman to fall in love with each other or to feel really married. Most new parents begin to fall in love with their baby sometime during the first month. Usually the first fleeting smiles of contentment on the baby's face are what clinch it. Sometimes having to care for a sick baby arouses concern which grows into love.

POSTBIRTH DEPRESSION

In anticipating birth, it might be valuable for a mother to know that after delivery she will probably experience an emotional down. More than just fatigue, she might feel depressed. This feeling too is natural and should not cause her to worry.

Postbirth depression has many causes. It may be due to the hormonal changes that follow birth. (It is for this reason, as well as for having lost the baby, that women experience mild depressions after miscarriages and abortions.) Also the mother experiences a peculiar sense of loss at having her baby physically parted from her. In addition, she might feel depressed because the hospital staff separates her from her baby except for short visits, frustrating her need to see and smell and feel her baby. Or she might feel down because now that she has given birth at last all she has to look forward to is coping with house, mate, and baby. (This would be even more true if she didn't want to have the baby.) She might feel depressed that she has lost her big belly and her excuse for being overweight —but not her excess weight.

Another and more subtle source of postbirth depression is the possibility that the mother might actually be afraid of her baby. The baby is still adjusting to a new environment— undergoing changes in temperature, breathing irregularly, eating erratically—and seems fragile. She might feel that she must be extra careful in lifting, holding, or moving the baby, taking care not to hurt him or her or cause damage accidentally. A baby is a totally helpless being with no language to express wants or needs. This initial period can make the mother feel tense and unsure.

She might also feel depressed when the baby's continuing demands exasperate her even though she knows she should not feel angry: it is not the baby's fault. This too could be particularly true if she or her husband were ambivalent about having the baby in the first place. The solution would be to face her feelings and try to understand that they are natural. Adaptation would become easier for her.

Postbirth depression can last up to six months. From time to time there might be a few days when a new mother feels tearful. At such times, it might help to get together with a friend undergoing a similar experience. Talking about it helps revive flagging spirits.

If she feels continually depressed and the depression is a profound one, it would be a mistake to hide it or think she can work things out for herself. She, her husband, and the baby would benefit if she sought professional help early.

THE MOTHER SHOULD TAKE GOOD CARE OF HERSELF

In any event, it would help the mother to talk about her feelings, whatever they may be. The postbirth period is a time when she has the right to expect aid from everyone in her environment—husband, pediatrician, friends, relatives, even close neighbors. She might seek out those who will be supportive of her without trying to control and direct her life. She should try to get plenty of rest and sleep, take care of herself, let the house be untidy for a while, let unimportant things go, and not try to be helpful to others. Her husband can take care of himself, and if he is not capable he should learn.

Giving birth may be statistically common, but it is an uncommon experience for each mother. Her best course is to take it easy and get back to being her old self again—to save herself. She might have to change her routine in some respects, but that doesn't mean that she must stop living or give up her interests. Creating a new being does not mean cessation of her own being. It does mean suspending many former responsibilities, which she cannot immediately resume.

2

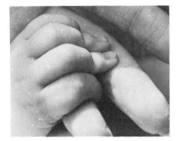

The
Newborn

"Above, the heavens, below, the earth—I alone am the Most Honored one."... Buddha is supposed to have declared this directly as he came out of his mother's body.... We all make this cry, but have forgotten it.

D. T. SUZUKI

Unique in the animal kingdom, the newborn human is totally helpless for the first weeks of life. Food, protection, and warmth must be provided by another person. Even to move from one position to another, the baby needs help.

Indeed, for the first day or two, a newborn can register sights and sounds but has no perception: perception implies a *consciousness* of seeing or hearing. Shortly after birth, however, perception makes its appearance, so effortlessly that we tend to think of it as being there from the moment of birth.*

TOUCH

In the hours following birth, babies sense much more than they perceive, predominantly through touch. Touch is dormant at birth and is awakened by the mother's holding and caress-

---

*René A. Spitz, *The First Year of Life,* New York, International Universities Press, 1965, p. 4. The late Dr. Spitz, a psychoanalyst who made some of the greatest contributions to the study of infancy, commented in a footnote that from birth (and even earlier) the infant *responds* to external stimuli, but because there is no consciousness yet, these responses are a mere "reception" of the stimuli.

Most of the material in this chapter, as well as some of the material in Chapters 4, 5, and 9, is based on the cited work and on Spitz's *Genetic Field Theory of Ego Formation,* New York, International Universities Press, 1959.

ing. Washing the baby after emergence from the uterus helps quicken the infant's sense of touch.

Although touching is a much more limited sense than seeing or hearing will eventually become, its distribution over the entire body serves the baby well at the very beginning. Feeling the mother is a baby's first contact with her, providing a sense of belonging with someone. It also provides a sense of being loved. In infancy to be touched and fed is to be loved. Touch is a durable sense. Long after sight, hearing, speech, and even mental faculties have been lost or impaired in old age, the sense of touch remains.

The mother's touch becomes a method of communication for an infant. If she wants to communicate that her nipple or the bottle is available, all she needs to do is touch the baby's cheek with it. Instinctively, the baby will turn his or her head in the direction of the touch. Similarly, if the baby is feeding and the mother touches the outside cheek, that may puzzle the baby. It is confusing to an infant to have both cheeks touched at once: the baby wonders which way to turn when the stimulus comes from opposite directions.

THE GRASPING REFLEX

If you place your finger in a newborn's hand the baby will sense it and grasp it tightly. Grasping is not a purposive action but purely a reflex of skin and tendons in response to the stimulus of your finger. As long as grasping remains a reflex it has no meaning: the baby merely closes his or her hand on a sensation. The sensation happens to be your finger. It is the baby's way of practicing grasping for later use, when there will be a need to pick things up or to hold on to you. Only when the baby is about six months old will grasping be done intentionally, under the control of the mind.

Grasping often accompanies feeding. The baby's hands "grasp" air in response to a hunger pang. Then, as the hunger is satisfied, the hands relax.

By the fifth or sixth month the baby can reach out for objects like a teething ring or a string of wooden beads and pick them up. The new ability to see an object and grasp it indicates that eyes and hands are coordinating well and that the cortex has begun to function. The eyes see a thing and the hands know how to go to it, carefully enclose it in fingers, and bring it near. That ordinary event is an achievement when you consider that, only a short while before, the baby could only look at things with a wandering gaze and aimlessly move two uncoordinated arms. Now internal organization is more advanced. The baby can actually alter surroundings, even though only in a limited way.

This stage of development requires greater supervision in parenting. The baby who has learned to grasp objects can pick up safety pins, scissors, and baby powder, all of which may go into the mouth because they look, feel, smell, and taste interesting.

In infancy to be touched
and fed is to be loved.

Toward the end of the first year the care with which the baby will make a delicate pincer of thumb and index finger is impressive. If the baby fails to pick up a desired object — for example, a straw fallen from a broom — the thumb and finger will slowly close on it again. If the second attempt fails, the baby, not feeling the frustration that an adult might feel in a comparable situation, will once again with patience and concentration slowly close thumb and finger on the object — until finally the object is grasped.

THE "PRIMAL CAVITY"

To a baby the most important part of the body is the mouth. Everything that can be held goes into it. In the earliest weeks of life it is through the mouth that the baby forms his or her principal relationship with the environment. It may seem to us that mouth contact is a circumscribed way of "learning" the world, but to a newborn the entire universe is nothing more than an oral and intestinal sensation. Slowly, however, babies learn to distinguish among the different shapes and textures of objects by their mouths just as adults do by their hands. Babies use the mouth as a sensing device, and so important is the mouth to their functioning that Spitz refers to it as the "primal cavity." According to brain physiologists, the human brain serves the lips and mouth more than any other body part, with the hand a close second.

A baby's mouth has three functions. It is the body opening through which the baby experiences the world. It is part of the baby's means of nourishment and survival. And it is an erogenous zone: the nourishment gives pleasure. This premium of pleasure awards the mouth a place of psychological prominence for the first year of life and a clear ascendancy over all other body parts. Even the most casual observer would be convinced that this period of infancy is decidedly oral in character.

SIGHT BECOMES PERCEPTION

In addition to sensing through touch, babies learn about the world through seeing. As we have said, newborns have sight but not visual perception. They have not yet learned to interpret and understand the visual stimuli they receive. They see simple shapes, colors, and patterns, but these have no meaning: they are not organized or intelligible. The random impressions are like unprocessed information fed to a computer that is not programed for it and makes no sense of it. One confirmation that humans do not automatically begin to perceive but must learn to do so is the reaction of blind persons who through surgery gain sight for the first time. They don't know *how* to see. The world is so chaotic to them that, according to Spitz, some have even asked to have their blindness restored.*

The point is that visual stimuli must become organized before visual perception is possible. This organization converts the stimuli into images of the world that begin to make sense.

The mother (or mothering person) helps transform stimuli into images with meaning, and the way she does this is through a "dialogue" with her baby. She interacts with the baby, responding to cues. As Dr. Margaret Mahler explains cueing,† the baby tries a variety of means to express need and tension — sounds, looks, hand movements — but the mother, purely spontaneously, responds *selectively* to them. The baby learns which gestures and sounds bring the desired results, and the mother in turn learns to understand more accurately what the baby's needs are and to respond to them more effectively.

*Spitz, *The First Year of Life,* p. 40.
†Margaret S. Mahler, *On Human Symbiosis and the Vicissitudes of Individuation,* New York, International Universities Press, 1968, p. 18.

For example, if the baby cries and the mother thinks the crying might be caused by hunger, she offers her breast or a bottle. If her response effectively deals with the tension (hunger), the correctness of this action demonstrates to the baby that his or her needs are being communicated and understood. The mother's action is need-fulfilling and therefore "makes sense." Thus a nonverbal language develops between them.

A more subtle and quite common example is this: A baby who is several weeks old notices that at times he or she is picked up in a certain way and with a certain look on the mother's face as she does something with her blouse; the baby knows that the mother is going to feed, and if he or she had been crying quiets down and becomes expectant.

To a newborn the entire universe
is nothing more than
an oral and intestinal sensation.

This visual "language" develops between mother and infant without either of them necessarily being aware of it as language. The mother holds and cradles the baby in a special way and smiles: that means she just wants to hug and be playful, which the baby looks forward to now with joy. Or if she lays the baby on a soft blanket and does something with the diaper while bending over to talk, the baby knows it is time for a diaper change. Thus stimuli become organized. They change from *general stimuli* to *signals that have meaning*. That, according to Spitz, is how sight becomes visual perception.

THE INCREASING VISUAL FIELD

After the first three or four weeks of life a baby is increasingly able to perceive a nearby face as the form and configuration (gestalt) of a face. Thus in addition to mouth perception the baby has eye perception, opening the way to learning more about the world. As eye perception develops, the baby's visual perspective deepens to include more things of the world. The baby can now view objects across the room, for example, and seeing becomes a subtler and more comprehensive form of touching.

A heightened visual perspective is a revolutionary advance:

it creates space. It becomes obvious, however, that the sense of space is still faulty when you see the baby attempt to reach for something in the next room, seen through an open doorway. That some objects are near and some far is not yet real to the baby. To see and like a thing is to want to touch it. It is not your nose or eyes or hair, not a painting on a wall or a brightly lit ceiling or the house across the way. To the baby it is an undefined yet interesting sight to take hold of, feel, sense with the mouth and tongue, taste, and play with. It is a fascinating new world, and the baby delights in every bit of it.

Perception is a complex phenomenon. In your lifetime you may have seen hundreds of toys, rattles, and objects of all sorts for children, but it was not until you yourself had a baby or were expecting one that you became aware of which toys or rattles would be appealing to or safe for a baby. Perception is selective. You tend to perceive what has importance for you at a given moment. (There is much truth in the joke "I'll see it when I believe it.") When you have a letter to mail you perceive mailboxes, but once you have posted the letter you stop noticing mailboxes. If everything in your broad perceptual field were of equal importance you would be confused by the profusion of stimuli.

According to some psychologists, persons over thirty years old tend to perceive themselves as ten years younger than they actually are, despite what they see in the mirror. It is not surprising, therefore, that infants perceive themselves in an even more grossly distorted way. The baby's brain is still being formed daily, cell by cell. At birth the brain and nervous system are the least developed parts of the baby—are in fact incomplete. For them to be wholly formed, nine months of postbirth development are required.* We can assume, therefore, that a baby sees a world different from ours, fuzzy, indefinite, dreamlike. The baby's brain is not capable of functioning well because it lacks the interconnections that make thought possible.

Perception can be subverted by emotion. There are times when a baby cries hard because of hunger, but the rage caused by the hunger pangs interferes with the perception that the breast or bottle is available, even if the mother puts the nipple into the baby's mouth. It would be best for her not to force the issue but wait for the crying to slacken from fatigue or because

*The nine months of gestation seem matched by the nine months of postbirth development of the brain, locomotion, and teeth.

she is holding the baby in her arms and then reoffer the nipple. After calming down, the baby will feed contentedly. An enraged baby's rejection of the nipple is not a rejection of the mother. A baby who is cared for and loved is not a rejecting creature.

At this earliest stage, much of an infant's life is visceral. Still in a womblike state of being, a baby feeds, sleeps, eliminates — feels content or miserable according to the state of the stomach and intestines. The periphery of a baby's body, where the sense organs are, and the developing brain are secondary. A newborn's life is governed by the digestive tract, and every feeling is a "gut reaction." A newborn has few other reactions to life, and certainly no more sophisticated ones.

THE BABY'S PERCEPTION OF YOU

How does a baby perceive you? In fact, does a baby perceive you *as* you?

To a baby you are only a face, and a face that has no separate existence. It will be weeks before the newborn begins to perceive you *even in part* and many months before you will appear as a separate, whole person — as you.

What makes this misperception possible is that a baby has no conception of inside and outside. Even mother's breast does not feel like something outside. To the baby it is all "me."* At times there is something that adults call a hunger pang. That sensation comes from some part of the "me." Then there is something that adults call a breast (or bottle), which provides the needed satisfaction: a baby accepts the breast or bottle not only as "me" but as a "good" part of "me." A baby's perception of the world needs extensive correction.

THE BABY'S OMNIPOTENCE AND PSYCHOLOGICAL DEVELOPMENT

Whatever a baby is aware of feels like the self. The self and the world are one. Up to the age of three months, no distinctions are made. A baby "knows" no boundaries. A baby feels omnipotent, alone, eternal, cosmically vast, and self-sufficient. A baby's "self" experience is godlike.

Thus all humans begin life in a delusional state. Each baby

*Spitz, *The First Year of Life,* p. 35n.

"thinks" he or she is the universe, is immortal, needs no one. Some never altogether outgrow that delusion but unconsciously maintain it in some form throughout adulthood.

Some of the most powerful feelings of nostalgia, which is the wellspring of much art, come from the gradual acknowledgment of personal mortality and the "loss" of omnipotence. This acknowledgment is made beautifully explicit in a statement by Joseph Conrad: "I remember my youth and the feeling that will never come back any more — the feeling that I could last forever, outlast the sea, the earth, and all men."

What makes an infant feel omnipotent? When a baby experiences hunger and begins to cry, a "good enough" parent satisfies the need without fail. Because the whole world is "me," however, the baby experiences the feeding as a *self-feeding*.

A baby who is cared for and loved is not a rejecting creature.

Over the next several months, the baby slowly perceives that apart from "me" there is a "not-me." Because this dimly understood external reality reliably provides satisfaction, it is felt to be good. The "not-me" does not fight the baby's expressions of omnipotence, which are chiefly crying and gesturing, but with minimum frustration satisfies each need dependably. The trust that the baby builds from this experience encourages him or her to begin relinquishing the omnipotence. The "me" has no further need to be all-powerful if the "not-me" is reliably helpful.

The slow unfolding of development is the best development, and growth is never better consolidated than when feelings of satisfaction belonging to each of its stages are fully experienced. If the parent does not offer sufficient satisfaction to the earliest infantile needs, the baby will tend to hang on to the delusion of omnipotence. *A baby has a psychological need to feel omnipotent until reassured that the omnipotence is not necessary.* If this need is frustrated — if, for example, the baby is allowed to cry helplessly for a half hour or more because of a feeding schedule in order "not to spoil the baby" — the baby's feeling of omnipotence is prematurely ended. The delusion does not slowly give way to reality, which is the healthy outcome, but is suddenly shattered, which leads to problems. A premature awareness by the baby of his or her helplessness creates enormous anxiety and permanently scars development. It is an overdose of reality.

THE MOTHERING PERSON AND MEMORY

How far back does memory begin? Are babies born with a memory, or do they develop one?

Through the first month and most of the second month of life, a baby does not recognize milk or bottles or nipples or breast. A hungry baby will respond to the sight of the breast or bottle as to a cue. But when there is no hunger, the visual "cue" means nothing. This is evidence that a six-week-old baby has no memory. Each event, no matter how often repeated, is a new event.

All humans begin life in
a delusional state.

Memory develops toward the end of the second month. One of the things a baby begins to do at this age is distinguish between an inanimate background and the human being in it because the human being moves. This is especially true when an adult approaches the baby. If the baby is hungry, the mouth will open at the approach. When the baby feels tension inside (hunger) he or she begins to perceive outside (the adult). Tension fosters perception. Our mailbox example demonstrated that perception is anchored in need. With successive recognitions of you, the baby begins to store away all the perceptions of you, and that storage is memory.

Observations made by Spitz suggest that it takes a baby two months longer to recognize the bottle than the human face. This is true even though the baby might see the bottle many times a day, touch it, and drink from it. The baby seems to be innately responsive to the configuration of the face. Recognition of the human face comes first, recognition of objects second. Breastfed babies stare very steadily, almost thoughtfully, at the face of the mothering person, but bottlefed babies stare inconsistently. (Is it because some mothers hold the bottle away from their breast, making it inconvenient for the baby to see their face?) Breastfeeding, which lays down a better memory trace of the mothering person as a pleasurable gratifier of needs, would therefore seem to foster a more efficient development of memory.

The baby begins to like the human face for just this simple reason: the face is present on each occasion that needs are gratified, and the baby soon learns to associate human features with pleasure and wellbeing.

PSYCHOLOGICAL BIRTH:
THE GOAL OF EARLY CHILDHOOD

Like physical birth, psychological birth has its period of gestation, in this case beginning with the first feedings of the newborn. The face that brings pleasure gradually becomes a person, but only over a long period of time: three years. First it is only a face. Then the face is part of a person. Only slowly does the part-person become a complete and separate being. When the child feels that he or she and mother are two separate persons, the child has reached "psychological birth." Psychological separation is possible only when there is an outside person to separate *from.*

As we deepen our study of human beginnings we will note a curious reversal. At first the baby forms a strong bond with mother (to a lesser extent father). Then he or she begins to loosen that bond. The reasons for both events are identical. In the first year the baby, helpless and dependent, forms strong ties for survival and wellbeing. Parents, especially mother, are quite literally a life-support system. By the age of three, however, the baby loosens those ties — but again, for survival and wellbeing.

It is the developmental task of infancy and early childhood to lead to psychological independence and autonomy by the end of the first thirty-six months. Birth was merely a physical separation from mother. By three years, if all has gone well, the child will have achieved psychological birth and become an individual. Much development will take place in the attainment of this goal: learning to feed, think, speak, discover the difference between wish and reality, and love others — abilities that we will examine as we go along, beginning with feeding.

3

Feeding and Human Development

I famish and I pine.

SAPPHO

Once we understand that to a baby feeding is not just survival but is the first expression of love, the quality of feeding assumes great importance. Because hunger and sucking are the earliest needs of life, how and to what extent these needs are gratified establish in the baby lifelong patterns. All subsequent need satisfaction will tend to be based on these patterns.

To the brain and nervous system, no experience is ever lost: they react to and register each event. To employ an image that Freud used in another connection, it is like the "magic" pads on which a person writes and then lifts the transparent overlay to make the writing "vanish." Closer inspection reveals that traces of the writing remain permanently inscribed on the wax pad beneath the overlay. Similarly, experiences leave traces on the psyche in permanent "inscriptions," which form the person's behavior patterns. The experiences of feeding and sucking, because they register first on an almost blank pad, are the most permanent.

THE TECHNIQUE OF FEEDING

The eating habits of very young babies are similar to those of adults in at least one respect: sometimes they want just a snack and sometimes a lengthy meal. The feeding baby may pause briefly, then look for the breast again — perhaps stop and start many times, even dozing for a moment between feeds. Feeding is one of the baby's major activities and a source of much pleasure. A baby eats with passion, making noises of lusty satisfaction, and after the more insistent pangs of hunger have been satisfied he or she may begin a leisurely sucking again, as if the feeding were a meal of several courses.

As a "good enough" parent you go along with the baby. You don't rush the feeding or grow impatient by thinking the baby is dawdling on purpose, nor do you attempt to force-feed by inserting the nipple into the baby's recoiling mouth. The baby would fight such an attempt and you would understand, just as you would resent it if someone were to force you to eat because of that person's needs or daily agenda.

In the beginning you may not know how long your baby needs to feed. At first the baby does not know either. In the uterus feeding was regulated automatically. It generally takes two to four weeks for the mother's milk supply and the baby's demand to match. And it also takes time for mother and baby to adapt to each other as persons. With experience, each feeding might grow a bit longer and less of a stop-and-start affair as needs and capacity increase. For the first several months the tissues of a baby's body grow at a great rate, and repeated feedings are required to supply the need.

We say "you feed the baby," but all you really need to do is hold the baby in your arms and simply allow the baby to feed. The baby is born knowing what to do and requires only a little practice and minimal help from you. The baby will swivel the head from side to side until the mouth encounters the nipple. You merely place the breast or bottle close to the baby's face. The baby's cheek, swiveling back and forth, encounters the nipple, and the mouth, guided by instinct, closes on it.

In the first weeks of life the baby may eat as often as ten or twelve times in a twenty-four-hour period. A normal, healthy baby savors each meal like a gourmet. But unlike a gourmet, a baby sometimes continues to eat until overtaken by slumber.

The feeding experience is a time for parent and baby to get acquainted. The breastfeeding mother might hold the baby in a way that allows good physical contact between the baby's face and her breast. If the weather is warm she might enjoy holding the baby's naked body against her exposed torso.

Feeding the baby is an intimate experience, not some correct thing to do. It would be best if the mother felt comfortable and unrushed and enjoyed the feeding for the sensual experience that it is. Perhaps this pleasure, like the intense pleasure of intercourse, is nature's way of ensuring the survival of the species.

Bottlefeeding, to a lesser extent, can also be a sensual experience for the mother, as she cradles her infant and enjoys watching the sucking motions of the baby's mouth. The mother who bottlefeeds can feel just as maternal as the breastfeeding mother.

It is most important that the breastfeeding mother should feel right about her method of feeding, because if she does not —if she is tired, anxious, or nervous—her feeding could have an adverse effect on her letting down her milk. ("Letting down" milk is a neurohormonal reflex that expels milk from the tiny sacs in the breast called "alveoli," each the size of the head of a pin. The baby's sucking stimulates the mother's pituitary gland to secrete oxytocin. Her milk sacs, by tightening, squeeze milk into the passageways called sinuses. When the milk lets down, the baby can get it by exerting pressure around the nipple.)

Because letting down is a reflex, it may be inhibited if the mother is upset or uncomfortable. In the case of some women the presence of relatives or strangers inhibits letting down, but others say that it takes much more than that to inhibit their reflex. To ensure good letting down, breastfeeding is best when the mother feels content and is free from any serious problem or stress. Rest produces milk. Anxiety diminishes the supply. The mother hugs the baby gently, makes soft sounds, and smiles down at the tiny face—the face that after the first few weeks begins to gaze so steadfastly at her while feeding—and makes the baby feel loved and happy. The mother feels secure, easy, and at peace, and so does the baby. The mother feels— and perhaps the baby too in a fuzzy way—that there is between them an inexpressibly deep and satisfying relationship.

FEEDING, LEARNING, AND HUMAN RELATIONS

That face gazing upward: so much is going on when a baby does that while feeding. As the baby mouths the nipple and stares at you, touch perception blends with visual perception. The baby may seem distracted or busy eating, but he or she is learning about you and getting acquainted with your features, which will soon seem beautiful. Associating your face with pleasure and gratification will reinforce the baby's love for you. The baby is learning to read your facial expressions, your voice, and the way you touch, hold, smile. The baby notes when you frown or speak curtly and when you are pleasant and soft-spoken. The baby can tell the difference between your making a feeding a chore to be gotten through impatiently and feeding as a slow, loving occasion that provides more than just the bare necessities. The baby feels whether you treat him or her as someone you value or merely as someone whose obvious needs you tend to before plopping him or her down in the bassinet again.

Sometimes the baby stops eating and concentrates on your face, reaching out to feel it, fingering your mouth and nose, studying your features and trying to understand you. The baby is forming the first human relationship ever—relating and being related to. No subsequent relations will have quite this effect. This bond with you will become the model for all human relations. The quality of later demands for affectionate companionship will depend in part—in considerable part—on the outcome of this earliest one. If the baby feels you are a dependable source of satisfaction, he or she will feel content and will form a picture of the world as a place where beings are generally good and pleasant things happen. If there is little emotional gratification now, according to this pattern there will be little expectation of it in adulthood, nor will tenderness and companionship be offered then either.

If a parent were out of tune with the baby's needs and rushed things or stopped a feeding too soon, the baby would become anxious and uncertain. If that should happen repeatedly, the baby might feel that it would be better to rush impatiently through a feeding before it is taken away, like adults who display the feeling that they had better grab things while the grabbing is good.

The baby's feeding is an emotional experience and a foundation for all psychological life. For the baby to drink the milk you give is much more than filling the stomach, much more than a sensual experience. It makes for nothing less than a psychological set. The baby is held, touched, spoken to, made warm, rocked gently, and smiled at, and the reactions to this contribute to—*form*—the baby's outlook on life. When the feeding experience, which is more complex than anyone used to think, is not as complete as it should be—when the baby is kept full, warm, and dry but no more than that—areas of "hunger" are left, which leave their mark on character. It makes sense to speak of having an "appetite for life" when appetite has led to satisfaction, physical and emotional.

DEMAND OR SCHEDULED FEEDING?

Should the baby be fed on demand or on schedule? The question is abstract. If we phrased it more concretely, the answer would become obvious: should one feed a baby who is hungry?

Physiologists say that the stomach of a newborn becomes empty about an hour and a half after a feeding. Moreover, because of a smaller stomach, a six-pound baby may require less food but more frequent feedings than a seven-and-a-half-pound baby. Thus a baby who is fed on a schedule of two, six, and ten o'clock may nap after the two o'clock feeding and reawaken feeling hungry at three-thirty or even earlier. According to the schedule, the baby has awakened two and a half hours too soon and, tearful or not, must wait. The trouble is that a newborn is psychologically not developed enough to tolerate the delay. There is nothing in the baby's experience to inform him or her that relief is eventually forthcoming. A baby who cries on and on for food feels utterly abandoned, and the paroxysms of screaming are the expression not just of pain but of despair. To the baby the vigorous hunger contractions will go on forever. The anxiety and despair are a terrifying experience in the unconscious life of an organism scarcely days or weeks old.

Being hungry and abandoned feels
the same to a baby as
inhabiting a cold, unpeopled world.

Despite the pain and crying, no relief comes. It is not the scheduled feeding time, and the baby is left to rage hopelessly. When this happens repeatedly — and that is what does happen if the baby is put on a schedule — it becomes one source of depression in adulthood, as becomes clear in the analysis of adults. "Hope deferred makes the heart sick." The baby's experience is that life is preponderantly hurtful and pleasure is not to be relied on. There is little use in wanting something, because no effort will succeed in getting it. And the baby builds on these unhappy feelings. Better to wish for nothing than to go through life with the agony of wishing and not getting – and it is better not to depend on others. We have all met adults who retain these feelings throughout their lives. Most were probably schedule-fed. It was the fashion in the '20s through the '50s to schedule-feed babies. Even now, many pediatricians continue to recommend it, and mothers trustingly go ahead with the recommendation.

We might better appreciate the importance of demand feeding if we looked at it from a baby's point of view. To the baby an important part of feeding is the mother's presence and the quality of the experience. Hunger gnaws and the baby wants the pain stopped. The mouth instinctively opens to find the nipple. If the breast or bottle is unavailable the baby cries and, in a reflex, pushes the fists somewhere near the mouth (if hand-to-mouth coordination has not yet been achieved). The crying, in reaction to pain, intensifies if a feeding is not offered.

An infant whose deprivation is prolonged begins to experience what an adult would describe as panic. The panic added to the pain of the gnawing in the stomach begins to overwhelm the baby. When this happens often, as it does in scheduled feeding, the pain and anxiety have a devastating effect on the baby. For the convenience of adults, the baby placed on scheduled feeding is condemned to privation, distress, and the beginnings of emotional difficulty.

The continued privation imposed by scheduled feeding makes the baby fearful and builds so great an unconscious feeling of helplessness that he or she may not be able to overcome it later. Being hungry and abandoned feels the same to a baby as inhabiting a cold, unpeopled world. Some adults who were subjected to this early experience have the unconscious dread that they will live the last years of their lives alone, poor, and unloved, fearing what they in fact once actually experienced, although they cannot remember it.

When the feeding finally does come, the baby's reaction is comparable to the immense relief a drowning person must experience who, after having given up all hope of survival and prepared to die, unexpectedly sees a rescue ship.

In contrast, let us see what demand feeding is like. The baby, feeling a gnawing in the stomach due to hunger contractions, swivels his or her head from side to side "looking" for the nipple. If it is not there the baby cries. The breast or bottle is offered, and the crying stops because the need is filled. Feeding begins, and slowly a look of contentment comes over the baby's face as the gnawing sensation gives way to satiation. After a leisurely feed the baby falls asleep. No severe frustration, no deprivation, no panic.

It used to be argued, and some still believe, that letting a baby cry builds character and that one should not spoil the baby by catering to every whim. And besides, crying is good for the lungs.

It would be a mistake to assume that the baby behaves and reacts in the same way adults do. To attribute adult motives to the baby or read adult meanings into a baby's acts is the error of adultomorphism. If the baby cries and you think that the crying is an attempt to order you around, that would be adultomorphism. In reality, the baby is merely responding to internal stimuli, with no knowledge of a "you" to order. The crying is due to the pain of hunger.

Hunger is a physical need requiring satisfaction, not a "whim" that adults should avoid catering to. How can feeding, which alleviates the hunger, spoil a baby? If a baby's pain or discomfort is removed by a parent's care, the baby does not demand a continuation of that care once he or she is feeling better. And as for "building character," to believe this one must make the assumption that character is built purely through deprivation and pain. And that is false. Satisfaction, gratification, contentment, and love—these more than anything else are the building blocks of character. Only a baby who is several weeks old can tolerate frustration in more than extremely small doses.

Selma Fraiberg, a psychoanalyst and teacher of child analysis at the University of Michigan Medical School, describes the effects of scheduled feeding:

> Our experiment in getting babies' stomachs to contract at orderly intervals produced some unforeseen consequences. A struggle over food was set up in the earliest months of infancy and very often the battle over food was waged over the family dinner table for years afterward. Eating problems were high on the list of complaints to pediatricians and child guidance clinics in the 20's and 30's. The thwarted instincts got their revenge.

> Today's baby is fed when he shows signs of hunger, and if this seems trite to the contemporary reader, let me remind

him that twenty years were devoted to the reform of infant stomachs before we emerged with the cliché. Today's baby, with his unreconstructed stomach, shows every sign of flourishing under this regime. His relationship with his mother is more harmonious than that of the clock baby because his mother satisfies his hunger.*

If these early experiences have such a profound effect on development, why don't nurses in hospitals feed on demand? Scheduled feeding was not devised by nurses, nor would it be up to them to adopt a new policy. The reason for scheduled feeding is a quite practical one. Nurses have a difficult job, with a variety of chores to do all day long, so the blame is not theirs for the little time they can devote to each newborn. They must impose a routine on their daily activities merely to get through them all. It was for this reason that hospitals welcomed scheduled feeding when that idea was first proposed some forty or fifty years ago. And now hospitals find it difficult to give up even though they know that demand feeding is psychologically better for a baby. Even though in recent years there has been a declining birth rate, nurses in most hospitals still have a dozen babies to feed, and it is easier for them to give feedings on a schedule of two, six, and ten o'clock rather than when each baby wakes up hungry.

Satisfaction, gratification, contentment, and love—these more than anything else are the building blocks of character.

We have scheduled feeding almost universally in the United States today simply because in the last forty years or so more and more women have decided to have their babies in a hospital rather than at home. Hospitals demand conformity to their rules, which are based on administrative convenience, not natural method. That fact tends to get lost to view. To some, medical help in childbirth, once intended as an aid to nature if and when needed, has come to be regarded as the "natural" or normal way to have a baby.

Having a baby in a hospital first became popular after Ignaz Semmelweiss, a nineteenth-century Hungarian obstetrician

*Selma H. Fraiberg, *The Magic Years,* New York, Scribner's, 1959, p. 73.

working in the General Hospital of Vienna, dramatically reduced puerperal fever (childbed fever) and maternal mortality, from nearly 20 percent to 1 percent, by introducing stricter sanitary measures.* The medical profession then began to regard pregnant women as patients in its province ("maternity cases"), and the feelings of omnipotence that some doctors seem to have — or that are sometimes ascribed to them because of their power of life and death over lay people — spread unconsciously into a new and subtle area: it is the *doctor* who "brings the baby into the world." (Freud once remarked that obstetricians are frustrated mothers.)

When you are choosing a hospital (if you have a choice), you might ask if its policy is to insist on scheduled feeding despite a rooming-in arrangement. Most hospitals do insist, and it may take several tries before you find one that will go along with your wishes and permit demand feeding.

THE BOTTLE OR THE BREAST?

Is breastfeeding better than bottlefeeding? Nutritionally, yes, but psychologically, not necessarily. It depends on how the feeding is done.

More and more women, especially young adults, are opting for breastfeeding. Young parents no longer uncritically follow the recommendations of hospital staffs. There are even signs that breastfeeding in public might someday again become acceptable, as it was in former times in parts of Western society and still is today in many areas of the world.

Nutritionally, breastfeeding is unsurpassably better because the substances in mother's milk are ideally suited to the baby's needs, supplying protein in its most assimilable form and a fat content that formulas and homogenized cow's milk do not have. Human milk protects against upper respiratory infections, gastrointestinal infections, eczema, asthma, hay fever, and dental caries when the teeth come in. Prepared formulas can approximate the substances in breast milk, but they are by definition only an approximation. Science is not advanced enough to know what protective elements there might be in mother's milk that artificial formulas and heat-treated cow's milk do not provide.

Furthermore, formulas and processed cow's milk can pro-

*Semmelweiss's reward for this benefaction, despite its demonstrated efficiency, was such ridicule from the medical profession that he was driven to suicide.

duce such undesirable side effects as diarrhea, constipation, low blood sugar, and colicky behavior. Breastfed babies are less likely than bottlefed babies to contract skin disorders and infections of the lungs and throat, and they develop far fewer allergies.

In the first two or three days after birth, the mother's breasts are filled not with milk but with colostrum, a thick, yellowish fluid rich in protein, minerals, vitamins (especially vitamins A and C), and disease antibodies, which immunize the newborn against infection and allergic reactions after leaving the protection of the mother's body.

Colostrum is mildly laxative and helps clear the baby's digestive tract after birth. The proportion of colostrum in the milk gradually decreases and the fluid thins, until at the end of the first month the breasts produce milk alone.

The protein in breast milk is completely used by the baby. In contrast, half the protein of cow's milk is excreted. This means that a baby has to take in twice as much cow's milk as mother's milk to get the same amount of body-building protein. Some of the plumpness we sometimes see in babies is early obesity from taking in extra amounts of cow's milk to supply the need.

There are signs that
breastfeeding in public might
someday again become acceptable.

Good nutrition is important during infancy, especially in the first nine months, when the brain and nervous system are developing rapidly and need an ample supply of protein. Adequate amounts of essential nutrients are a necessity for optimal physical and psychological development.

Nutrition is important for the mother too. Although most women are careful about their diet during pregnancy, they may not be aware that their nutritional needs are almost as great during breastfeeding. A pregnant woman needs two thirds more protein than one who is not pregnant, and a breastfeeding mother needs 50 percent more protein than normal. Some breastfeeding mothers who supplement their diets with extra protein, vitamins, and minerals find a noticeable alleviation of postbirth depression, which is occasionally caused only by fatigue and less than adequate nutrition.

The very last swallows of breast milk are especially rich in milk fat, and it is this fat that gives the baby a contented, well-fed feeling. A baby who is not breastfed and therefore does not get that fat content at the end of a feeding tends to become hungry sooner even if he or she has drunk a larger than usual quantity of formula or cow's milk.

Besides, nowadays we take into our systems enough artificial ingredients and chemicals without starting so soon after birth. As for the argument that human milk has a higher level of DDT than cow's milk, that level is not dangerous — so far. The allowable level of DDT in cow's milk is 1/10,000 the dose needed to produce illness. Although the level in human milk is higher than that, it is nevertheless within safe limits.* Furthermore, the nutritional advantages of human milk far outweigh the disadvantages of DDT. (A more intelligent solution would be to stop all use of DDT and the other chlorinated hydrocarbons more recently developed as DDT substitutes.) During nuclear testing several years ago cow's milk was found to have eleven times as much strontium 90 as human milk.

Breastfeeding is also easier for mother and baby. It is convenient, spontaneous, and natural. Bottlefeeding, on the other hand, entails a procedure. Apart from the washing up and sterilization, there are other nuisances. Sometimes the rubber nipple of a bottle does not function properly because the hole is too small or too big. In the case of the oldfashioned bottles, to maintain milk flow, air frequently has to be let in by standing the bottle up.

The tendency is to emphasize the means of feeding — bottles, rubber nipples, mixing, sterilization, and apparatus — which creates a subtle change in the quality of the experience. Even with the newer types of bottles, which have an inner bag to eliminate a vacuum and ensure a continuous milk flow, the mother may tend to become more involved in the devices than in the baby's feelings and needs and her own natural responses. What was to be a tender, relaxed, intimate, and above all spontaneous experience tends to become a process.

---

*Marvin S. Eiger and Sally Wendkos Olds, *The Complete Book of Breastfeeding,* New York, Bantam, 1973, p. 33.

BREASTFEEDING AND THE BABY'S
EXPERIENCE OF REALITY

There is also the psychological aspect of breastfeeding. The baby gets milk from a bottle by sucking but gets milk from the breast by pressing the gums to the areola, the darker-skinned area around the mother's nipple. (The baby gets hardly any milk from the nipple itself but sucks to hold the nipple in the mouth as an anchor.) Feeding is hard work. The baby sometimes actually breaks into a sweat—but that is caused mostly by the liquid passing into the bloodstream and being distributed around the body. And the baby's work is psychologically beneficial: it takes time to get milk. Gratification does not come too easily, which would be unreal, nor is it unusually hard to attain either. That would be equally unreal.

In contrast, feeding the baby milk through a rubber nipple with a large hole in it may make feeding a too easy, passive swallowing experience for the baby and thus might tend to encourage the baby to hang on to a passive mode of functioning. A baby could, in fact, develop the unconscious expectation that pleasures flow without effort—and become unhappy when reality proves otherwise. It is precisely through these subtleties that a baby gradually develops a sense of the quality of living in the world and learns how to adapt to it for his or her greater wellbeing.

BREASTFEEDING AS AN EMOTIONAL EXPERIENCE
FOR MOTHER AND BABY

Perhaps most important, breastfeeding as an emotional experience seems to have the edge over bottlefeeding for both mother and child—although, as we shall see, bottlefeeding properly handled can hold its own quite well psychologically. For the baby who was once part of the mother and now feeds from her body, breastfeeding provides a soothing continuity. The baby feels the mother's heartbeat and rhythms, which may give him or her some deep sense of satisfaction. What the baby wants is not the correct food at the correct temperature in some clinical dosage but mother's warmth, closeness, and enjoyment in feeding. Her pleasure comes across as love. A baby who feels loved not only loves in return but loves himself or herself as well. We never feel so good about ourselves as when we are loved by another.*

Some women are afraid that breastfeeding will tie them down to their baby. But most mothers speak of feelings of joy in nursing their baby and feel that nursing can be consistent with their self-fulfillment, although it may mean temporarily postponing a structured career or redesigning a work schedule.

For the nursing mother there is the physical pleasure of breastfeeding. Though relatively rare, some women even experience an orgasm while nursing, a clear demonstration that breastfeeding is an intimate part of female sexuality. There is an additional psychological pleasure: breastfeeding is something that only a woman can do.

Some mothers welcome breastfeeding because it compels them to sit down, relax, and take time off from all the chores that need to get done. Breastfeeding becomes a rest period, a quiet interlude in an otherwise hectic day.

An occasional bottlefeeding may supplement breastfeeding so that the father can participate and give the mother time off. These supplementary bottlefeedings also help on those occasions when a babysitter is used. If too many feedings are skipped, however, the mother will feel discomfort in the breasts similar to engorgement.

The mother who has no objection to breastfeeding finds that it offers a side benefit. Breastfeeding releases oxytocin, a hormone that causes the uterus to contract rhythmically as the baby sucks the breast. This helps bring her figure back to normal faster. She can actually feel her body tightening up. If the mother breastfeeds her baby on the delivery table, which she can do if she is not drugged, the sucking on her nipple stimulates her uterus to contract in expulsive waves that push out the placenta easily and quickly.

Breastfeeding also has the effect of reducing fertility as if doing things the natural way has the psychologically benign

*In this connection, we cannot help noting the advantages of prepared childbirth. Some medications typically given during labor interfere with a baby's ability to suck *for as much as four days after birth*. If a mother tries to breastfeed a baby who has been unintentionally drugged through her placenta, she may experience the sadly common frustration of seeing her new baby not respond to her offered breast. When this happens mothers mistakenly assume that they are in some way at fault or fear that there is something wrong with their baby or assume that they were wrong to insist on breastfeeding, that their friends or the hospital nursing staff who tried to persuade them to bottlefeed were right after all. Meanwhile their unrelievedly engorged breasts make the experience even more depressing and usually painful as well.

result of spacing children. Nursing suspends the menstrual cycle if the baby breastfeeds exclusively and frequently.* *But it would be best not to count on breastfeeding as a method of contraception.*

Although for nearly all women it takes weeks or even months to fully recuperate from labor and delivery trauma to tissues, studies indicate that women who nurse show an earlier interest in sex in the postbirth period than mothers who bottlefeed.† This may be due to the earlier return to size of the uterus and the stimulation of the breasts.

If a mother's dislike of breastfeeding is strong, her baby would probably be psychologically better off with bottlefeeding. Also, if she knows she must return to work after only a few months, it might be better to start with the bottle rather than switch abruptly on her first day of work. Breastfeeding should never be done unwillingly because it is "better." It is not better if a mother hates it while she is doing it. It is important, however, for her own growth and satisfaction to be in touch with the reasons for her decision.

If a fear of sagging breasts is responsible for her aversion to breastfeeding it might be helpful to know that it is pregnancy that enlarges breasts hormonally, to prepare them for milk giving, not breastfeeding. Therefore, engorgement may occur even in women who do not breastfeed. With breastfeeding, the darker pigmentation disappears and breast size returns to normal once nursing ends. In fact, according to some medical opinion, breasts that have never been used for feeding are more likely to lose their shape or droop. Good bra support and exercise during pregnancy and lactation will protect lengthened breast muscles.

If a woman has deeper fears about breastfeeding, she might use the following checklist to discover what those fears might be. Insight into fears coupled with information about the realities of problems is sometimes enough to resolve them. Verbalizing these fears to her pediatrician, her husband, a close friend, or especially someone who has enjoyed nursing can help to dispel them.

---

*In areas of the world where mothers nurse as a normal part of their daily routine, the menstrual cycle may be suspended for as much as eighteen months, so that babies are naturally separated by up to two years or more, which generally benefits both mother and children, since she can make each her central concern for a longer period.
†Eiger and Olds, *The Complete Book of Breastfeeding*, p. 136.

Would she be embarrassed if her parents or other relatives saw her breasts exposed? She could ask to be allowed her right to privacy.

Is she afraid her husband might become jealous? She could discuss his feelings with him.

Is she afraid of breast cancer? Breastfeeding does *not* cause breast cancer. In fact, there is evidence to suggest that women who breastfeed have a lower incidence of breast cancer than those who do not.

Is she afraid she might enjoy physical pleasure in breast-feeding, feel sexually stimulated? That is virtually universal and perfectly natural.

If this is not her first child, is she afraid that breastfeeding the baby will make an older child jealous? Since time immemorial children have watched their baby brothers and sisters being breastfed without themselves suffering any harm.

Is she afraid that she might do a bad job? The first few feedings might be awkward for her, but practice will make it easier.

Is she afraid of the pain of biting or abrasion? It will be many months before the baby can bite, and her pediatrician can explain ways to avoid abrasion.

Some women are afraid that their breasts are too small to produce enough milk to nourish their baby. But size is irrelevant. Small breasts can produce surprisingly large quantities of milk. Even flat-chested women can breastfeed successfully. If the mother maintains regular and frequent breastfeeding with only an occasional bottle in between, her breasts will continue to produce milk at a rate that keeps up with her baby's needs—even if she has twins or triplets. The baby's sucking stimulates the breasts to produce, aided by an increased intake of liquids (and protein, calcium, and iron supplements to supply the mother's body needs).

BOTTLEFEEDING CAN BE PSYCHOLOGICALLY JUST AS GOOD AS BREASTFEEDING

In feeding, what matters most is not whether breast or bottle is used but the spirit in which the feeding is done. There is no better reason to bottlefeed than an emotional preference for it. If a mother were to breastfeed as a duty, her dislike of it would be communicated to her baby. For both, bottlefeeding would certainly be preferable to breastfeeding if breastfeeding were done angrily, resentfully, or mechanically. Feeding as an emotionally cold act would be as dissatisfying to a baby as making love coldly would be to an adult. What a baby needs almost as much as a supplier of needs is a cheerful and loving friend, and that means that a mother must feel comfortable with whichever feeding method she chooses. What is essential is that she enjoy watching the baby eat and fill up on the warm milk she gives and that the baby take pleasure in being fed by her. But whether she breastfeeds or bottlefeeds, it *is* important that she feed on demand.

Feeding is an emotional experience. It is *the* emotional experience of infancy. It is important, therefore, for the mother to feel good about her particular way of feeding her baby. If she prefers bottlefeeding, that would be psychologically just as healthy as breastfeeding provided that she does the bottlefeeding as though she were breastfeeding. That is, even after the baby can hold the bottle without help, she snuggles the baby against her exposed breasts rather than against clothing and allows the baby to gaze up at her face, not away from her. It is this simulation of breastfeeding that makes bottlefeeding a psychologically acceptable alternative. This kind of bottlefeeding gives the baby the same feelings of love, closeness, and security that breastfeeding does, the affectionate physical contact whose importance in early infancy cannot be overstressed.

One serious problem of bottlefeeding is the temptation to prop the bottle up and allow the baby to feed alone and without contact. Bottleholders are available for this purpose, and they are even worse, for they make it possible for the mother to leave the baby for short periods of time. But that is strictly the mother's advantage. The infant will feel anxious at her absence. The baby receiving that kind of mechanical feeding will long for closeness. This seemingly trivial experience could have the effect of lessening the infant's (and later the adult's) feelings of love, tending to make him or her into someone whose responses are emotionally cold and distant. As has become clear from the psychoanalyses of many adults, the sense of being unhappily alone in babyhood leads *invariably* to some degree of depression in adulthood.

It is important for a baby's psychological wellbeing to be held and comforted while feeding, to look at mother and have her look back, to take in her face and good feelings along with her milk. The experience of eating alone is not too different from the adult feeling of dissatisfaction at a solitary meal in the impersonal atmosphere of a cafeteria as compared with the pleasure and warmth of eating at home with someone whose company is enjoyed.

Another problem with bottlefeeding is that the washing up and sterilization procedures need advance preparation to avoid the frustration of delay for the baby. But what cannot be done in advance is heating up the milk or the formula. That must be done while the baby waits. Bottlefeeding makes visiting and traveling a nuisance too.

As an adult you can manage to take care of your own needs because you are capable of tolerating delay in the gratification of those needs. A baby's needs depend on the parent: gratification may not be postponed for too long without damage. If feeding is a problem for the mother—if her baby does not respond the way she would like or feeds for too long or too short a time—rather than feel resentful or confused about her role, she should consult her pediatrician or seek professional advice from a counselor or from members of La Leche League.*

Feeding is *the* emotional
experience of infancy.

BRINGING UP THE BUBBLE

After and often during a feeding, a baby needs to be burped to bring up any air bubbles that might be trapped in the stomach and that could cause extreme discomfort. More than just physical pain, colic can cause psychological distress. If from time to time during a feeding you hold the baby in an upright position, whether facing away from you or leaning against you with face over your shoulder, the air bubble will generally tend to come up by itself, although you might gently rub the baby's back a little to help. Or you might lay the baby

*La Leche League was founded in 1956 by a group of mothers to help teach other mothers how to breastfeed successfully and easily. Today the League comprises over 1,000 groups around the world, with many doctors on its medical advisory board. If you live in a large city, you can find a branch of the League listed in your telephone directory. If not, you can write to La Leche League International, 9616 Minneapolis Avenue, Franklin Park, Illinois 60131, for information about the branch nearest you.

in your lap on his or her stomach with the head to one side. In this position a bubble comes up more easily. If after several minutes there is no belch and the baby doesn't seem to be in pain, there probably is not much air in the stomach.

Occasionally a baby stops feeding because he or she feels full after a small amount. It may be that air has been swallowed and the stomach is bloated. If you bottlefeed, to prevent the baby from swallowing quantities of air, tilt the bottom of the bottle up to make sure the nipple remains full at all times. Ready-made nipples sometimes have too large a hole and *pour* milk down the baby's throat. It is better to buy a nipple without a hole and make your own hole in it. After you have burped the baby, if a large bubble has come up, try offering the breast or bottle again. With the trapped air gone from the stomach the baby may want more food. But don't insist. With breastfeeding less air is swallowed and less burping needs to be done.

Sometimes the belch is a very loud one, almost raucously adult-sounding. It is a good precaution to put a towel or diaper over your shoulder because very often the belch is accompanied by a small quantity of milk, usually curdled and — especially with formulas or cow's milk — strong-smelling. Curdled mother's milk never smells unpleasant.

Some mothers arbitrarily burp their babies every so often in a businesslike way, even though the baby wants to go on feeding. One such mother was observed burping her baby for half the "feeding" time, administering well over 1,500 pats on the back.*

THE NEED FOR SUCKING

Even after a feeding has been completed a baby's mouth will continue to make sucking movements. Babies also suck during sleep. After a month or two they discover their hands, and when they learn how to bring their hands to their mouths they begin to suck their fingers and thumbs. All babies have a need for the pleasure of sucking — merely sucking, entirely unconnected with nutrition. It is a need for the lips and mouth to work in a kind of muscular satisfaction.

In fact, according to some authorities, the emotional tension

*Sylvia Brody and Sidney Axelrad, "Mother-Infant Interaction: Feeding and Tension Tolerance at Six Months," a film with commentary, presented at the New York Psychoanalytic Society, May 13, 1969.

created by insufficient use of the mouth is actually greater than the tension created by delaying a feeding. If there is no nipple to suck on, a baby will naturally suck on a corner of a blanket or a thumb or finger. Thumbsucking is so natural that it sometimes begins in the uterus, where the thumb sometimes finds its way into the baby's mouth. Babies have been known to be born with a calloused thumb.

The sucking instinct is strongest in the first three months of life. The longer a baby's feeding sessions last, the less sucking is needed on thumb or object. Babies who are not held and fondled, which reassures and satisfies them, show more need for thumbsucking, which is a way of reassuring and satisfying themselves.

Because the baby makes no distinction between the mother's body and his or her own, thumbsucking is to a baby no different from sucking the breast. When the mother is not present, the pleasurable sensations of sucking her breast are substituted by thumbsucking. The discovery that the baby's own hand "is always present whereas the mother's breast periodically disappears probably serves as the first distinction between a body of one's own and an outer world."* Thumbsucking is a step toward independence.

Breastfeeding satisfies the sucking instinct better than bottlefeeding does, because with bottlefeeding the mother can see when the bottle is empty and will generally take it away, whereas the breastfeeding mother, not knowing when her breasts are empty, tends to let her baby suck contentedly for a while longer even though the baby may not be getting any more milk. Thus the baby not only gets a sufficient amount of food but temporarily exhausts the need for sucking.

IS THUMBSUCKING BAD?

Although babies who are not held and fondled show more need for sucking, thumbsucking does not in itself indicate emotional disturbance. *All children suck their thumbs,* and most of them are happy and have no problems.

Generally the need for sucking diminishes in the second half of the first year. After that, thumbsucking is often not just an indication of a need to make sucking motions but also a way of providing self-comfort or pleasure. Here too its persistence is

*Anna Freud, "Infants Without Families," in *The Writings of Anna Freud,* Vol. III, 1939–1945, New York, International Universities Press, 1973, p. 600.

not a cause for anxiety. Thumbsucking usually disappears spontaneously by the time the child is between three and six years old, *usually the latter.* It seldom persists beyond the growth of the second teeth.

Attempts to stop thumbsucking are generally futile: the urge will merely take some other form of expression because the need to suck is instinctual. Sometimes the attempt to stop thumbsucking only increases it. Nobody likes to be told what to do, especially not a baby. A sudden and premature prohibition of an instinctual pleasure might make the infant rebellious and more of a thumbsucker. Or the prohibition might make the baby anxious, and he or she may seek to allay the anxiety through, ironically, the comfort of thumbsucking. The attempt to stop thumbsucking by applying something bitter-tasting to the thumbs and fingers or by putting on mittens develops in the child complicated feelings about pleasure and your love.*

Thumbsucking is a step toward independence.

Some parents, because of their own upbringing, become anxious and try to stop the baby from thumbsucking or sucking the blanket because they fear the baby will not outgrow it. Prematurely thwarted, the sucking instinct remains clamorous, and the baby tends to need these transitional objects for a longer time. Of course, when this happens the parent mistakenly feels that the thumbsucking should have been stopped sooner. The baby got used to the thumb or blanket and now can't do without it. The reverse, of course, is more likely to be the case. The parent might have let the thumbsucking go on longer and the baby would have outgrown the need, with no great problem about giving it up.

Some attempts to stop thumbsucking appear to succeed — until it is discovered that the child has developed nailbiting instead. Or bedtime rituals make their appearance. Reading before sleep, for example, if it is compulsive, is a later substitute for the comfort of thumbsucking.

*The importance of the thumb to human psychological functioning might be better appreciated by knowing that the area of the brain serving the thumb is as large as that serving both lower limbs. Gordon Rattray Taylor, *The Science of Life,* New York, McGraw-Hill Book Company, 1963, p. 204.

As long as behavior happens at an appropriate age it is generally best to let it play itself out in its time. The appropriate age in thumbsucking is the first six years of life. If you keep taking the baby's thumb out of the mouth, you will frustrate the baby to no avail. That will not put an end to thumbsucking. If you force matters, you will succeed only at great psychological cost. The instinct will find other paths for expressing itself. Instincts can only be diverted into new paths, not stopped.

If the child still thumbsucks after the age of six, you can help the child to relinquish the pleasure by explaining that it is acceptable to suck one's thumb but it is not an adult thing to do. Grownups don't suck their thumbs — something the child will now become aware of because you are pointing it out. This is not condemnatory and it makes the child think about it.

Maybe some time much later — say, two years later — you might casually mention the subject again, *once*. You have on your side a desire on the child's part to emulate you and join the world of grownups. You provide the incentive to think about not sucking the thumb any more. Eventually, as the child begins to view the matter in this light, and as the instinctual need to suck diminishes, the thumbsucking will stop for the best possible reason: not out of a fear of incurring your annoyance but more positively, out of a wish to be grown up. In the great majority of cases, thumbsucking goes away by itself, whereas coercion causes problems. Forbidding behavior only forces it underground.

But don't be surprised if your child occasionally thumbsucks long after you thought he or she had given it up. We all regress in moments of stress. An adult encountering a situation of stress might pour himself a drink, light a cigarette, or bring fingers to the mouth as though "thoughtfully." Those are "adult" expressions of thumbsucking.

PACIFIERS

Some authorities believe that pacifiers are not intrinsically bad and even have the advantage of being easier to give up than the thumb because they are less satisfying. Also they are less "autoerotic": they at least are an *outside* object. But we have already seen that a baby does not distinguish between the self and outside objects. Others say that providing a baby with a pacifier lowers any incentive to explore the world. Although it might be argued that early satisfaction could make for less inquisitiveness, we might wonder if satisfactions extinguish curiosity.

Pacifiers are like thumbsucking: both are transitional. The transition is from the baby's feeling him- or herself a part of the mother to feeling separate and independent. To discourage either pacifiers or thumbsucking would be to deal with a symptom rather than the cause. The baby has continuing needs, in this case to feel soothed and comforted, and when those needs have exhausted themselves, the external expression of the needs falls away.

Some mothers have been known to put a pacifier into the baby's mouth as a means of silencing the baby. This could of course run counter to developmental needs by encouraging and therefore artificially prolonging this earliest mode of satisfaction and by using the pacifier as a substitute for mother's attention, which is what the baby might really be needing at that moment.

FEEDING IS LOVE

A baby needs both milk and love. In a sense the baby needs neither one more than the other. In the beginning milk is virtually synonymous with love.

As we have said, it is not breastfeeding as opposed to bottlefeeding that is of the greatest importance psychologically but rather the climate of feeling, and that is why the mother's pleasure is quite important, as is everything relative to the baby's mouth and feeding. Feeding should above all be a pleasant experience, filled with a quiet contentment for both mother and baby. She reclines on a couch or sits in a comfortable chair or rocking chair, with a soft pillow under her arm to help support the baby's body. She looks at her baby and finds this tiny new creature fascinating. Every one of the baby's movements and sounds while eating are exciting. At times she is moved by the experience. And when the baby's lips broaden into a smile at her while they attempt at the same time to continue sucking, she feels a thrill of pleasure and wants to laugh happily. This emotional "feeding" she gives the baby (they are really giving it to *each other*), which the baby feels as warmth and love, will help the baby grow to be a warm and loving person. Feeding and love are not separable at the beginning of life. Both are nutrition, physical and emotional. Food is love.

Mere feeding and physical protection make it certain that the baby will survive, but life is more than survival. A baby fed in a cold manner — whether in a bassinet with propped bottle in the mouth or at mother's breast for a "dutiful" feeding — would be left "hungry" by being deprived of the emotional side of the feeding experience, the warm interaction. The baby not only enjoys being hugged and talked to and smiled at while being fed, he or she absolutely requires it. Fortunately for the baby — and the world — most mothers enjoy the same things and are quite willing to meet the need.

WEANING

Weaning is the transition from sucking to get food from the breast or bottle to feeding from cup or spoon. It is a mistake to think of weaning as "taking away" the breast or bottle. Much more positively, weaning means introducing a baby to new foods and a new method of eating. It is a step forward, not a deprivation.

Nutritionally and psychologically, weaning should begin between the seventh and eleventh months, preferably the latter. (Breastfed babies do not require solid foods as early as bottlefed babies because the nutrition supplied by mother's milk is superior.) It is regrettable that many pediatricians recommend earlier weaning, sometimes for reasons so flimsy ("It's good for the baby to begin to get accustomed to new tastes") that they sound like a kindly attempt to "indulge" the breastfeeding mother at the expense of the baby. If the mother has been breastfeeding, waiting to wean until the baby is ten or eleven months old means that the baby can go directly — but *slowly,* of course — to the cup or spoon (not fork) without the interim step of bottles. To go from breast to cup in a direct way is psychologically more beneficial to the baby — the fewer changes and steps to get used to, the better — and physically the more practical for the mother. At less than seven months, the baby would have trouble with cup or spoon, and weaning would be more difficult. By nine, ten, or eleven months, enough teeth have come in to make weaning to solids feel quite natural.

Dr. Winnicott says that an indication that weaning can be

achieved without adverse effects is when the baby begins to throw toys from the crib or playpen onto the floor. Toward the end of the first year a baby seems to delight in hurling objects. He or she takes an obvious pleasure in getting rid of things, and Dr. Winnicott suggests that this indicates a readiness for the baby to "get rid of" the breast, at least for some of the time.* Perhaps, the last feeding of the day might be at the breast because at night everyone tends to regress, and as Dr. Winnicott says, this regression is in the rhythm of life.

According to those who advocate breastfeeding most strongly, weaning should last from the time the baby is nine months to two years old. Although nutritionally there may be good reasons for so long a transition, and although mothers who enjoy breastfeeding do not find a long weaning process tiresome, from the psychological standpoint a few months of weaning are probably good enough. It is important to bear in mind that weaning is an individual matter. Some babies need more sucking than others. Some are conservative and others are quite adventurous and daring. Both patterns are normal.

Food is love.

When you give the baby a cup to drink from, drink from a cup yourself. Mimicry is the most natural way to learn at this age.

TEETHING AND THE IMPORTANCE OF TRANSITIONS

When a baby is between three and seven months of age the first teeth begin to come in. Teething is an uncomfortable time for the baby and also for the breastfeeding mother. Now, in addition to flailing and crying, the baby has a new means of displaying aggressiveness: biting. To a breastfeeding mother this often seems like a good time to wean, almost a "natural" time. A bottlefeeding mother might find that she needs new rubber nipples quite frequently.

But weaning at this time would be wrong for two reasons. The baby could place the biting and the weaning in a cause-

*D. W. Winnicott, *Mother and Child,* New York, Basic Books, 1965, p. 91.

and-effect relation with a wrong conclusion. The baby might feel that he or she is being weaned because of the biting and that therefore self-assertiveness is "bad," punishable by the loss of the breast or bottle — which is felt to be a loss of love as well.

Secondly, a baby needs a transition, time to see that, although he or she may be biting, the mother doesn't stop loving or feeding. If the biting chafes the mother's nipple, she might switch the baby to the other breast. In this way she allows a healthy self-assertiveness to emerge confidently, according to a new developmental thrust, which to the baby feels natural and right.

If the biting actually hurts the mother, she should not be afraid of reacting — provided that she continues the feeding. The pain is real, and it is good for a baby to learn that it is not acceptable to hurt anyone. However, she must take care to *react without rejecting.* The mother's reaction is the baby's first knowledge that some actions are wrong or "bad."

Precisely because a baby tends to see cause and effect where

Weaning is an individual matter.
---

none exists, it is critical to time the occurrence of the psychologically important events of life. If any important events happen very close together, they might be misunderstood as necessarily connected. ("Important" refers to the baby's experience.) Therefore, it is best not to wean the baby when the parents are about to go off alone on vacation or even for just a weekend, leaving the baby with a grandparent. That could have a devastating effect. The baby might associate weaning (in fact, *development*) with losing the mother.

A gradual transition is always best. The baby needs time to adapt to new experiences. In the first six or nine months, much of the baby's life is taken up with oral pleasures. The baby is getting used to living in the world, is more at ease with the parents, and has worked out a rapport with breast or bottle and the small amount of the family environment that he or she perceives. The baby feeds in confidence, becomes interested in all that goes on, and in general enjoys what is now a familiar routine.

Why stress these details—allowing the baby to take the breast when *the baby* wants to and let it go from the mouth when *the baby* wants to, breastfeeding even after teething has started and not stopping abruptly? It is because all subsequent development builds precisely on these details and on the baby's reactions to them. When walking becomes possible the child will soon want to dart off from the parents. Of course the child will fully expect you to be there the moment he or she reconsiders and runs back. This darting away is a forerunner of eventual independence. It is like practicing being alone in the world, even if only for a few seconds and only to go just a few feet away, a fearful distance for a very young child. If the child can accomplish that with a minimum of anxiety, he or she will be encouraged to try to prolong the time "away" from you.

This behavior has a forerunner in feeding. Darting away and back again is a repetition of the earlier experience at the breast, where the baby turned away from the nipple for a moment and then found it again. The baby's confidence in refinding the nipple helps in the later experience of physically leaving mother with no anxiety that she might be lost forever. That is one reason why weaning is best done gradually. It establishes an excellent pattern for growth.

If the mother has been breastfeeding and no longer wants to do so, even though it is best to go gradually from breast to cup, it would do no harm to switch to the bottle for one of the baby's meals each day (and preferably simulating breastfeeding), later increasing that to two or three bottles a day. Those who believe in breastfeeding as dogma regard this suggestion as a dubious compromise. But if it makes the mother feel better, it is a psychologically acceptable compromise provided that the changes are made gradually and the bottlefeeding is as intimate, pleasant, and warm as the breastfeeding was. Perhaps each meal might end with some breastfeeding. That also helps to satisfy the sucking instinct, which continues to play itself out.

4

The Developing Personality

I am my possibilities.

GABRIEL MARCEL

The quality of feeding, so critically important, is the first in a succession of events that form the baby's personality and character. Although thumbsucking, walking, speech, and the other events of infancy and early childhood arise out of innate causes, the impact of the environment, principally the mother, plays a significant role. What is innate and emerging is experienced by the baby in the specific context of your parenting. This interaction of the innately programed and the quality of the environment that you provide shapes the specific personality of the baby.

FEEDING AND SECURITY

In addition to being a nutritional and emotional experience, a baby's feeding is a learning experience. The baby learns something about the nature of the world, to which he or she begins to adapt. When a baby sucks milk, lets go of the breast or bottle, and returns at leisure, the impression builds that it is rather a pleasurable world and one that can be relied on. Good as the breast or bottle is, the baby can let it go without fear of not getting it back. The "good enough" parent doesn't force the nipple into the baby's mouth or take it away prematurely but provides what the baby needs in an atmosphere of calm availability. This calm availability instills in the baby a feeling of security.

FEEDING AND PSYCHOLOGICAL SEPARATION

As early as the first weeks of feeding there was a foreshadowing of the baby's psychological separation by the age of three. If feeding experiences have gone smoothly — being fed on demand, letting go of the breast or bottle and finding it available again when needed — the later letting go of the mother as a person is made easier. The child will be able to let go with confidence, knowing that, just as the source of food was once not lost, mother will not be lost.

FEEDING AND EMOTIONS

If a feeding can be relied on and satisfaction is consistently forthcoming, even though the baby is dependent on a dimly perceived outside person for the gratification of needs, he or she feels reassured that the needs *will* be gratified. The baby begins to feel that expectations have every chance of attaining fulfillment. The feeding experience establishes a pattern of trust and confident expectation. The environment is dependable, and gratification is predictable. The baby whose needs are satisfied has no reason to feel otherwise. In this way, the satisfaction of *physical* needs leads to a positive *psychological* outlook.

Insufficient gratification of a baby's needs gives rise to the opposite feelings, pessimism and distrust. It also leads to feelings of hungry yearning for unattainable things, a vague and indefinable dissatisfaction that extends into adulthood. It is the view of most psychoanalysts that many complicated problems in adult life — alcoholism, drug addiction, compulsive overeating, and other forms of self-defeat — have their origins in large part in consistently poor feeding experiences in the first few months, whether scheduled feeding or premature or abrupt weaning.

THE ORIGINS OF CHARACTER TRAITS

All but the most severe genetic or chemically based psychological problems have their origin in postnatal life, as do character traits as well. Babies are not *born* selfish or generous, for example, nor are they born with emotional problems or a fixed personality. Their experiences in life help create these problems and characterological traits.

It is true that there are constitutional givens that affect character development. But they do not themselves form the whole of character. Psychological problems and character traits are formed by a blend of what is innately given, the parents' influence on the child, and the child's subjective experience of the parents.

Where there is no genetic disorder, the parents are the element having the greatest influence. The mother is the baby's first experience of the world and reality. When the mother responds to the baby she thereby "interprets" the world by reacting to the baby's needs. She "teaches" the baby something of what the world is like. This opportunity is without parallel: never again will the life circumstances of the baby allow of such carefully tailored, growth-promoting influence.

The satisfaction of
physical needs leads to a
positive *psychological* outlook.

The second and third factors—the baby's subjective experience of the parents and the baby's genetic endowment—are related. The parents may provide all that the baby needs, but because of innate physiological and psychological differences, each baby experiences parental care uniquely. That is why the same parents may have two children with strikingly different personalities. All the parents can do is to make themselves available to each baby. It is up to the baby to "make use" of the parents.

THE INFLUENCE OF THE ENVIRONMENT ON CHARACTER

If feeding is not done in a way that consistently satisfies emotional needs, the baby might become anxious and remain in a tense and helplessly expectant state. From this condition feelings might grow that would crystalize as character traits— for example, voraciousness or greed, the feeling that one can never have enough, that the world owes one a living. Or the child might show signs of resentment, being quick to get angry and finding signs of withholding on the part of others even in the absence of any withholding. Or if the feedings are too long delayed, the child might develop the trait of impatience.

Another trait that can develop from poor feeding experiences is impulsiveness — not enjoying things in any deeply satisfying way but grabbing them on the run. A baby experiencing poor feedings might tend to give him- or herself poor "feedings" throughout life, literally eating poorly, as self-deprivation and to undermine health, or eating the wrong things and perpetuating the suffering by the self-denying struggle against obesity, or living an unfulfilling life.

If the parent crams food into the baby, deprives, feeds coldly, shouts, and dumps the baby into bed — or if the parent feeds in a leisurely way, gives affectionate hugs, and enjoys playing, spending time, and talking with the baby — these are what the baby will respond to unconsciously but habitually, and the responses will form the baby's character. There is nothing mysterious or preordained about a person's character and personality.

We noted that consistently poor feeding experiences and the agony of going hungry despite cries for help, if prolonged, can lead not only to a generally pessimistic response to life but to bouts of depression in adulthood. Such experiences build the feeling that to avoid disappointment one should expect nothing. This exaggerated caution joins easily with a feeling of distrust of others, that it is better to rely on no one. Hope doesn't automatically spring eternal. At the beginning of life, it can be destroyed or badly damaged.

Not all character traits are formed in this oral stage of psychosexual development. Some come from later stages. Character traits that derive from the anal stage, for example, are miserliness, excessive orderliness, and stubbornness. When we discuss toileting we will see how the events of that stage of development might give rise to these traits. In the next stage of development, the phallic stage, when boys and girls become aware of their genitals, the traits of competitiveness and envy make their appearance in both sexes.

FUSION

One other psychological development of crucial importance — fusion — should be mentioned, even though its relevance is not immediate.

Freud's dual-instinct theory, although still occasionally attacked by some, has never been satisfactorily superseded. According to this theory, the human infant is born with two instinctual drives, love and aggressiveness.* Whatever the baby may do in life, *all* of it will be powered by these two drives. Every act, every thought, every wish, every fantasy — the impetus of the entire gamut of human behavior is love or aggressiveness.

Neither force operates in a pure state. By the time the child is six months old, each is alloyed — *fused* — with the other. If a person could feel raw aggressiveness with no tempering admixture of love, his or her behavior would exhibit great hatred and violence, as in murder.

Poor feeding experiences can lead
to a pessimistic response to life.

In healthy functioning, feelings of love predominate over aggressive feelings. How does this desirable predominance come about? When the baby's earliest needs are consistently gratified by a loving parent, feelings of love are nurtured and brought out. If, on the contrary, the baby is badly frustrated, a hostile form of aggressiveness erupts in an untamed and unmanageable manner. Both gratification and frustration occur in life at one time or another, of course, but a "good enough" parent, attuned to the baby's needs and tolerance, especially in the all-important first three years, makes certain that the gratifications, offered in an atmosphere of consistency and reliability, outweigh the frustrations. In this simple way feelings of love win out over aggressiveness. Those in whom a healthy fusion has taken place tend to love more than they hate — to be forgiving and understanding. We have stressed so heavily the quality of the feeding experience in the first months because it offers the first and best opportunity to

*As a psychoanalytic term, "aggressiveness" does not share with "aggression" the connotation of destructiveness. "The U.S.S.R. aggresses against Czechoslovakia" implies the military destruction or subjugation of one country by another, but to say that a baby is aggressive implies only that he or she is capable of striving in a healthy way. Even the act of walking requires a degree of psychological aggressiveness: *to make the move.* "Aggressiveness" might be thought of as self-assertiveness — which is, psychologically, a healthy characterological trait.

establish this desirable balance. Nothing fosters psychological development so well as the predominance of love from the outset.

HOW GROWTH HAPPENS

Development is making actual what was only potential. A baby has innate forces that are as inexorably forward-moving, as purposive, and as suited to the task of living as a baby chick's industrious cracking open of its shell and, cocking its head and staring wonder-eyed, stepping out into a fascinating barnyard world. No one needs to explain to the chick how to do that. It instinctively and efficiently does everything it needs to do in order to start in life, and it does so at a level "beyond understanding." In some respects, the human baby does the same.

A brief overview of human psychological development at this point might help clarify such day-to-day events of a baby's life as the feeding we have talked about and, later on, toileting — in fact, all the steps of growth.

The three components of a baby's growth are these: (1) physical maturing, (2) psychological development, and (3) the environment. The three come together and synchronize.

For example, as a baby's leg muscles grow strong (*physical maturing*), the baby feels a *wish* to walk (*psychological development*), and at the first faltering attempts the parents smile encouragingly (*the environment*). Physical maturing is necessary but by itself not enough. Babies who are orphaned in the second half of their first year have maturing leg muscles but, being parentless and cared for in the impersonal atmosphere of a hospital, they lose all desire to move, let alone walk.* They learn to walk much later than normal. Along with the physical maturing there must *at the same time* be the wish to walk. Psychological development and physical maturing must coincide. What facilitates the appearance of the wish at the right time is a welcoming and loving environment — the parents.

Another common example: by approximately two and a half years of age, the anal spincter muscles finally become capable of control (*physically mature*). The child wants to do things in a more adult way (*psychological development*), and therefore, to please the parents (*the environment*), learns to use the toilet.

*René A. Spitz, *The First Year of Life*, New York, International Universities Press, 1965, p. 278.

INNATE FORCES

The child's physical maturing and psychological development are programed by the genetic code, just as an ivy seed is programed to become an ivy vine and no other kind of plant. The genetic code determines the shape of the leaves, the pattern of their spacing, their middle crease, their curl, their ability to cling, and so on. Long before there is any growth at all, these highly specific qualities are present in the seed. They make their appearance in due course, requiring only sun, soil, and rain.

The genetic code is what accounts for your having the same bump on your nose that your mother has on hers. You may have your nose surgically altered, but your son might nevertheless have a similar bump on his nose, because human growth too is genetically programed in the seed. The length and musculature of a person's arms when fully grown, his or her adult height, the appearance and pattern of body hair in adolescence, the quality and pitch of the mature voice – all these aspects of physical maturity are determined within the first half hour of conception, inherited through the genes and chromosomes, and appear in life according to an inner timetable. Similarly, the wish to walk, the need for closeness, the readiness to love, the thrust toward mastery over abilities – in potential form these aspects of psychological development are also determined a half hour after conception. The two processes are reminiscent of those tiny Japanese shells placed in a fish bowl that slowly open to form intricate flower arrangements. The intricacy is there from the start, in potential.

PARENTS ARE THE BABY'S ENVIRONMENT

The environment is the element that varies: you can shape behavior for better or worse. You can modify the development of genetically determined characteristics, thwarting or fostering their unfolding. For example, if you thrust a growing child away from you when there is still a need for closeness, the child will be dependent on you longer, delaying – or blocking forever – the appearance of the innate ability to do things without help.

There is one crucial difference between physical maturing and psychological development. Physical maturing is not so vulnerable to disruption as psychological development. Cells can multiply, glands secrete, and muscles retain *some* degree of tone even in adverse circumstances. But *a baby cannot develop fully psychologically without a benign environment — without you.* Full psychological development absolutely requires the *continuing* presence of loving, guiding parents (or other caretaking adults).

It is not enough for you to tell your child you love him or her. The child must *feel* loved by you, feel surrounded by an atmosphere of love. A baby who is several months old may not think rationally but can sense with remarkable accuracy whether you are happy, depressed, angry, upset, or loving. The baby picks these moods up from the way you talk or look or move your body or pick the baby up. If you are unhappy you might not feel very loving at the moment, and the baby will feel rejected.

Perhaps the saddest creature in the world is a baby whose parents were unhappy to have had a child, or who angrily fight in front of the child or secretly hate the child for causing them to stay together. The child feels unwanted and unloved even though most of the time, when they are not openly fighting, these parents try to hide their feelings. An experience of this kind could make a child smile infrequently, talk seldom, learn little. The child would tend to be anxious and withdrawn. Feeling unwanted would badly affect his or her development, slowing it down or even halting it. The child could develop self-hatred through feeling hated by the ones from whom he or she naturally expects love.

A child has no choice over parents and their personality but is stuck with them for better or worse. Therefore the quality of parenting is decisive: growth comes from an inward thrust but happens always in relation to others who are significant, principally parents. It is impossible to live emotionally unrelated to others in the formative years and develop into a human being in the full sense of the term. Although during gestation the mother creates her child physically, after birth she (and the father also) "creates" the child in a far more subtle way. The mother's and father's own unconscious needs stir to life those particular potentialities in their child that reflect the parents, their abilities, their preferences, and their limitations. Thus a child becomes the specific child of specific parents.

THE ORDERLINESS OF DEVELOPMENT

There is an appropriate time for certain feelings and events. A feeling of omnipotence is normal at three months whereas in adulthood it would be pathological. Experiences belonging to a particular stage of growth promote further development most effectively if those experiences occur in that stage. For the best development, events should happen neither too soon nor too late. Each stage of development builds on the successful completion of the preceding stages.

If some experiences were to come too soon, for example, they would be difficult for a baby or a child to handle and would feel burdensome. To "toilet-train" a baby by the age of one year would be a disturbing experience for the baby, not a growth-promoting one, because the baby's anal sphincter muscles are not yet capable of control. Experiences that come too late or out of sequence may complicate subsequent development. To delay weaning for several years, for example, would work against a child's growing independence, sabotaging it, in all likelihood forever.

Full psychological development requires
the *continuing* presence of loving,
guiding parents (or other caretaking adults).

Some experiences cannot be made up for later on. For example, if you feed a newborn only every four hours and let the baby spend part of each day crying futilely, switching to demand feeding at the age of six months would not undo the psychological damage or significantly alter character traits.

An ordered progression in development means that the events of life are never so haphazard as they seem. They build on each other, an earlier event shaping the direction and outcome of a later event. If in the early days of life a baby experiences consistent gratification of the instinctual need to be fed when hungry and is given love and attention, the imperative quality of that need diminishes: the need peaks out — and then lessens. The baby can move on to the next phase unencumbered by an ungratified need that continues to clamor for satisfaction.

But if in that early stage something should go wrong — if the baby were to be deprived of food and suffer prolonged pains of hunger—that would make the toileting phase more difficult because the baby would arrive at it with feelings of dissatisfaction, unhappiness, and, as a result, complicated feelings toward you. The baby would express the dissatisfaction and unhappiness as a counterforce to your suggestion that he or she use the toilet and would fight you with unexpected stubbornness. Learning to use the toilet would be a lengthy, exasperating affair.

Emotional difficulties never just fall away. They persist unconsciously and use each succeeding phase of development as a possible avenue of solution even if, as frequently happens, the new avenue cannot possibly lead to the satisfaction of past needs. For as long as a problem remains, it continues to seize on any available expression, any channel, any means to work itself out unconsciously.*

That is how emotional problems proliferate until they seem complicated and unfathomable, defying rational sense. Thus in the toileting phase a feeding problem will try to resolve itself through anal pleasures and functions. This is not possible, of course, which is precisely what creates difficulties. Such an attempt only complicates toilet functioning—and this, in *its* turn burdened and complicated, affects the character of succeeding stages of development. And so on through life. If we consider that we are leaving out here the lengthy process of identity formation and such other subtle areas as the development of conscience (superego) and the part played by unconscious fantasies, we can begin to appreciate the intricacy of human growth.

A feeding problem could eventually burden a love relation. If the individual is dependent and never satisfied (feeding problem) and stubborn and argumentative (toilet problem, as you will see), these infantile needs, still clamoring for gratification and still seizing any channel that presents itself, try to work themselves out through another person. "You're supposed to satisfy me—and do it the way *I* want! It's been weeks since you've given me a present!" A love relation thus taxed usually breaks down. There may be no stronger argument for taking extra care in childrearing during the first several years than the knowledge that the deepest happiness in life comes from an enjoyable, lasting relation with another.

*According to Marcus Aurelius, "What prevents a work from being completed becomes the work itself"—a one-sentence summary, incidentally, of the obsessive-compulsive neurosis.

It is useless to try to induce development. A child will do things as he or she becomes capable of or interested in doing them. And certainly it is not advisable to force a child to keep up with a neighbor's child. Although there are definite stages of development and although we have spoken of an inner timetable that applies to all human beings, each child passes through the stages a bit differently from all others. No baby ever develops exactly according to descriptions in books. And living as we do in a conformist society, it is well to remind ourselves as often as we can that a person's uniqueness is the most valuable part of him or her.

THE TRANSMISSION OF PROBLEMS THROUGH GENERATIONS

Problems are transmitted from one generation to the next. In order to break into the cycle, it is important for parents to understand how their own past psychological development affects the psychological development of their child. They might be unconsciously repeating the childrearing patterns laid down by their parents, even though they hated their own upbringing, unless they understand that problems are being passed on in direct or modified form.

A person's uniqueness is the most valuable part of him or her.

Consider the case of a highly intelligent father who was so badly frustrated as a child that his predominant emotion in life became anger, expressed in part as a perpetual contrariness. The anger was so strong in him that he felt threatened by its power and therefore bent over backward to appear a likable, pleasant person. The anger did show in his relations with his six-year-old son: in the guise of "preparing him for the future" the father was quite severe in his demands and seldom spoke to the boy except to give orders or criticize and disapprove. When his wife confronted him with this observation, he claimed he was providing his son with a good preparation for life, whereas she would only coddle and spoil him. He did not understand that the "moral fiber" he was building, as he called it, was merely a pattern of frustrating his son as he had once been frustrated, and that this pattern was not the guidance he thought it was but an expression of the lifelong anger he had so thoroughly covered over.

The little boy grew defiant and rebellious and burned with anger too, developing the symptom of bedwetting and falling back on a sure form of self-comfort: he would surreptitiously fondle his penis for hours, through his pants pockets. The father's parents created problems in the father, and the father in turn transmitted problems to his son as a result. Once begun, the cycle is difficult to interrupt because, as is clear from our example, the transmission of problems is done unconsciously. Possibly the only way, and quite probably the best way, to end the passing of emotional difficulties through the generations is psychotherapy.

IN NORMAL DEVELOPMENT, THINGS FIT

Nothing is more obvious than that these remarks are oversimplifications. But the justification for including them is that they offer a glimpse into some of the complications of psychoanalysis, whose goal is the reduction of the "unfathomable proliferation" of emotional problems to their earliest, simplest component parts, which then permits them to move forward freely with a more natural "fit."

In normal development, things fit. One of the first of these fits in life is the consonance between the baby's need for much loving care, to survive, and the mother's generally powerful feeling of love for the baby in the first months.

Another example from the earliest period is this: if the baby breastfeeds at birth, the colostrum in the mother's breasts clears the mucus from the baby's digestive tract, thus opening the way for better feedings and ensuring minimal gas pains. The mother in turn begins to produce milk a day or two earlier, and it gives her pleasure to see her baby drinking her milk. This good level of lactation in turn increases the release of a hormone called "prolactin," which stimulates the outflow of maternal love.* The mother's pleasure stimulates even more

*"Prolactin causes the mammary glands to produce milk. It also seems to have psychological effects, since laboratory experiments have found that it can induce motherly behavior, even when artificially administered to virgin animals." Marvin S. Eiger and Sally Wendkos Olds, *The Complete Book of Breastfeeding,* New York, Bantam Books, 1973, p. 41.

milk to be let down, and this contented breastfeeding produces oxytocin, causing her uterus to contract rhythmically and return her figure to normal sooner.

Another fit: a newborn cries because of inner distress. The quality of the sound is peculiarly irritating to adult ears, a signal they cannot easily ignore, which forces them to respond, and the baby is cared for.

Later, a baby who has just learned to stand up and walk trips and falls easily. The baby is not bothered by these spills, and no one worries about them, because of another fit: the falls come at a time in life when bones are soft and the body flexible. In old age they could be fatal.

One more example of fit is the transition from demand feeding to the eventual eating more or less on schedule. A baby's feeding on demand may be perfectly acceptable to a new mother, who for the many months of pregnancy might have wondered how it would feel to offer her breast to the mouth of a baby. But after a time the novelty wears off and she tires of breastfeeding. When the baby is five or six months old, every once in a while she might try skipping a snack that she feels the baby only halfheartedly wants but doesn't really need. The baby's increased readiness to adapt to a schedule and budding capacity for a small degree of independence fit in with her need to be less tied down.

A natural fit is like skin on flesh—unquestioned, taken for granted. There is thus an easy complementarity in the mother's eventual wish to be free of her child at times and the child's increasing ability and desire to be less dependent on her. This particular fit works so well and so naturally that the mother avails herself of it without necessarily being conscious of it. If she should ever get the feeling that things are too much for her, she doesn't ignore it as "unworthy" of a mother but respects it and takes time out to do things for herself. The baby, equipped by nature to do so, adapts to her, and she feels good about that. This relaxed attitude is not selfish of her—far from it. Her easygoing feeling refreshes her, which helps her to continue the work of mothering with a sense of renewal.

5

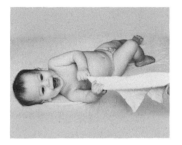

Completing the First Three Months

A smile is a language that even a baby understands.

Popular saying

The first three months of life constitute the most impressive transition a human ever undertakes—from nonbeing to being, from womb to world, from physiological structure to biological organism—and the shadowy beginnings of a psychological self. They are also the most formative months. Whatever the baby's experiences are during this earliest period, whether painful or pleasurable, each will leave a lifelong, indelible stamp on the baby's psyche.

FROM DEMAND TO SCHEDULED FEEDING

Demand feeding ultimately settles into a more or less scheduled feeding pattern. What was desirable at an earlier age may not be desirable or appropriate at a later one, because an individual's needs seldom remain exactly the same. At the very beginning of life it is better for a baby to be fed whenever feeding is needed, night or day. Beginning around the third month, however, it is easier on everyone, including the baby, for the baby to eat rather more regularly, on a schedule that loosely fits the family's lifestyle. The baby learns to wait for increasingly long intervals between feedings, which makes it possible for a feeding schedule to be arranged gradually, based on the baby's new abilities, not imposed by theory. The effect of loosely scheduled feedings at the age of three or four months, when the baby can tolerate delay (because he or she has become accustomed to a degree of frustration and in addition knows by the parent's signs that a feeding in on its way), is quite different from the effect that the same schedule would have had at the age of three or four days. Then it would have been painful starvation.

At six weeks old, if the baby is gaining weight and looks healthy, the feeding in the middle of the night might be eliminated. As a first step, you might begin by not responding immediately to the baby's crying. (Rushing to pick a baby up at the very first moment of crying would indicate anxiety on your part, and that would be communicated to the baby, who would feel that whatever he or she is crying about is terrible.) You might let the baby awaken and cry a bit. If the sounds are not desperate or angry, you might let them go on a while longer before responding. If the crying stops in a moment or two, perhaps the baby's need was not great. If, however, the crying persists, you might feed after all and next time let the crying go on a bit longer. In two or three weeks the baby will be able to forgo the feeding in the middle of the night.

The tolerance for frustration
fosters psychological development.

If the baby can tolerate your not responding for short periods of time, encourage this new ability to wait. Meanwhile, you will get more sleep, and the early-morning feedings will begin to approximate your normal breakfast schedule, a change that the baby will find congenial and that will fit your needs as well. As you get more sleep and feel refreshed for the next day's work, your feeling of wellbeing will benefit the baby too.

TOLERANCE FOR DELAY

Tolerance for the postponement of pleasure is acquired by the baby between two and six months of age. At the outset of life, the baby only clamored for his or her needs to be met and you were prompt in responding to those needs, making sure that there was consistently more gratification than frustration. In fact, it was precisely the consistency that made it possible for the baby to learn to postpone gratification: consistency made for predictability. The baby became able to put off pleasure, knowing that it would be forthcoming because you had always been reliable up till then.

The ability to tolerate delay is remarkable. It is impossible at the beginning of life, yet only a few months later and long before the brain is fully formed the baby achieves the ability to endure the discomfort of hunger pangs. A parent's role undergoes a change to reinforce the new ability. Earlier, before the baby knew about cues, it did not matter that he or she saw what you were doing as you prepared to give a feeding. Your movements had no meaning related to eating. Now the baby reads the signs showing that you are aware that the baby is hungry and that you are preparing to feed. And the baby begins to be expectant. To nurture this new ability to wait, you become sensitive to the baby's expectancy. By your movements and activities — making sounds that are familiar, getting the bottle ready, opening the refrigerator door — you give indications that food will soon be on the way. And in fact you do offer it soon. It is this meeting of expectation and looked-for gratification that convinces the baby that you are both on the same wavelength and consolidates the ability to wait.

The tolerance for delay is remarkable for another reason. It amounts to an ability to withstand the frustration of an instinct with all the power of its drive — no small achievement. And it is worthy of note that a baby is capable of attaining this even before being able to sit up. This growing capacity to deal with increasing amounts of frustration leads to greater adaptability in dealing with the real world, especially later, when frustration will be encountered in abundance. The tolerance for frustration fosters psychological development by compelling the child to call on inner resources to deal with problems — to try to work things out on his or her own. Immediate gratification is no longer an absolute necessity.

The value of frustration, if it is not of overwhelming intensity, is that it emphasizes a highly important fact about the real world: achievements require effort. Things don't happen merely because a person wishes them to. Wishing is a pleasant but by itself wholly futile activity.

The ability to delay pleasures has a far-reaching outcome in mental functioning. A person who cannot tolerate delay *must* act immediately and according to whatever will bring the quickest pleasure, however detrimental that pleasure might prove to be. But a person who is capable of delay and can tolerate a degree of discomfort can weigh consequences and consider alternatives before choosing the most advantageous route to longer-range pleasures. Thus the person who can delay becomes capable of somewhat more extended thought, which facilitates the exercise of judgment. Judgment, as a faculty, is perhaps one of the most important benefits that derive from the ability to postpone pleasure.

The ability to postpone pleasure also offers a benefit to parents. A baby learning to tolerate larger and larger quantities of tension can wait for increasing periods of time before the frustration becomes "too much." This makes life easier for parents in that the baby's demands become less imperious and less frequently voiced.

THE POSITIVE USES OF FRUSTRATION

None of this means that parents should deliberately set out to frustrate a child. Life itself is a succession of frustrations. The very first frustration is the baby's emergency need for oxygen at birth, which "forces" him or her to use the lungs. This is soon followed by the frustration of hunger, which "forces" the use of mouth and lips to suck. Later comes the frustration of weaning, which "forces" greater physical separation from mother – and so on. Each of these frustrations, coming in its natural time and in an appropriate dosage, teaches a baby something more about living in the world. Manageable frustrations impel change.

To take a familiar example, we said in Chapter 1 that although during pregnancy you may have doubts about whether you are mature enough to be a parent and feel frustrated at not being able to cope easily, the responsibility of caring for a baby forces you into a new and unsuspected level of maturity. Frustration is like the periodic dry spells that force plants to grow longer roots to reach the moisture at deeper levels of soil. As a result, the plants grow stronger root systems and flourish more than ever.

Another, more subtle reason that frustration is beneficial to a baby's development is that it causes the baby to experience him- or herself *as* a self. Frustration has the special feature of emphasizing the separateness of the baby – the gratification of needs *must* come from outside. There *must* be another person, because if that were not so, the baby could gratify his or her own needs, and frustration would never be experienced.

THE TAMING OF AGGRESSIVE FEELINGS

Frustrations arouse hostile feelings, but if frustrations are kept low, feelings of love toward others begin to predominate over all other feelings. Slowly the baby's powerful instinctual drives — especially the aggressive drive — become more tamed and gentle, though no less strong because of that.

Psychic energy exists in a raw state at birth. Through taming, the energy becomes converted into a form that the baby can use for further psychological development. The energy no longer discharges explosively: it becomes productive by working through channels. If psychic energy were to remain in an untamed state, it would be like an automobile that is not in gear: the motor may be accelerated but it can only roar uselessly. Its power is wasted. Untamed aggressiveness reveals itself in adults who fight, become enraged (even if the rage is permanently suppressed), or feel hatred toward those around them — and toward themselves. They expend psychic energy unproductively.

As aggressive feelings become tamed, even though feedings may be delayed, the baby's love for you, being the predominant feeling, will outweigh any anger or aggressiveness he or she might feel, because the baby doesn't perceive you as a frustrater but as one who more often than not fills needs and offers love. The baby's high threshold of frustration enables him or her to overlook many frustrations that a baby treated differently might react strongly to and resent in a form of pathology known as "injustice collecting."

THE PROTECTIVE SHIELD

It is difficult for a baby to get used to living outside mother's body. After birth — and to a lesser extent throughout early childhood — the mother acts as a protective shield, a tough psychological skin between the baby and the world that enables him or her to become accustomed to stimuli and demands, growing stronger in the process, finally taking over without outside aid.

In the most obvious form of protection, the mother protects

the baby by clothing him or her appropriately and by warding off excessive outside stimuli. She also helps the baby to deal with inside stimuli by reducing the baby's own tensions: feeding whenever the baby is hungry, changing wet diapers, responding to all complaints with some appropriate action before the frustrations intensify. By acting as a buffer against the harsher pains of the world and regulating frustration and gratification, the mother fosters the baby's development. The baby who never feels overwhelmed and powerless enjoys growth and change.

It is difficult for a baby to get used to living outside mother's body.

If the baby were to encounter obstacles too great to deal with, he or she would feel inadequate or confused. Bearing in mind that one of the goals of a baby's life is to learn to do things alone by achieving mastery over mental and physical abilities, the mother (and soon the father too) tries to create a harmony between the baby's needs and the baby's abilities at any given point. Keeping inner tensions comfortably low reduces the possibility of conflict. And without conflict there can be no problems. The baby never gets the discouraging feeling that life is too much to bear or that events are bewildering or frightening. Development takes its best course — slow, unhurried, unpressured. And so the baby moves developmentally forward step by small step, with few disturbances and never any feeling of helplessness.

THE "SMILING RESPONSE"

Beginning as early as the first week, expressions appear on the baby's face that resemble smiles. In fact they are not smiles but only accidental movements of facial muscles in response to internal stimuli.

In the second month, there are occasional "smiles" due to satiation. Smiles in response to another person come only during the third month, and these are considered true smiles because they are conscious gestures, willed acts, indicating that the baby recognizes the configuration of the human face.

"Except for the infant's following the human face with his eyes in the second month, this smile is the [baby's] first active, directed, and intentional behavioral manifestation."* To parents seeing this smile on their baby's face for the first time there is no comparable thrill. Few events in life give as much joy as a baby's smiles offered to you.

This first real smile means that considerable psychic organization has been taking place within the baby. A once poorly perceiving, unthinking, grossly distorting, helpless organism now recognizes the configuration of the human face and shows delight by smiling at it. The baby forms a tie of love with this face — the first tie of love ever. The baby is no longer totally passive: the smile indicates a capacity for psychologically active behavior.†

Keeping inner tensions comfortably low
reduces the possibility of conflict.

Until now, the baby has not differentiated between him- or herself and the rest of the world, but this first smile reveals that the baby has begun to make some small distinctions and, equally important, has become capable of a human relationship. Human relations are aided by memory, which has begun to be a strong component in functioning: the baby remembers the mother's face and smiles at seeing it. (If breastfeeding promotes earlier development of memory, as we have suggested, it promotes the earlier development of human relations as well.)

The smile marks the end of the period of greatest helplessness in life. The baby has begun to perceive that mother and father are separate beings — but has *just* begun to perceive that, and only fuzzily. There is yet a long way to go in differentiating the self altogether from mother, the principal nurturing person. Indeed, the baby is far from perceiving that there is a "she" to be differentiated from. At this stage "mother" is only a face. Feeling loved by that face — the "face"

*René A. Spitz, *The First Year of Life*, New York, International Universities Press, 1965, p. 86.
†In shifting from passive feeding in the womb to "active" feeding at the breast, the baby was still functioning instinctively, not intentionally.

that feeds, clothes, hugs, and talks — the baby beams a smile at it. Sometimes the smile is so intensely mirthful it looks as if the baby, overwhelmed with delight, were saying, "You and I know such a marvelous secret that it tickles me to pieces." But that, of course, would be to read into the smile. The smile, as far as anyone can tell, is an expression of pure love for that wonderful, pleasure-giving face and expresses a huge and uncomplicated joy in living.

Development takes its best course: slow, unhurried, unpressured.

The "smiling response" marks the end of the first stage of human development. The baby's internal organization since leaving the uterus is impressive.

Although everything seems to be occurring *inside*, the baby has begun to perceive that there is some dim, incomprehensible *outside* too.

Memory traces have been laid down in the mind.

The baby has made a shift from the passive mode to the active, from the instinctive to the intentional.

Relations with another human being have begun.

Finally, as we have seen, there is a major change that has great implications for human growth and happiness. At three months, no object will provoke a baby to smile intentionally. Not even the bottle will induce a smile, nor food, even though the baby is hungry and may respond eagerly to the cue of the bottle and may reach out awkwardly to touch it. The nurturing person's face, however — which the baby has learned to associate with pleasure and reliable gratification — easily elicits a smile.

6

The Discovery of the World

The process of advancement is interesting. It isn't that you get bigger to fit the world; the world gets smaller to fit you.

T. S. ELIOT

THE DUAL UNION

To the newborn, mother and child are one undifferentiated person. Indistinguishable from each other, they form a "dual union." This symbiosis is fostered by the mother's supplying what the baby needs and the baby's supplying what the mother needs.

The mother feels fulfillment in nursing and playing with her baby, and the baby picks up her happy mood and feels a sense of wellbeing. The mother responds to the baby's smile with a smile of her own and with soothing sounds. In this simple way, they mutually stimulate each other. A bond of love is formed between them that, consciously or not, will last the rest of their lives and will never be quite duplicated with anyone else.

For the baby especially, this bond of love has permanent psychological importance. A baby who feels securely loved by mother has a much better chance of growing up contented and of developing to full potential. As Freud remarked a long time ago, a baby or child who feels loved by his or her mother grows up with the conviction that success is easily attainable.*

---

*"I have found that those persons who consider themselves preferred or favored by their mothers manifest in life that confidence in themselves and that unshakable optimism which often seems heroic, and not infrequently compels success."

A baby who feels this love, expressed by the good first experiences in life we have been describing, especially by early satisfying feedings and care, will in all likelihood grow up to be a person with self-confidence and the capability of creating a happy personal life. If later on that person should suffer the frightening consequences of war or the pain of personal tragedies, the original confidence, as well as a pleasure in being alive, will protect against severe trauma — against the possibility that any psychological shock will have a lasting debilitating effect on emotional life. Even if handicapped by poverty and racism, such a person might bend but not break.

STIMULATION

Although the stimulation of child and parents is reciprocal, the parent's part is naturally the greater. Providing stimulation to the child is a way of promoting growth. As the psychologist Jean Piaget says, "The more a child sees and hears, the more he wants to see and hear." Stimulation through play develops the baby's intelligence. You crawl on the floor with the baby, give the baby a ride on your foot or your back, sing a simple tune, and make funny sounds. The baby loves all this and looks forward to more. You enjoy it too. Even if you have had a hard day, playing with the baby is a good way to relax for a few minutes.

The mother supplies what
the baby needs, and the baby
supplies what the mother needs.

Stimulation takes many forms. Sometimes it is just holding the baby and having a "conversation." Or the baby discovers that you have fingers and that fingers taste interesting and might be placed in the mouth from time to time. Later it might be your playing games with the baby's fingers and "clapping" his or her hands. The baby's delight is unbounded at that. Or you might pick the baby up in your arms and walk around the room, pausing to look at different objects. Because babies are unable to move around on their own, they need help in getting more and more stimulation to satisfy a growing demand.

Or the baby might spend time playing with a string of colorful beads or bells tied across the crib. They occupy the mind for long periods and teach something more about the world—colors, shapes, sizes, and sounds. Objects that hold attention help satisfy stimulus-hunger, which is a very real hunger. Still later, the stimulation might take the form of your humming and singing or telling stories. It doesn't matter if the words are not understood.

To the growing baby the world is fabulous, strange, and wonderful. From the stroller the baby hears the leaves of trees make a rustling sound. How interesting that is! If you live in the country, colorful flowers sway in the breeze, and a baby might stare at such an event with the fascination of a poet. In city streets, fire engines go wailing by, and a cat darts across a sidewalk. Indoors, curtains blow in with a gust of wind, and sometimes rain splatters against windows beaded with drops that become erratic rivulets.

Your stimulation and your love and attention further the baby's psychological development, but they also seem to help physical development. It has been found, for example, that babies who are not stimulated enough by their parents—who are not held, lovingly spoken to, or offered distractions—are more susceptible to infection. Even as adults their general health is relatively fragile, making them more prone to illness than others.*

In extreme instances where loving, continuing contact with parents has been absent, babies have actually died. Spitz describes infants who, because of wartime conditions, were separated from their mothers between six and eight months of age. The babies were fed, clothed, and kept dry in a hospital setting, but they were not picked up, held, talked to, or smiled at, as they had been up until then. The babies gradually withdrew into themselves, stopped smiling, lost weight, and languished. All those whose mothers did not return died while still less than a year old. Spitz describes this illness, which he calls "hospitalism," as "total emotional deprivation."† It un-

*Boston Children's Medical Center, *Pregnancy, Birth, and the Newborn Baby,* New York, Delacorte Press/Seymour Lawrence, 1972, p. 250.
†René A. Spitz, *The First Year of Life,* New York, International Universities Press, 1965, especially Chapter XIV, "Emotional Deficiency Diseases of Infancy," pp. 267–84, and Chapter XV, "The Effects of Object Loss: Psychological Considerations," pp. 285–92.

derlines the literally vital importance of the continuing presence of the *same* mothering person, even if only part time, in the first year—or more—of life.*

There should be neither too much stimulation nor too little. Parents generally sense that overstimulation is not good: shouting, blaring radios, people constantly moving around the baby, too many people playing with the baby at the same time, tickling the soft little body—this sensory overload would be difficult for a baby to deal with. A baby could adapt to it, but that would not foster the sense of relaxed wellbeing that contributes so much to health. It would tend to make the baby high-strung and tense and create a need throughout life for continued strong doses of stimulation.

Fondling a baby's genitals, whether as a way of pacifying or just giving pleasure, can create considerable problems. For one thing, it would make for an erotic relation with members of the family. This would in time have the additional side effect of blurring strong lines of identity. A boy might ask himself as he grows up, for example: "If my mother is being seductive with me, am I her son or her lover? And who, then, is my father to me?" A girl might ask: "If my father is seductive with me, maybe he prefers me sexually to my mother. That gives me special pleasure, but it also makes me feel guilty toward my mother." And so on.

Besides, a baby is a gentle thing, with quiet needs and a need for quiet. Too much stimulation, such as tickling, might in the short run appear to be delightfully welcome to the baby but in the long run might set up a need for still greater stimulation. And psychologically speaking, the long run is always more important than the short run. There is also the danger of making the baby, in Freud's words, an "erotic toy" of the parents, which would rob the baby of development and any normal life.

---

*The concept "total emotional deprivation" seems to be true of other species too. Not very long ago the New York Aquarium rescued a baby pygmy sperm whale whose mother had apparently been killed. Although the whale seemed to do well in the aquarium, where it was treated with special care and given a diet that increased its weight, it soon began to lose that weight and one day, after a month of being motherless, simply stopped breathing and died. Behavior of this kind raises questions about the so-called will to live. How much of "will" is the feeling of being loved—originally by mother?

THE BEGINNINGS OF SELF-IMAGE

At the beginning of life and for the first several months, a baby has no self-image whatsoever—in fact, has no "self." If a baby has any sense of his or her own being, it is of something boundless. There is no "self" that feels distinctly apart from everything else, and therefore there *is* nothing else. It is as if he or she were global and timeless, with neither beginning nor end.

As the child begins to perceive some indistinct external world, the idea of separate physical being begins to form. Much of this self-image is body image. A baby exploring his or her own head, torso, and limbs gradually perceives boundaries and limits: "All this is me. All the rest is the world."*

The child who perceives that things happen not by his or her wishing for them but because of another's aid discovers that there are other limits as well: "I am not omnipotent." Progress in life might be described in one sense as the discovery of limits. It is also true, however, that our continuously growing sense of reality leads to widening horizons. The discovery of limits only means seeing things more and more as they really are rather than in wishful distortion. It does not mean a narrowing of life but a life of greater possibilities.

THE LIMITS OF THE SELF AND THE LARGER WORLD

It is not long before this initial period has run its course and the baby begins to make finer distinctions between the self and the world, the "I" and the "not I." A painful sound is outside and "not I." Hunger pains are inside and part of the "I."† These

---

*If you surreptitiously pat a two-year-old's behind the child will turn to try to discover what is there. If you repeat your action, the research won't be given up until the child establishes finally that it is not his or her body that is causing the sensation but you.

†The emergence of the distinction between "I" and "not I" is discussed by, among others, Spitz, *The First Year of Life,* pp. 330–35, *idem, No and Yes,* New York, International Universities Press, 1957, pp. 113–16;. D. W. Winnicott, "The Theory of the Parent-Infant Relationship," *International Journal of Psychoanalysis,* 41 (1900): 585–95.

According to Freud, however, at the very beginning a baby relegates hunger pains to "not I" on the egocentric grounds that whatever is pleasurable is "I" and whatever is unpleasurable is "not I." This is untenable, but it takes a lot of experience to trim a baby's narcissism. Also: "An infant at the breast does not as yet distinguish his ego from the external world as the source of the sensations flowing in upon him." Sigmund Freud, *Civilization and Its Discontents,* Standard Edition, Volume 21 (1930), London, Hogarth Press, 1961, pp. 66 ff.

distinctions are learned at first from simple events, like the baby's tasting fingers and toes. It takes some time for the baby to realize that the hand he or she sucks on and the hand that occasionally moves back and forth in front of the face are the same object. Many months later, in the second year of life, as the baby learns to speak, the words "I" and "mine" assume importance as expressions of self. After that, feelings about the body, so closely tied to feelings of "I," lead to high esteem for the products of the body, feces and urine. All these feelings combine to form a sense of self as distinguished from the rest of the world.

There should be neither too much stimulation nor too little.

Let us look once again at how frustration leads to an increased sense of the separateness of the self. The baby cries in hunger and is fed. But occasionally the breast or bottle is not immediately available, because mother happens to be in another room. With this small frustration, the baby begins to suspect that the satisfying feeding experience may not be spontaneous but may come from somewhere else, from something "outside."

This is a momentous discovery. It is not only a heightening awareness of boundaries, it is an increasingly convincing discovery that the world is not just "I," that there is more, that there is another person. True, the other is a person in part only: at first the "other"—the entire world, in fact—is merely mother's face and breast (or the bottle). But that is at least a first step toward comprehension of the vast reality outside. So we see that there is a subtle shift from viewing the "self" as omnipotent to viewing the breast and mother as omnipotent. The view is still wrong. But it must be considered a step forward.

Curiously, it is when an infant is most helpless, in early infancy, that he or she feels most powerful. But we know of course from the psychoanalyses of adults that it is when the baby (preserved, so to speak, in the unconscious) feels utterly helpless that he or she is tempted to fantasize being all-powerful. The wish overthrows the truth.

The baby's exploration begins to extend to more of the world. The baby sometimes stares fixedly at objects and people — sometimes to the discomfort of strangers, who wilt under so inflexible a regard. A rattle with a decorative drawing on it might rivet a baby's attention for minutes at a time. The baby is seeing everything for the first time. To us it is all the same old world. To the baby it is the first confrontation with existence.

INSIDE AND OUTSIDE

The baby's neck muscles are among the first muscles to develop, so that by the third or fourth month he or she can hold up the head and turn to look at something or to respond to a sound. Around this time all babies go through a brief experiment: they turn their heads 180° to one side to look at an object across the room, then swing their heads all the way around and look off in the other direction. Then they turn back to the object across the room again. A baby might repeat this several times, and if you are watching you might feel mystified unless you understand that the baby is learning to distinguish what is real *out there* from what is real *inside*. A baby has to learn that feelings, sensations, and "thoughts" are inside and objects are outside. By staring at inanimate objects, looking away, and then finding them again, the baby repeatedly confirms that they remain where they are, independent of the baby's actions. They don't go away as an internal sensation might.

The long run is always
more important than the short run.

In this way a baby learns the difference between those things that can be touched or seen and those things that exist only in the self. Inner and outer realities are kept clearly separated even though they are experienced as interrelated.

REPRESENTATIONS OF THE SELF AND OTHERS

Identity is complex. It is composed of sensations and mental images of the body as well as a sense of the self as distinguishable from the world. It is, in fact, a sense of the self as a *uniqueness*. The self has constancy but it changes too. As Sartre says, we develop and change "within a permanency." That permanency is our identity.

Philosophers have suggested that we don't really see others but only our images of them. Psychoanalytic theory is in agreement with this view. A baby begins by having no picture of you. Then the baby perceives "you" and takes "you" inside. By thus internalizing you, the baby "creates" you, stores away images of you one by one until there are tens of thousands of images, like an archive of photographs, moving and talking and smelling and touching. These myriad images together form "you" in the baby's mind.

The growing child carries around this personal "version" of you inside. After a period of absence from you, his or her image of you may need to be reinforced. In time the absences can grow longer, until finally the inner version of you becomes a permanent feeling of having you inside.

We change "within a permanency."

The baby's image of the self develops similarly. The baby "takes in" him- or herself bit by bit, image by image, sound by sound, movement by movement, until it adds up to an ongoing subtotal. (The total could come only at death.) The sense of self — identity — is intimately involved in this process: the baby differentiates between the images of others and the self-images.*

An important part of a baby's taking in these thousands of images is the sorting of them. First the sorting takes the form of large categories. For example, a baby might distinguish between an image that is "I" and one that is "not I." Then the sorting becomes more refined — perhaps, at age four, something like "I am a girl." Then even more refined — for example, in adolescence: "I am like my mother in that I enjoy being self-assertive and feminine, but I am like my father in that I enjoy being lazy sometimes and am not very handy with tools." The distinctions become more subtle and more numerous, and they

*This section loosely paraphrases, in quite simplified form, a portion of Edith Jacobson, *The Self and Object World,* New York, International Universities Press, 1964.

contribute to an ever increasing sense of identity and separateness as a person.

The child builds in images of mother so that even when she is absent there is still that all-important sense of her nevertheless being "there." The child takes in her looks, voice, feel, expectations, fears, love — all — and makes them a part of the self. It is when he or she can "carry mother around," or "internalize" her, some time after the age of three years, that the child is able to explore another part of the house without the presence of mother or to go it alone on the first day of nursery school. It is through this process that the child moves toward independence.

THE DISCOVERY OF THE BODY AND SEX

As any observant parent knows, a boy has erections from the beginning of life. In fact, studies show that erections occur within the uterus. Some time after the first year, as part of the experience of touching the body, the baby eventually discovers that a certain part of it produces more pleasure when touched than all the others: the genitals. Particularly in warm weather, when they go around lightly dressed or nude, children tend to touch their genitals (little boys relatively more, perhaps, because the penis protrudes and is more accessible). Most mothers ignore this self-fondling, knowing how harmless it is, neither encouraging it nor discouraging it.

Until Freud, people spoke of the "innocence of childhood," meaning that that period of life is without sexual feelings of any kind. Freud upset this notion — and quite a few people — by stating that the sexual drive is there from birth and changes only in its form of expression, evolving through stages from oral pleasures to anal pleasures to phallic pleasures, and finally to a specifically genital stage, or maturity. He also noted that mild feelings of pleasure are derived from the genitals even in the earlier phases, as witness the occasional erection of a little boy and his pleasurably handling his penis and a girl's snuggling her hand between her legs to rub her genitals.

There are still some parents who are disturbed when they see early manifestations of the sexual instinct, as though any instinct could be "bad." Perhaps their own upbringing was repressive: sex was regarded as dirty or (the same thing) not to be talked about. Or perhaps sex has unconscious incestuous significance for them. Their guilt or fears might be difficult for them to deal with, but to acknowledge that their reactions might be the problem and not their child's free expression of feelings would prove helpful to both.

Their fears are in any case misplaced when it comes to a baby. A baby hasn't the slightest idea of what is socially acceptable or not, what is morally "reprehensible" or not. A baby merely responds naturally to drives, to the glandular rhythms of the body. A baby's body (as well as a child's and an adult's) is at all times a busy, active physiological factory working at full steam, with muscles responding to nerves, glands secreting, and cells multiplying. If a little boy gets an erection, it is quite unintentional and, in the earliest months, not even a reflection of erotic feelings toward anyone. His erections have even less significance than the erections that all men get several times every night, even though they are seldom aware of it, in rhythm with their dream cycle. If a little girl snuggles her fist between her legs and likes it because "it feels good" it is not because of some problem or an evil nature but because she has good working glands and is healthy enough to enjoy pleasure.

SPLITTING UP MOTHER INTO "GOOD" AND "BAD"

Adults see that the same mother or mothering person sometimes gratifies and sometimes frustrates the baby. To the baby this is more "reality" than can be comprehended. All the baby knows is that there appears to be a gratifier of needs and there appears to be a frustrater of needs. In moments of frustration it is extremely difficult for the baby to consider that there are other moments when the frustrating person also gratifies. Therefore, the baby loves "one" and hates the "other" quite as though they were two different people. In other words, the baby splits mother into two mothers, a "good" one and a "bad" one — and wants to keep one and get rid of the other.

This splitting is so universal that it forms the basis of all those myths and childhood tales in which there is a "good fairy" and a "witch." As a child grows up he or she comes to see what adults already know, that the "good" and the "bad" mother are one and the same person at different moments. In advanced levels of literature too we see the same correction: there are no pure villains or heroes, because a good writer knows that even a "villain" has good points and every hero has flaws. People are human. And so are mothers and fathers.

The erroneous split is corrected — the two "mothers" are seen to be one real Mother — when the baby notices over the many long months of the first year that it is the same person who provides gratification and occasionally causes frustration. The baby therefore revises the earlier theory to make it agree with a more accurate perception of reality.

What motivates the baby to do so is an increasing awareness that survival requires the aid of another person. For this reason alone the baby would be willing to put up with frustration to get the needed gratification from that person. In time the baby views parents as whole persons, providing both gratification and frustration.

Although to describe it in this way makes the matter sound rational and simple, there can be considerable reluctance even among adults to heal this split. Some adults unconsciously persist in the belief that some persons are "good" and some "bad." And because they see themselves as among the good, the moment anything goes wrong in their lives they are quick to blame the nearest person, who becomes one of the "bad" ones. They fail to perceive that everyone is capable of both good and bad.

7

Crying

I want! I want!

WILLIAM BLAKE

Crying is one area of childrearing in which the parents seem to need at least as much care and guidance as the child. The baby's crying is their greatest single source of frustration and distress, and part of their frustration is in not always understanding *why* the baby cries.

CRYING AS DISCHARGE

At no time in life will crying again occur so frequently as it does in infancy. We might be tempted to infer from the sheer amount of crying in the early months of life that it serves more than one purpose. But it doesn't, not at the beginning. In the first days and weeks, crying is simply a method of discharging feelings of tension or anxiety. It is a reaction to an internal state: a discomfort or pain makes a baby cry long before the baby knows the parents exist. The crying is *not* intended as communication.

It is quite important to note this fact. *The baby does not cry with the intention of annoying you.* The baby is not "demanding" anything, not "ordering," not "controlling," or any of the other adultomorphic interpretations of a baby's crying you may have heard.

As discharge, crying can actually be pleasurable to the baby, because the baby's body is doing something in reaction, and *any* way of using the body feels good to a tiny infant. The baby is learning about him- or herself through "self" sensations, and it feels good to be capable of "action" in response to pain and discomfort. Dr. Winnicott says: "Screaming and yelling and all forms of crying must be definitely exciting. The importance of our recognizing this, the value of crying, is that we can then see how crying works as a reassurance in time of trouble. Babies cry because they feel anxious or insecure, and crying works. We must therefore agree that there is something good about it. Later comes talking" as a form of discharge instead of crying.*

Some parents have been told that the baby cries in an attempt to control them, that if they respond to the crying the baby will become a tyrant ordering them around, and that the best thing to do, therefore, is to ignore the baby. Fortunately, these parents are increasingly in the minority. What is curious about these views is the assumption that a baby is born knowing quite a bit about human behavior: dominance and submission, annoying others, and so on. It is even assumed that from birth a baby knows about communication, knows that there is a "you" to communicate with. There is another assumption too: a baby is a tyrant who has to be "broken," as though a baby is born evil.

The baby does not cry with the intention of annoying you.

Of course there is no truth in any of this. Yet even while the mother was in the hospital she no doubt heard some "experienced" mother, having her second or third baby, advise her not to "give in" to the baby — for the baby's sake. "You'll *spoil* the baby. You build the baby's character by ignoring the crying."

CRYING AND THE BEGINNINGS OF MORALITY

Even though to a baby crying is purely a discharge, parents generally respond to it as if it were a communication. ("The baby must want to eat.") Therefore, what begins as a discharge process gradually *becomes* communication — which, incidentally, aids the work of building relations between the baby and the parents.

*D. W. Winnicott, *Mother and Child*, New York, Basic Books, 1957, p. 58.

In the beginning, screaming in response to an internal state may give considerable satisfaction to the baby. But it soon becomes clear that the crying alone does not relieve needs. Only another person can bring relief. As this slowly becomes understood by the infant, from the second month on, the baby, *to ensure survival*, modifies his or her behavior and learns to develop satisfying relations with you. The paramount importance of human interaction is thus driven home in one of the earliest learning experiences in life, the recognition that the baby must take care not to arouse great or lasting displeasure in you, if he or she wants needs to be met. It is not difficult to discern in this recognition what is perhaps the most primitive expression of the moral injunction "Do unto others as you would have them do unto you." According to Freud, the "original helplessness of human beings is . . . the primal source of all moral motives." A fact emerges from this state of affairs that must surprise those who believe that babies are controlling creatures whose one aim is to be spoiled by parents: we see that the baby, far from attempting to manipulate the parents into submission, feels on the contrary a need to please them and, if necessary, would go a long way to placate them.

COMMON REASONS FOR A BABY'S CRYING

There are some common reasons why most babies cry. A baby's needs are often imperative and will remain imperative until the baby understands that help is always at hand and there is never a need for panic. Those needs are relatively few and generally are the same as an adult's: love, food, warmth, protection, and, not very many weeks after birth, communication. And, like an adult, a baby wants the immediate cessation of a pain.

For the first several weeks of life, the cry of a newborn almost always means hunger. The pin-sticking-into-the-baby theory does not hold up too well for these weeks. That *might* happen, but it is a rarity.* If not hunger, then crying means that the baby is uncomfortable. You might try changing the baby's position or picking the baby up.

As the baby gets a bit older and becomes accustomed to the ways of life, he or she will sometimes cry merely in anticipa-

---

*If you can afford the new tape-on disposable diapers, pins are no longer needed — so much for them.

tion of a discomfort, as when you begin to change a diaper: from past experience the baby knows that that means there may be an unpleasant cold feeling for a few minutes, if it is winter.

There are other reasons. If the crying is due, for example, to the discomfort of a bright light, you might notice that the baby will turn his or her head to one side, away from the light or the glaring sun. If the pain is due to hunger, once hand-to-mouth coordination has been acquired, the baby might stuff a fist into the mouth. With colic, a baby might double up and cry.

A six-month-old baby might cry out of rage at the frustrations of life, where things don't happen automatically as they did in the uterus, and, illogically, the baby might want to be rid of *you* as the frustrater, completely unaware that you satisfy needs more than you frustrate. The baby still, for a while, tends to think of you as that face out there that merely happens to be around while his or her needs are getting satisfied.

This gross distortion of the facts is also characteristic of some adults, perhaps those who did not have their distortions of reality fully corrected back in the early months of life. For example, a husband might angrily stomp out of the house and "get rid" of his wife ("Who needs *her?*") by spending an evening at the neighborhood bar and then, when he is drunk and begins to feel lonely, docilely return home to be with his wife again. He sees no contradiction in this. We can conclude that emotionally he is still a baby.

The cause of some crying is hard to identify. The baby is dry, there isn't even that famous pin sticking into the baby, he or she has recently been picked up, is warm (you check), you have tried rocking, there's no brightly glaring light—yet the baby cries. This can be especially annoying if in addition the baby has just been fed to the groggy point.

The strange fact is, however, that babies do cry sometimes just after being fed. The crying in this case might be due to fatigue—the exertion of feeding plus, perhaps, having been awake for a long stretch before that. An especially active baby might in fact *generally* cry before falling asleep because a good cry is calming and sleep-inducing.* Or the crying might be due to a bubble or to colic or to lack of stimulation and boredom.

*Benjamin Spock, *Baby and Child Care*, New York, Pocket Books, 1968, p. 185. His section on crying, some of which is paraphrased in this chapter, is well worth reading.

Eventually, when there begins to be a "you," the baby might occasionally cry in an attempt to manipulate you. Very often this type of crying sounds false to an experienced ear. This happens only when the baby is many months old, probably in the second year, and by then you are fairly well acquainted with each other.

IS CRYING GOOD FOR THE LUNGS?

It used to be asserted that crying is good for the lungs. But this view ignores the fact that breathing, kicking, and other movements are good for the lungs too. Against the lung-development theory must be weighed the possible psychic damage if crying is allowed to go unheeded too long because it will "do the baby good." Crying futilely on and on out of desperate need will actually do the baby considerable harm. It is not an exaggeration to say that ten minutes are a large and significant portion of a newborn's lifetime. It is important *not* to let a baby cry too much because that could build a sense of utter helplessness, which if prolonged could lead to despair.

No one can deny that crying helps the baby's lungs to develop, but that is true chiefly at the very beginning. The baby's first breaths of air are the most difficult ones in life. The lungs, like mechanical bellows, must overcome inertia all at once. Filled with fluid only minutes before, in the uterus, at birth the lungs need to have their thousands of tiny air sacs cleared of mucus and opened to air in order for them to function. Crying helps this clearing process — although babies who have been anesthetized need to be slapped and shaken for as much as a whole minute to begin breathing. The lungs begin their lifetime task of breathing, while continuing to clear themselves of fluid for another day or two. (That is the reason for the puzzling amount of sneezing a very young baby does. It is not the beginnings of a cold but a natural process.)

With umbilical life behind, blood circulation is rerouted to begin its work. Blood is distributed to the lungs, the stomach, and the brain, and when this happens the brain becomes able to take over the function of dealing with internal and external sensations. The first cry of the baby, which used to be induced by a slap on the buttocks administered by the doctor or midwife and is now more humanely induced simply by holding the baby upside down and rubbing the back, is really an emergency, crash breathing exercise. It is a way of getting the organism to begin functioning, like shaking a watch to start its movement. Suddenly the diaphragm makes its first contraction, thereby squeezing from the lungs the no-longer-needed fluid, and then, like a balloon puffing up, the lungs expand as they suck in oxygen. With that first lungful of air the baby has started a life of his or her own, and conception, after nine long months, has finally reached fruition. It does seem a miracle.

The baby's very first
breaths of air are the most
difficult ones in life.

To hear the baby go on crying when there is no apparent reason is extremely frustrating to parents. But in the beginning even the baby is unspecific about his or her needs or about what is causing discomfort. A baby reacts to every passing tension or pain with a single global response — crying — whether hungry, wet, bored, anxious, colicky, overstimulated, or uncomfortable. However, some time after the first two months or so, the baby's various cries begin to sound a little different from each other, with subtle shadings in tone, and when that happens the parent learns to distinguish between them.

WHAT TO DO ABOUT THE BABY'S CRYING

If you are in doubt about why the baby is crying, various possibilities might be considered. If you haven't picked the baby up recently, try that first. Babies cry less who are picked up often, talked to, and held close. If you haven't fed the baby in a while, you might try that — without insisting. If the baby cries before a feeding and stops afterward, the crying was due to hunger. If the baby cries *after* a feeding, it might mean fatigue or colic (gas).

If the crying is caused by colic, gently hold the baby in a position that will get up any bubble that might be there, perhaps laying the baby on his or her stomach across your lap, rubbing the tiny back with care and talking soothingly. To handle a baby roughly or speak loudly at a time like that would only increase the misery. Colic can be excruciatingly painful, and a colicky baby needs sympathy.

If you have tried everything and the baby is still crying, put the baby into the crib, wait a while, and then gauge the sounds. If the crying doesn't get worse — become frantic or absolutely enraged — but softens a little or begins to sound lazy and maybe even rhythmic and musical, in a stop-and-start, questioning-listening way, it may well be that it was due to overstimulation and fatigue, and there's nothing you can do about that except to let the crying lead to sleep.

It is most important that you not get alarmed or worry that you are doing something wrong. If the mother has been breastfeeding, she might at a time like this feel tempted to lose her convictions and decide that the solution is the bottle. That would be a mistake.

The baby's various cries
begin to sound a little different
from each other, with
subtle shadings in tone.

Despite these tips, you may sometimes feel miserable, even anxious, if you still don't understand the reason for the crying and therefore feel inadequate as a parent. That in turn could make you feel helpless, which could lead to your becoming angry at the baby for frustrating *you*.

However, before you let your anxiety carry you away, remind yourself that *sometimes absolutely nothing can be done* except to weather these bad moments and hope they won't recur too often. Feeling guilty doesn't help. If nothing else you do stops the baby's crying, it might be helpful and reassuring just to hold him or her in your arms.

Some parents, especially mothers, become so attuned to their baby's needs that it almost seems as if the needs are communicated telepathically. That ability, however, comes only later, when parent and baby know each other well. But *fairly* soon you learn to read most signals well enough to know what the specific need is and understand the source of pain or discomfort.

If you have been doing a moderately good job all along as a "good enough" parent, sometimes the best course in childrearing is just to allow things to happen. There will be times when the baby is only mildly upset and will react by crying. Must you necessarily rush to respond? If there is nothing seriously wrong and the crying does not sound desperate or enraged, you might let the baby cry for a few moments.

CRYING AT DIFFERENT AGES

Time is on your side. Although your baby may cry often at first, your love and care will reduce the need for crying. If you feed on demand, crying will be minimal. (In fact, if in spite of the advantages of demand feeding that we cited you choose scheduled feeding, you might reevaluate your decision, asking yourself at this time if you *want* to hear so much crying.)

Crying begins to be used as a means of communication when the baby is three months old. Once there is memory and past gratifications can be recalled by the baby, crying is used to call out to the parents. This is not the same as "ordering them around." Crying is a baby's only means of summoning help.

Babies cry less who are picked up often, talked to, and held close.

A five- or six-month-old baby can tolerate crying much more than a newborn and doesn't need to be picked up each time. In fact, picking up a baby who is six months old or older each time at the very moment the baby begins to make sounds might convey the message that crying is an acceptable way of getting attention. Another danger is this: if you respond each time only after prolonged crying, you thereby train the baby to cry a lot to get a need satisfied. This precaution does not apply during the first three or four months. After that, use your judgment.

At eight or nine months old, the baby might cry just after being put to bed or on awakening in the middle of the night. Don't necessarily respond immediately. Let the baby fret or cry, and listen from time to time. The baby may go back to sleep. At that age a baby can cry for quite some time — ten minutes, by now — without suffering bad effects. If the crying gets louder and goes on longer, there may be a real need to be met. Pick the baby up and see if burping is what is needed. If it isn't, rock the baby in your arms until the baby falls asleep again. You might expect that to happen if you are visiting friends and put the baby to sleep in a strange bedroom. But again, as long as the crying is not desperate, there is no harm in ignoring tears of this kind, at least for short periods.

By the age of one year, nighttime feedings have long since ended, but the baby may continue to wake up at six in the morning and want to be fed. At this stage of childrearing parents are often utterly exhausted, and these early-morning demands make them grumpy. The baby, however, fully awake and rested after a night of sleep, feels talkative and frisky and wants to be near them. Part of the difficulty is that "talkative" at this age means loud yells and cries. Under the pressure of hunger pangs, babies don't know how to moderate their voices: volume is all-or-nothing. When they want to "say" something, they simply let blast. They pass in an instant from contentedness to what sounds like a shrill cry of despair. It is an extremely trying time for parents, and the yearning to get away from it all is never so strong as now. However difficult those early weeks were, they were easier than this.

This is a time for husband and wife to help each other out.

Sometimes the best course
in childrearing is just
to allow things to happen.

As father feeds breakfast to the baby, mother showers, dresses, and enjoys a precious fifteen minutes of liberty, during which she braces herself before taking over again for a while.

SOME BABIES CRY A LOT

Some babies are more tense than others, especially in the first few months. That is no reflection on the parents. Doctors and psychologists don't know why, but some babies get irritated over apparently nothing, cry for a while, and then stop.

Sometimes it may seem that the baby is deliberately trying to make you feel bad, as though he or she hates you and finds you intolerable. But to think that would be to make the mistake of adultomorphism. The baby's rage is only a reaction to inner discomfort or pain.

If your baby is having difficulty of this kind, the first few months will be a bit harder to get through. But you can only do your best. And if you feel you have honestly done so, try to slough off any guilt feelings and let your spouse, mother, grandmother, or anybody else you trust take over occasionally while you go to a movie or visit a friend.

Colicky babies are hard for anyone to take. As often as you can, try to get away, leaving the baby with your mate or a sitter. If you can't and the crying just won't stop no matter what you do, put on some music or turn the TV up a bit – for a while. It might help to know that colicky babies usually change their behavior after they are three months old – and often turn out to be bright, alert children. Above all try to keep yourself from feeling angry, resentful, or depressed. If you do feel down, talk to your doctor, husband, friends – anybody. It almost always helps.

Some babies are more tense than others.

Fortunately most babies are not the difficult kind who frequently cry on and on for no apparent reason. Most of them cry out of a real need and stop crying when the need is taken care of. A somewhat older baby cries less often simply because the baby is used to living in a world of temperature change, hunger pains, sounds, and lights – and used to the parents and their ways. The need for crying also diminishes when the baby learns to speak. Speech serves to discharge inner tensions and becomes the preferred mode of communication. And at the same time, during the long months of the first year, you develop unawares the ability to screen out some of the baby's crying. Between the baby's crying less and your increasing tolerance, life becomes easier.

8

Eating

Unrest of spirit is a mark of life.

KARL MENNINGER

Beginning in the second half of the first year, eating problems seem to appear all at once. Quite unexpectedly, the once docile baby becomes contrary. What accounts for this turn of events? In this chapter we will try to gain insight into the typical causes of eating problems to see how they might be resolved. Perhaps our understanding of the psychology of infancy and early childhood will enable us to perceive that certain patterns of behavior that appear to be problems are part of normal development and not cause for concern.

There are times in a baby's life when many exciting things seem to happen all at once, and mealtimes after weaning are among those times. The baby can sit up now and have the fun of a high chair, making him or her feel big, or sit on a plastic infant seat placed near the parents. Eating at a table or in a high chair is exciting. You want the baby to eat the food, but the baby has just recently discovered how wonderfully warm and mushy it feels. Besides, to the baby it is not food that you're offering but something that's more fun to squeeze than eat, something new to study and learn about. Mashed lima beans are not a vegetable: they are a green blob. From the seventh month on and for two or three years afterward, the baby likes to play with solids. While eating, the baby beats the food on the plate with the flat of the palm or grabs a handful of food and rubs it on the tray of the chair or on the face or head.

You sometimes feel that the baby would rather wear food than eat it. But the baby is only discovering the things of the world and what can be done with them. On occasion the baby's hair smells ripe from old mashed potatoes, especially in summer, but you will be giving a bath soon anyway. You let the baby have the fun, as long as he or she goes on eating from the offered spoon, because you know that this phase, like all phases, will end.

A baby is accustomed to sucking to get food, not sliding it from a spoon, which is why the baby sucks during the first attempts at spoon-feeding. Weaning therefore is tantamount to a retraining. At first the baby resists, then makes clumsy efforts. It helps to go slowly, putting a dab of food on the baby's lower lip and letting him or her lick it off, to see that spoon-eating can be quite tasty, almost adventurous. Once the baby becomes accustomed to the spoon, put the food deep into the mouth so that the baby swallows it as a reflex. If you put food just inside the mouth, the baby will tend to reject it — another reflex — or let it dribble out.

In the beginning, the baby does not know that there is a connection between a spoon and eating. That is why the baby will grab the spoon away from you and then complain that you are not putting food into his or her mouth. Understanding what the baby is doing might help in those moments when you feel exasperated at such "unreasonable" behavior. One solution would be to let the baby hold one spoon while you feed with another.

MEALTIMES: EXCITEMENT AND EDUCATION

To the older members of the family, dinner is just another mealtime, but to the baby dinner, like everything else, is a learning experience. The baby is learning what it feels like to have people sit all grouped together, what mother and father do at the table, how different foods taste. The baby bangs things to learn the sounds they make. Some objects clack when hit against the floor or table, others chock, some thump, some bong.

The baby is even learning what the mouth is — that hole in the face into which you slip in all *your* food. The baby might not have given this much thought before now, partly because it is only in recent weeks that more and more thought has become possible. The baby is learning about the constancy of gravity. How fascinating that a piece of orange that leaves the hand journeys all the way to the floor! How interesting that it then stops and merely lies still.

It is difficult for a child to understand why one must sit at a table to eat food. Dining at a table is an advanced degree of socialization and feels unnatural to the child. To a child, eating can be enjoyed anywhere, even on the street, and moving around and fussing are a part of eating too. Also a child does not understand meal *time.* That too is a highly sophisticated concept. To a child, eating should take place whenever one feels hungry, whether before, during, or after "mealtime." Between the ages of one and four it is natural for a child to want to eat four or five times a day, nibbling on snacks rather than eating meals. Too much parental strictness too soon in this socializing process could create an "eating problem." The child in this case would be the victim of the problem, not the cause of it. Very often the "baby's eating problem" turns out to be the parent's lack of sensitivity to the child's developmental needs.

Eating at this age takes a long time because to a baby more is involved than a meal. *Nothing* in the world is taken for granted by a baby. As with all the events in life, everything about eating a meal is new and exciting, and eating itself is the least part of it. The baby is learning, for example, that it is impossible to blow and swallow at the same time. The parents' patience is taxed while the baby discovers that fact through trial and error. In ways such as this, the baby's knowledge increases. Usually as the meal progresses and the appetite gets satisfied, playing and experimentation increase. When the playing outweighs the eating, most parents consider the meal over no matter how much food is left on the plate. To persist in the face of disinterest would be to invite problems.

Each taste is entirely new too. To a grownup mashed potatoes may be just mashed potatoes, but to a baby they are a white fluff that mother is asking him or her to mouth, and this fluff, the baby discovers, happens to be hot, and not only hot but creamy-soft (strange that the baby doesn't have to suck to get it, though), and it goes down the throat in a smooth way. Also, it tastes radically different from milk, and what*ever* it is, everyone else is eating it too. *That's* new. Mashed potatoes might even taste better than the thumb, although a thumb still gives longer-lasting satisfaction. But the thumb is certainly superior to the mashed carrots at the last feeding which had *so* unusual a taste that all the baby could think to do with them was mush them around the mouth once to give them a try, dribble them out, grimace, and cry at the unbelievable awfulness of it.

It takes time to get used to new tastes. "We grownup people do the same thing when we eat strange food. We smack our lips —make faces—laugh—talk about the food. . . . That's what the baby is doing. He plays and makes a game out of eating."*

If the baby appears to be eating very little, it usually helps to have him or her eat apart from the other members of the family. A family eating together around a table can be so exciting an atmosphere that an eight- or ten-month-old baby is unable to take the eating part seriously. To a baby fun is *fun* whereas eating is merely eating.

A child does not understand meal*time.*

Generally, if the breast- or bottlefeeding experience was satisfactory to the baby and he or she feels loved, cared for, and protected, and if until now there has been no struggle between baby and parents, there will be no conflict now. In the oral stage of development, conflict very often takes the outward form of an "eating problem." The child who has few problems with parents will have few problems with food.

LIKES AND DISLIKES

A child doesn't like every food offered at every meal any more than you do. Some children positively hate certain foods from the start and never learn to like them. Or a child might love broccoli and then suddenly grow to dislike it. If a child hates a food, it is better not to force matters. The nutrients that the rejected food contains can be gotten from other foods. If the child is forced to eat, he or she will continue to hate the food and perhaps will hate you too and begin to develop complicated feelings about eating. We learn best not when we are forced to learn but when we learn pleasurably.

*Erma Brenner and Symeon Shimin, *A New Baby! A New Life!* New York, McGraw-Hill Book Company, 1973, p. 81—a brief but excellent book on child care.

During the child's whole life up to this point eating has been equated with love. Therefore, a parent who force-feeds would appear inconsistent. Up until now the parent has been easy to please. But because the child spits up some broccoli once, mother yells, "No!" or "Don't do that!" Where does she stand? Why does she shift in her feelings toward the child? Is she going to prove difficult to get along with? This behavior is puzzling to the child.

No child loves every food that is nutritionally good. It takes time for tastes to develop. Meanwhile, if a child loves certain foods, and they have some nutritional value, they should be served often. A child does not get sick or die from a lopsided diet but eventually gets bored and begins to want something more.

To a baby fun is *fun*
whereas eating is merely eating.

Another cause of conflict is to deny a child the food he or she likes until the rest of the meal is eaten. To say to a child, "If you don't eat your squash you can't have pie" would make squash a punishment, not a food. Besides, children don't know what a "meal" is: all they know is that they are hungry and naturally reach for what they like best. (Older children can sometimes eat a piece of candy just before a meal without at all losing their appetites.) Babies and young children have no conception of main course followed by dessert. It is all food to them. It would also create conflict to insist that the child eat all the food on the plate, as if there were some recommended quantity to be ingested rather than an appetite to be satisfied.

Furthermore, "Eat this little bit for Mommy" offers the baby a way to refuse food and conveys the message that eating is a method of earning love. Some children grow to adulthood using food as a substitute for love or compensation for a frustration, and end with a problem of overweight.

Mealtimes are psychologically healthier when they are pleasant occasions. If eating is a tense and nervous time, the baby becomes tense and unhappy about it. The more parents insist on the baby's eating, the more they tend to encounter a surprising intransigence. Force is met by counterforce. If parents can relax about meals and remember that much of the benefit of meals is the *pleasure* of dining, both parents and child will have an easier time of it. That is why the children of mothers who are not strict about the quantity of food eaten often have better appetites. Children who are taught to eat, trained to "good eating habits," or nagged into table manners struggle against these attempts and end by losing their appetites. Meals become a duty, not a pleasure.

Some parents mistakenly interpret the child's reluctance to eat as defiance of their authority. They insist that the child, whether hungry or not, eat all the peas on the plate—which doesn't make sense on the face of it. That can create difficulties. If the child is urged to eat despite his or her feelings, the child will quickly catch on that not eating is an effective means of frustrating the parents. A child doesn't stop to think that eating is a necessity. They are conveying the message that the child has to eat for them. If the child feels a need to control them or get back at them—for example, because of scheduled feeding back when the baby was only a month or two old—the child will seize on this opportunity to make eating a power struggle.

The child who has few
problems with parents will
have few problems with food.

Parents who insist on feeding an unwanted lunch when the child is old enough to climb out of the little seat sometimes fall into the trap of trailing the baby with a plate of food and an extended spoon. The child only enjoys the parents' frustration and powerlessness. It would be better to forget that meal and plan for an earlier dinner than usual—and to expect no problem of appetite.

A child may *seem* to dawdle and stretch meals out, but children naturally eat slowly. They have not been conditioned to rush through meals the way many adults have. An adult might go through a meal in five minutes. But a baby might easily take a leisurely twenty minutes or more, which was how long the feeding took at the breast or bottle—still a recent experience.

Adults take eating for granted. We might even eat an apple as we stroll, but to a child who is just able to walk, it becomes a matter for decision: to eat an apple *or* walk. Eating on one's own and walking are both relatively new abilities, and each still requires concentration. A child who eats and walks down a street will do both *very* slowly.

Sometimes "eating problems" are a case of misunderstanding on the part of parents. To take one example, teething always plays havoc with a baby's eating habits and appetite, especially in the second year, when teething increases. We can sympathize with a very young baby, not so accustomed to encountering pain as we are (and so soon in life), for not wanting to eat when gums are aching. To force a meal would be to lack empathy.

There is another, very common reason for a baby's occasionally diminished appetite. In the second year of life the rate of a baby's weight gain is slower than in the first year. Therefore the baby tends to eat less, yet continues to thrive. Some parents, accustomed to the earlier rate of eating and weight increase, try at this point to stuff the baby, unaware of the change in need.

There are still other factors. Very often babies of the same weight and age have different appetites, and each has daily ups and downs of appetite as well, just as adults do. One way to get a baby to eat is to serve small portions. Even adults faced with a plate heaped high with food feel stuffed in advance, whereas a small first portion often leads to seconds.

A baby who doesn't feel stuffed, is not bothered by growing teeth, and is in a period of strong appetite has no "eating problem"— *if* the breast- or bottlefeeding went well. That's a big "if." In Chapter 3 we quoted Selma Fraiberg on the undesirability of scheduled feeding: "The battle over food was waged over the family dinner table for years afterward. . . . The thwarted instincts got their revenge." An "eating problem" has a history and is not the cantankerousness of the child.

The successful completion of each period of development makes the next period easier. If problems remain unresolved in a given period, they are carried forward to the next, where a resolution is attempted in a new setting or shifted from one sphere of activity to another. It is possible for an "eating problem" at the age of eighteen months to have nothing to do with meals. After all, why wasn't the "eating problem" apparent at the beginning of life, when eating and sleeping were the baby's two principal activities? The "eating problem" might instead be due to a premature attempt to teach the child to use the toilet. If the "eating problem" appears at this time it more than likely expresses a conflict over toileting transferred to (or continued at) the dinner table even though not otherwise connected with food or eating.

Another possibility might be that there has been a change in daily routine. Perhaps a babysitter or a new day-care person is being used for part of the day. Any change in familiar habits causes distress to a baby, and as a reaction the baby may develop an "eating problem" — a refusal to eat or perhaps a stomachache.

In the latter part of this oral period, toward the end of the first year, when the baby's teeth are rapidly growing in, the impulse to bite becomes strong. Biting feels good because it lessens the discomfort of teething. Around this time the baby goes through a phase of cannibalism, wanting to make things a part of the self by swallowing them — literally incorporating them. This includes mother. The baby would like to devour her so as to have her and *be* her, a fantasy that remains unconscious. (We know that babies have it because it makes its appearance in the psychoanalysis of adults' dreams and fantasies, which from context turn out to be infantile in their origins.) Because the self has not been clearly differentiated from mother, when the baby incorporates the mother it feels exactly the same as if the mother is incorporating the baby. They are the identical experience. A fantasy such as this, if it is pronounced, could cause eating difficulties. This sometimes becomes evident in the analysis of adults who have peculiar eating prohibitions — as, for example, a revulsion against eating eggs, because the person thinks of them as the embryos of chicks, or the chicken's *babies.*

Around this time and a little later, when language is being acquired, parents affectionately say to their baby, "I could eat you up!" To a very young child that makes sense as an expression of love. Loving a person and eating that person are the same at this age. Below the surface, however, it can be quite alarming. To a baby, "eat you up" is all too real and is unconsciously understood literally. Because babies and children in any case tend to misunderstand the intentions of adults, it would be much safer to say, "I love you so much!" or any similar equivalent.

"I could eat you up" is only one of many expressions in

English that clearly demonstrate the unconscious equation of love with food. Some acts demonstrate the equation too. In kissing, for example, we give another's cheek or lips a short, implosive suck. When guests arrive at our home we offer them food and drink.

CONTRARINESS

There is yet another psychological reason for what may appear to be an "eating" difficulty. At the end of the first year and increasingly in the second and third years, a child natural-ly begins to feel contrary. This contrariness is a highly impor-tant development. *Any* aggressive act toward you in this period is a thrust toward independence. The aggressiveness fosters separation. Differences of opinion, arguments, resistance, fights — everything suddenly becomes pressed into service if it leads to that desirable goal. If you understand these events and don't take them as a personal rejection or as a sign of a "destructive nature" in your child they are easier to weather, and parent-child relations become smoother.

Any aggressive act
toward you in this period is
a thrust toward independence.

There are times when more patience is needed than usual and when patience is the best help you can offer. ("Patience — that is action," according to Marianne Moore.) If you under-stand that your baby is building toward psychological inde-pendence from you, you can resist making mealtimes into a battlefield by compromising. For example, you give your baby those foods that are nutritious *and* enjoyable. There is always *some* food the baby likes that is also nutritious. You simply wait for the child to crave a more varied diet, because you know full well that when hunger returns there will be no denying it. It also helps meanwhile to withhold the nutrition-ally worthless foods — candy, ice cream, and soda.

Some parents tend to worry unnecessarily about vitamin deficiencies if a child's eating becomes erratic for a time. Dangerous levels of vitamin deficiency are extremely rare in our society. In any case, malnutrition has probably never occurred as a result of a baby's "eating problem."

From eight to sixteen months there are periods when the baby's contrariness takes the form of the demand to do self-feeding, a development that most parents encourage. It doesn't matter how sloppy the baby might be in the attempt to get a spoonful of food into the mouth—and onto the cheeks, nose, and hair, with most of it glopping onto the bib and making the high chair a malodorous swamp of drying vegetable mush. What is extremely important is the baby's wish to take over. That is part of an innate thrust toward independence and eventually being able to take care of oneself. In fact, independence may not happen later on if the baby's attempts now, in all their various expressions, meet defeat or discouragement. Some parents who complain that their children lack initiative are unaware that they themselves might have destroyed that initiative by thwarting early attempts of this kind.

9

The
End of
the First Year

Spoiling doesn't come from being
good to a baby in a sensible way,
and it doesn't come all of a
sudden.

BENJAMIN SPOCK

Second only to the baby's crying, parents seem to be most concerned about the matter of spoiling their child. They wonder if there isn't something they should be doing from the baby's birth onward to avoid spoiling, almost as if it were an inevitable experience.

CAN A BABY BE SPOILED IN THE EARLY MONTHS OR YEARS?

Think of this: you could live without a baby — that is what you were doing all the years before you had one — but except for minutes at a time, your baby cannot live without you. The baby is in the vulnerable position of absolutely needing you. You are in the position of advantage, getting to know and love your baby but without absolutely needing him or her, at least not to the same degree that you are needed. Also, you probably have a mate. To your baby, however, *you* (mother, father, or both) are the "mate." You are all the baby has in the world. It would seem, therefore, that a part of caring about the baby's psychological growth is to give him or her all the love you feel. That brings us face to face with the subject that concerns so many. Can a baby be spoiled through love? Is it possible to give too much love?

A baby, a new being, brings to the world no preconceptions or attitudes, no game playing, and, in the beginning, no complex behavior patterns. The baby does not attempt to manipulate you in a struggle to see who has power over the other. If a newborn cries loudly and long it is in response to the discomfort of inner processes rather than in an attempt to force you to do something. There is no "you" to force.

No newborn knows enough about life to fake needs. All needs are real. The baby may be tired or hungry or wanting to have a bubble brought up. Or he or she may want to be held and rocked. If you help satisfy the need, the need subsides. *Meeting a baby's needs is not "spoiling."*

Yet even though you cannot spoil a newborn or even a three- or four-month-old, there are still some people who advocate depriving and frustrating a baby to "build character," keep from "spoiling the baby," or "not allow the baby to tyrannize."

Those who hold such beliefs ought to examine their feelings to see if they are responding to a need of *theirs* to deprive the child or perhaps repeat with the child what was done to them. Of all the concerns that parents have about a baby it is curious that the matter of spoiling is spoken of so frequently. The ostensible motive behind parental concern is love for the baby. But when we see how ready some parents are to *withhold* their love "to avoid spoiling," it makes us wonder.

"You will spoil the baby" becomes a terrible self-fulfilling prophecy. These parents frustrate the baby's needs, which only makes the baby attempt even more desperately to satisfy those needs. That "proves" to the parent that the baby has *already* somehow become spoiled. They conclude that they should have deprived the baby even more or earlier.

Some parents mistakenly assume that to pick up a child on each request leads to spoiling. But this wish to be picked up might be the expression of a need—the need for more stimulation: a child can see and experience more when held in the parents' arms or on their shoulders. After the child has been held for a while the need might then develop to be put down again. A child who is picked up often will spontaneously request to be put down just as often. After the child is three years old the parents might begin to plead fatigue some of the time, but by that age children have a better understanding of parents' capabilities. Besides, another pleasure begins to take over by then. The child is happy in the thought that he or she is becoming too heavy for the parents, which only tells the child how big he or she is getting. Forever yearning to be big, children welcome every evidence of it.

If a little girl were to say to a parent while crossing the street, "Hold my hand," it would be a mistake to say, "Oh, you're getting too old for that." She would be asking for something based on a need, which she wants the parent to satisfy. She is also offering love and trust, which the parent would be throwing away by refusing the hand.

This important matter is worth emphasis. *If you do not meet an emotional need, the need will persist* and the child, seeking gratification of it, will remain attached to you. This may appear to be a problem of spoiling, but defining it in this way emphasizes the underlying truth, that *needs continue not to be met.* If you gratify an emotional need in its proper time, the appetite for it is appeased and the child's demands stop. The child is *not* spoiled.

Meeting a baby's needs
is not "spoiling."

If you are a giving person, the child will have no desire to manipulate you. The catch is in the word "giving." It means to give of yourself, to make yourself *emotionally available* to the child until each *emotional need,* as it appears, is gratified. Put more simply, it is not possible to give too much love. Love does not spoil and is never overabundant. Substitutes for love can spoil: excessive amounts of toys heaped on the child and loads of candy bought out of guilt may lead the child to expect and want still more. The toys themselves don't spoil, but the reason for giving them might. Giving toys out of love, not in place of love, doesn't lead to further craving. Love is what children need most. To spend more money on children than time with them is in fact to spoil: money and objects are not love.

On closer examination, "spoiling" often turns out to be a power struggle between parent and child, similar to some forms of "eating problems."

What most parents mean by "spoiled children" are children who demand often and seem never to be satisfied. Quite frequently these children whine a lot. But where this is the case the problem is invariably subsurface. As babies these children more than likely did not have their needs satisfied and as a result they nag their parents and experience persistent feelings of dissatisfaction. But a child whose needs have been met and who feels loved reacts quite differently. Such a child does not get upset if, for example, you refuse a request for candy ("Not now. After dinner.") or try to wear you down by annoying you about it until you either give in or become angry.

There is a subtle problem in discussing spoiling. We have said that a baby is not a controlling creature. Nevertheless there is a time in life when a baby makes every effort to control. It is worth dwelling on this, even at the risk of being repetitive, because of its importance to good development.

At birth and for the first several weeks, the baby does not try to manipulate you. You don't exist yet as a person to *be* manipulated. But the baby does have an innate need to feel omnipotent, in control over the self. In those first weeks control over the self is synonymous with control over the environment because one has not yet been distinguished from the other. It is absolutely essential to healthy psychological development that the baby *enjoy* this feeling of omnipotent control. Babies who don't enjoy this grow up to be compliant adults or constantly rebellious or angry.

It is not possible to
give too much love.

The baby's feeling of omnipotence is a very necessary delusion. The baby's personality begins to be shaped by the degree of success met by early efforts to influence the environment. The baby who feels that he or she *can* exert an influence on the environment feels effective and capable as a person. That is why you would not be spoiling a baby if you responded to the screaming and kicking by gratifying needs. If a cry "magically" brings gratification, the baby feels that *efforts are rewarded.* The baby does not feel helpless but instead feels capable of arranging matters so as to have needs satisfied. This has lasting influence on the baby's character. As the delusion of omnipotence continues to be met by the mother, the baby slowly relinquishes the delusion as he or she moves develop-

mentally forward. In time, the baby finds other, psychologically more advanced means of feeling effective and capable.

To frustrate this delusion of omnipotence through a power
struggle between mother and baby in some vain, misguided
attempt to avoid spoiling the baby would be to fix development
at this earliest need and thus in some way hinder all subsequent growth. Some children grow up to be extremely compliant persons as a result of having lost such a struggle at the
beginning of life. And compliance exacts a high price in
spontaneity and originality. These children become what some
call "maladjusted," but the irony is that it was the world (at
first the parents) that originally failed to adjust to *them,*
leaving them emotionally scarred forever.

Dr. Winnicott makes this very point when he speaks of the
"good enough" mother. According to Winnicott, the "good
enough" mother meets the baby's feelings of omnipotence as if
they were reasonable. She joins in that delusion for a while,
even *indulging the baby* during those early weeks, knowing
that the baby will outgrow this stage.

MORE CHANGES

Parents who are attuned to their baby's needs from the
beginning instill in the baby a sense that all is well and that
people of significance (mostly mother and father at first) are
helpful and cooperative. In time this feeling becomes so much
a part of the growing person that the child in turn becomes
helpful and cooperative to others and, perhaps more important, to him- or herself.

A baby evolves all the time. If the baby is going through a
period that is difficult for you, such as throwing food onto the
kitchen floor, it might be helpful to know that these miniphases will run their course and end spontaneously. This does not
mean that parents have to tolerate chaos. Most parents discourage excessive mess making, but they do so relatively
pleasantly, verbally, patiently, without hand slapping. To
teach a contented baby to obey is simple. (A baby who is
already discontented presents problems, however.) You hold
up an index finger, frown, and firmly say, "No." All babies in
the second half of the first year seem innately to understand
the significance of the gesture and, wishing to retain your love,
stop doing what you forbid. You might have to repeat your
order several times to get your point across, but hitting is

definitely not necessary. To make an unusual fuss over something that annoys you or to strike the child would only make the problem an issue, and the behavior would continue longer.

In the second half of the first year the baby begins to explore the world. Dr. Winnicott says that if you observe the baby closely, you will see that what at first appear to be random motions are attempts to understand experience. The baby sees a toy block, picks it up, mouths it, salivates over it with pleasure, looks up at you, puts the block up against your face so that you too can enjoy tasting it, suddenly whisks it back with a squeal of happiness, shakes it, and mouths it some more. After a while, the baby drops the block and turns to a wooden stirring spoon and enjoys banging it, throwing it on the table and picking it up again, and finally abandons it out of boredom. To the baby, none of that is random: each group of acts is a sequence adding up to a whole experience. These experiences are fun, but they are also learning bits. Cumulatively they become a body of knowledge about living in the world, knowledge that events have duration and are composed of parts.

The "good enough" mother
meets the baby's feelings of omnipotence
as if they were reasonable.

Not only is this an early form of education, it makes its contribution to the development of character too. If, for example, you were to take the block away from the baby right after the baby had picked it up and mouthed it, even though the baby was still interested in playing with it, and if you then also took away the wooden stirring spoon, and so on through the day, the baby would never feel the satisfaction of completing a whole experience. Instead he or she might feel that experiences are merely acts that have a beginning but no follow-through. One starts but never finishes them.

STRANGER ANXIETY

Between the third and eighth months, the baby has begun to perceive the face of mother (or mothering person) as a definite, specific face, no longer just anyone's. Before the baby reached the age of six months the mother could be relieved by a nurse or grandmother and there would have been no complaint from the baby. Anyone—or any "face"—could gratify the baby's needs.

From the fifth to the eighth month, however, the baby begins to recognize mother's face as a special one and wants to be taken care of by her and no one else. To be picked up and held by others at this age causes the baby to become tense, turn away, recoil, or refuse contact. The baby might even cry and scream. From the age of eight months on, being held in someone else's arms means nothing less to a baby than that mother has gone away. She might be standing only a foot away, but she has nevertheless been "lost" to the baby. The possibility of losing mother has begun to be a real and fearful one. Spitz calls this reaction "eighth-month anxiety," or "stranger anxiety," and he says that every baby goes through this stage.

If a mother were to hand over her newborn to others and return when the baby is eight months old, the baby would recoil from her as from a stranger.

Although "stranger anxiety" might sound negative, it has a positive aspect. It means that love of another is more possible for the baby because for the first time others are becoming real. In distinguishing among persons there is some glimmering recognition of them as different individuals. Stranger anxiety marks the very beginning of the baby's relations with others.*

Back at three months, the baby learned to recognize and respond to the human face with a smile. At eight months, however, *the baby begins to smile selectively*: he or she will smile only at mother's face, or the face of a familiar person, and no longer necessarily at just any face. The baby may, however, smile at a stranger if mother holds the baby and if the stranger does not come too close. If a stranger does move too close, then even though held in mother's arms the baby will feel threatened enough to turn his or her face away in avoidance.

THE DEFENSE CALLED "DENIAL"

Turning the face away in avoidance of reality is one of the earliest defense mechanisms—denial—and in its most rudi-

*René A. Spitz, *No and Yes*, New York, International Universities Press, 1957, p. 122.

mentary form at that: a person is not there if the baby simply turns his or her head away and, ostrichlike, *sees* no one. Some adults remain at this stage of emotional development, like the angry wife who on returning from an outing makes a show of warmly greeting the pets and pointedly ignoring her husband in an attempt at denying any involvement with him — which of course only emphasizes his importance to her.

This denial contradicts what the baby learned earlier, while doing 180° turns of the head, that objects (and people) remain where they are even when the baby is *not* looking at them. But the contradiction only attests the tenacious hold that wishing has over the demands of reality. At this age, in any dispute between wish and reality, the wish always wins.

CRAWLING

The baby's world of excitement in the second half of the first year is by no means limited to mealtimes. New excitements open up, among them the ability to crawl. The coordination of arms and legs with all the rest of the body becomes developed enough for the baby to move around unaided.

Stranger anxiety marks
the very beginning of the
baby's relations with others.

Ordinarily, at this age, the baby is confined to a playpen, which is not so restrictive as it might appear to adults but allows considerable freedom to play in a protected area. To a baby who has just barely learned to crawl, sixteen square feet is practically a world.

Another advantage of a playpen is that you don't have to keep rushing over to wrest objects away that are either dangerous for the baby or valuable to you. It is better not to let a baby get hold of things in the first place than to keep taking them away. Babies don't miss what they don't have, whereas if you keep retrieving objects from them they will, in a gross misunderstanding, feel you are depriving them and become angry and frustrated.

Some of the time you let the baby out of the playpen to

explore on all fours. And suddenly there are so many things to see and experience: not only table and chair legs but the fun of being *under* a table, that huge enclosed, mysterious space. The baby discovers wall outlets (safely plugged in advance with caps), a wastebasket, slippers, a lamp base, colors and shapes in the kitchen linoleum, the garbage pail, a plant, a moving curl of dust in the corner, a fly—all new things. Those that are dangerous now have to be put out of reach: bleach, cleansers, soaps, insecticides.

When the baby is out crawling in the living room or kitchen you keep a sharp eye out. If the baby finds an old key or a penny or a thumbtack you are alert to take it away swiftly and without fuss. Babies do not distinguish between a thumbtack and food, and you know that the thumbtack would go into the mouth in an instant.

It is a new period with new problems. In compensation, however, some old problems have been left behind. The baby's *total* dependence on you is perhaps the major burden to be outgrown forever, no small boon. You appreciate those half hours at a time when the baby can play safely and contentedly in the playpen while you go about your other work or possibly even relax.

THE FIRST STEP

Between the eighth and tenth months the baby begins to stand up while holding on to the playpen or furniture, some-times letting go the bars or a chair for a brief, daring moment before hanging on again and walking a step or two more. It is hard work to be standing up only to plop down suddenly, and sometimes it is a bit frightening. Occasionally the baby, tired after standing for a moment, begins to cry out of fear of plopping down too hard and so remains motionless, hanging on to the playpen in a misery of indecision until you release the grip and gently set the baby down.

The baby delights in the new ability to stand up and sit down and move around upright without anyone's help. After two or three months of this practicing, one day, with no special sign to announce its arrival, the great event happens. The baby lets go of the playpen or furniture altogether and, with concentrated self-observation, puts one foot carefully in front of the other, takes another tentative step—and swiftly grabs onto something and stops. The look on the baby's face is a blend of surprise, exhilaration, anxiety, and joy. The baby, in a momentous, evolutionary advance, has just taken the first step.

You clap your hands and say how *wonderful* it is. The baby, happy to see you so pleased and eager to try again, unconsciously experiences a feeling of even greater importance: "*I will succeed!*"

THE END OF THE FIRST YEAR

Looking back at this point, those first crushing weeks of childrearing were relatively easy once the routine got established. At that period the baby's activities were quite restricted. The baby moved, cried or made sounds, wet, put fists into the mouth, and played with a rattle or toy. That was the extent of the infant's independent activities. All of it happened in a limited space. Everything else had to be done for the baby by you or other adults: picking up, talking, fondling, feeding, playing, bathing, and putting the baby to bed to sleep. True, feeding an infant in the middle of the night after a tiring day was not easy. But compared to the difficulties of running after a twelve-month-old who can toddle around a room and open an unlatched door or head for the stairs, the care of the newborn was relatively simple.

"It is very important to remember that the time the baby needs us so much is short. Every few months brings a new stage of development. . . . As the baby develops and becomes more autonomous the total dependency on us lets up. This may mean more work for us at first. A baby's first attempts at self-feeding can be very messy. And a toddler beginning to crawl and then walk may seem to be 'into everything,' and does need more attention than an infant who sleeps most of the time, but the work becomes more rewarding as we see our children become more and more self-directed little people."*

This new level of interaction with the baby, although it might at times be physically quite exhausting to you, will have its psychological rewards for both you and the baby. This once sleeping, hiccuping, yawning, sneezing, crying, feeding, gurgling organism of incalculable potential is beginning to be more and more "human." That in itself is a welcome change. For the first time the baby can begin to express *gradations of*

*Paula Brown Doress, with Esther R. Rome, Wendy Sanford, and Norma Swenson, in The Boston Women's Health Book Collective, *Our Bodies, Ourselves*, New York, Simon and Schuster, 1973, pp. 210–11.

feelings, subtleties of mood that only short weeks ago he or she was utterly incapable of. There will be times when the baby feels angry, followed immediately afterward by an outpouring of joy. The baby will feel love for you and possessiveness toward a tinkling toy, then get enraged by frustration only to feel all cuddly and happy to be with you a moment later. The spectrum of reactions and emotions now becomes considerably enriched, as does your interaction with the baby.

THE EMERGING OUTLINES OF PERSONALITY

Thus we arrive at the end of the first twelve months of life, the "most plastic period in human development," in the words of Spitz. In this first year the baby has gone from a fetus to an upright, walking baby, recapitulating millions of years of human life. The baby has left a safe and secure uterus for a world of frustrations and gratifications, adapting to it in stride.

The baby has learned that letting go of something good does not mean losing it forever. There are pleasures and pains, but pleasures predominate, at least as the absence of pain. The baby has learned that there is an "I" and a "not-I." Beginning at first with feelings of absolute power and omnipotence, the baby has begun to perceive him- or herself slightly more modestly, as living in a shrinking but more real world in which there are limits. The baby has begun to have an early, dim awareness of self, of being not quite the universe.

The rational thinking processes are well under way, and although "magic" will fascinate for years to come, the baby will slowly be able to distinguish ever more clearly what is real. He or she has advanced to a point where a face is no longer just a signal that needs will be gratified but mother, father, friend, or stranger. The baby has gone from a passive receptiveness of things and people to active outgoingness toward them. The baby has learned to love and at times dislike mother as the principal gratifier and frustrater of needs, and has learned to fuse the two feelings together and come out loving her most of the time. The baby has learned that not all needs have to be met immediately, that even if gratification is delayed, he or she can expect it with confidence because in the past satisfaction has always come reliably. The baby has begun to build sturdy, lifelong defenses against the uncontrolled outpouring of instinctual demands, needing a little less help from parents in mastering feelings. The baby has begun to learn to walk and move around, explore more of a world that seems to grow larger by the week, and try different kinds of walks with the same concentration that an adult would devote to learning to walk on stilts. And, in some ways more important than all the rest, the baby has the earliest glimmerings that he or she is a separate person in that there seem to be others in the world and that they are rather more benign and helpful than not. As Spitz says, "Never again in later life will so much be learned in so short a time."

10

The Beginnings of Psychological Separation

I am the adventurer on the voyage of discovery.

EDWARD WESTON

The first year of life is remarkable for the variety of processes that unfold. But in the more intricate and complex second year, the processes subtly synchronize with each other as new interests and abilities feed into growth like tributaries into the mainstream. Principally, the baby learns to walk and run, begins to speak, moves from oral erotic concerns to anal ones, and learns to think. These abilities and preoccupations push the baby even farther toward psychological separation from mother (and father) in the instinctual thrust toward independence.*

Life is a series of separations. Although for the parents physical separation begins as soon as the baby begins to kick and react in the womb, for the infant birth is the start of separate physical being. At three months the baby's smiling at a human face signals the earliest beginnings of a separate psychological being.

In the second year, as the baby becomes aware of having a

---

*The discussion in this chapter and throughout the book of a child's psychological separation from mother is based on the work of Dr. Margaret S. Mahler, especially *On Human Symbiosis and the Vicissitudes of Individuation,* New York, International Universities Press, 1968, although the present simplified presentation cannot do justice to the subtlety of her contributions. The ideas are drawn from Mahler's work, but their applications are the author's.

self and inhabiting a world, he or she has started to become a separate social being.

But becoming a separate psychological being is by far the most complex of these developments and the most important task a baby faces. The smiling response may indicate the beginnings of separation, but the process doesn't really get under way until the baby is six months old, after which it continues until the age of three.

The child forms an extremely strong attachment to mother during those two and a half years. When the dependence on her reaches a peak of satisfaction and begins to diminish, separation follows. The more enjoyable and secure the relationship with mother has been, the easier the separation. If a mother would try to "encourage" independence by frustrating the baby's need for attachment she would only create a yearning for greater attachment, which would extend the need beyond its normal duration and perhaps even permanently. A child always moves to higher levels of need only after earlier needs have been sufficiently satisfied.

Physical closeness with their child may sometimes be wearisome for parents after the long first year. There are times when they yearn to get away from their child. But their feelings tell them it would be a mistake to thrust the child away if he or she feels the need to be with them. The child would inevitably experience that as a rebuff, and that would not only hurt the child but possibly backfire in the form of continued dependence on them.

Independence is not a matter of decision. It follows by itself after the child's dependency needs have been met and the process of psychological separation has been completed. It is quite important that the attempts at separation come *exclusively* from the child, not you. Coming from you they would be experienced as rejection. Coming from the child they are experienced as growth. The difference between the two is the difference between illness and health.

Nevertheless, matters can be arranged so that the mother can have freedom while meeting her child's emotional needs. There begin to be, for example, times of the day when the child is quite content to play alone, having been reassured over the months that mother would never simply disappear. The child feels secure and therefore able to tolerate her absence for brief periods. At those times the child can be allowed to play quietly for as long as no complaint is heard. Nearby but out of sight, the mother can take the pleasant and peaceful opportunity to relax, get done something that she has put off doing, or perhaps call up a friend.

For a growing child, this way of being alone, in an atmosphere of contentedness, is reassuring, not frightening. In fact, it makes being alone begin to feel desirable because it lets the child know that it is possible to do things alone and function quite well, a feeling that the child welcomes. The secret, of course, is that the child is not really "alone" but feels the mother's emotional availability. *The single most important feeling that a child can have in the first years of life is that the mother is emotionally available and that her availability can be depended on.*

FEAR OF MERGER

If closeness is carried to an extreme, it undermines the innate desire to separate psychologically. A cloying, smother love only makes a child impatient to get away. It works against the child's natural desire for a satisfying closeness that leads to the healthy wish to separate gradually.

A child always moves to higher levels of need only after earlier needs have been sufficiently satisfied.

Just as there is separation anxiety if a child feels that mother is not emotionally available or if she emotionally "abandons" the child, there is also anxiety over *merger.* Merger is a confusion in identity, which causes fear. The fear is not one of literally joining together but that the child's self will be swallowed up, so to speak, by the mother. Much like a child's differentiating him- or herself from the mother psychologically, merger is experienced internally.

We said earlier a child carries around a personal "version," or idea, of the mother that is composed of tens of thousands of images. Simultaneously, the child builds an inner "version" of the self as well, it too composed of tens of thousands of images. In normal functioning, these self-images and the images of the mother are differentiated from each other. The clear distinction between them helps the child to establish a sense of identity. With merger, however, the child's inner version of the mother becomes mixed with the inner version of the self. The two sets of images are not sufficiently differentiated from each other. This means that the child experiences no difference between self and mother — a threatening feeling once distinctions between the self and others have begun to be made. It is threatening because identity is blurred. Merger is feared as the loss of one's self. Merger is especially feared if the earlier relations between mother and infant were experienced by the baby as frustrating.

Differentiating the self from mother is closely related to psychologically separating from mother. Both aspects of development promote identity and individuality. Some parents unconsciously put obstacles in their child's path as he or she moves toward a clear sense of the self. The parents, responding to their own (usually unconscious) needs, defeat the child's progress toward independence by their intrusiveness — "Here, let me draw that picture for you" (which also makes the child a passive onlooker), or by their insistence on putting on a child's boots long after the child has learned to do so on his or her own, or by doing things like trimming the child's nails till the age of twelve. Or they reverse their roles: because of unfulfilling relationships in his or her own childhood or now, it is the parent who needs closeness with the child and doesn't allow the child to separate. A child's unconscious fear of merger is especially strong where a parent is the controlling kind.

Some mothers, in fact, get along well only with babies, not children. They don't feel threatened by helpless, passive creatures and either keep on having babies to maintain a fresh supply of dependent beings or go from being "good enough" mothers in the first year to mothers who continue to demand total dependence indefinitely.

The fear of separation combined with a fear of closeness leads to specific interpersonal problems in adulthood. The person, never having psychologically separated from mother, needs continuing closeness with others, but at the same time, fearing merger, needs distance. The two needs conflict with each other. This unstable state of affairs has been described as "porcupine love": close but not *too* close. "Open marriages" can be understood as attempts to resolve conflicts of this kind, although there may be other forces at work in individual instances. Some on-again, off-again relationships are unconscious attempts to avoid the feeling of being swallowed up by the other person. So too are bickering in marriage and infidelity. The closeness of marriage is unconsciously feared because it means loss of identity. It is less painful to break off a relationship than to lose one's identity.

AGGRESSIVE FEELINGS AND SEPARATION

In retrospect, it becomes clear that psychological separation started much earlier in many small ways. For example, when you held the baby in your lap there were indications that he or she wanted to do things independently: the baby stood up on chubby legs and then squatted and sprang up and down again and again. This jogging in place was partly to develop the leg muscles for walking. But partly too the baby was asserting a fundamental need to do things independently: you may be holding on, but the baby has an autonomous life, and there are some things that an infant wants to do without your help.

This move toward self-assertiveness and independence is powered by the aggressive drive. From the age of five months on, when you changed diapers the baby began kicking and rolling over, acting aggressively in obvious pleasure, even sometimes to your annoyance, as an expression of sheer joy in living and interacting with you. When the baby drank juice from a bottle, the drive toward independence occasionally took the form of the baby's insisting on holding the bottle unaided, to the extent of vehemently swinging it away from you if you reached out for it. Increasingly there were times when the baby wanted to do the feeding, be his or her own mother, and do without you.

The baby, who through most of the first year was a cute, loving, cuddling creature, began to bite your nose, hit your face and eyes, and even became angry and scolded you apparently over nothing. You understood that the baby did not hate you and you didn't get angry or scold back. These actions were a striving for independence. The baby struggled all the more, of course, in reaction to an unwished-for dependence on you, a state of being that the baby was becoming more aware of. Wanting to walk and get around alone, wanting to eat on his or her own, hitting you, biting your nose, and angrily scolding you – these forms of aggressiveness (self-assertiveness) helped toward psychological separation from you.

SEPARATION AND TRANSITIONAL OBJECTS

Like any developmental step of importance, the process of separation from mother is accomplished in stages. Partial steps make the ultimate move possible without strain.

We can view thumbsucking as a part of the move toward separation. Thumbsucking, sucking on a corner of a blanket or a pacifier, and hanging on to a favorite doll are a child's way of making separation more tolerable. The baby wants to move toward separation but still needs reassurance that he or she will not have the terrifying feeling of being utterly alone. To suck a thumb, the blanket, or the pacifier or hold fast to a doll is a child's way of not feeling lonely. It helps the child get used to the isolation and darkness of the bedroom, by keeping the child company, making it possible to tolerate your absence. The thumb and other objects to suck on or hug are substitutes for mother. Dr. Winnicott calls them "transitional objects." The transition is from a state of being merged with mother, as at the beginning of life, to a state of being related to her as a separate, outside person.

These transitional objects are loved for their texture and smell. To an infant, Raggedy Ann, more than just a doll, is an interesting-smelling, squeezable bit of stuffed cloth with a satisfying taste. Transitional objects get dirty, but because of their importance in reassuring a child, it would be a mistake to throw them out or replace them. When you go traveling, the child should be allowed to take them along. Eventually the child outgrows them.

SELF-INITIATED ACTIVITY AND DARTING AWAY

The child's learning to walk tremendously increases the ability to separate psychologically. A new phase begins in which the child becomes much more self-assertive. You not only accept that development, you might actually feel relieved by it, even if it *is* more work for you to contain the chaos and gently have to restrict him or her in the need to pull books off bookshelves and pots and pans out of kitchen cabinets. The more the child can do things without your aid, the more you can begin to see to your own needs. The two fit.

A child becoming accustomed to walking delights in discovering the world, which before could be seen in only a limited way. Now, attracted by a colorful cushion on a bed, the child is not obliged to stare at it in fascination from a distance or laboriously crawl to its vicinity but can walk across the room, get it, bite it, taste it, hug it, and fling it to the floor. A world of self-initiated activity has opened up.

Between any two developmental steps a transitional period is necessary. The child always takes one step forward and simultaneously hangs on to the past. As a step forward, darting away leads toward independence as the child leaves you behind and learns to do for him- or herself—practices being away from you. As a hanging on to the past, the darting away is never attempted too far from your side.* Whenever we take a major step in life we feel a tug toward the past, as if a slight regression helps ease the passage to the unfamiliar and new.

The thumb and other objects to suck on are substitutes for mother.

Life is filled with paradox. A child may toddle—or crawl—away to be rid of you, to make you disappear as if by magic, and when you are nowhere in sight, the child becomes terrified at being alone. Because children are not capable of objective perception, it is not surprising that even if it is they who run too far away from you, they blame *you* for abandoning *them.* They are right too. A child unconsciously gives you credit as an adult for being able to gauge how much anxiety is tolerable to him or her and to reduce it if it threatens to be excessive. And besides, full psychological separation is still in the future. You do not yet have a separate existence. That is why when a toddler gets hurt he or she is always surprised and dismayed that mother is not *automatically* at hand.

THE DREAD OF ABANDONMENT

As walking improves over the next few months the child begins to toddle away from you with giggles of joy only to dash right back. The child is testing whether—and learning that—it is possible to wander far away (it may be only a few feet, but to

---

*This, however, cannot always be relied on. Children do get lost: their reality sense lags behind in development.

a child it is the giddy edge of the world) yet not lose you. It is practice in psychological separation. A psychoanalyst named Manuel Furer has given this behavior the apt name "emotional refueling." The child wants to dart away from you (practice leaving you) because of an innate urge to increase the physical distance from you as a part of separating psychologically from you, which is thrilling. But it is frightening too, because at the same time another part of the child understands that life would be unbearable without you. After all, *you* might go away and disappear (a very real fear to a child) and that would be enormously painful. So, like a puppy retreating between the forelegs of the mother, the child touches home base for renewed confidence before darting off again.

Between any two developmental steps
a transitional period is necessary.

Unfortunately some mothers, not understanding the psychological subtleties of early development, soon learn the trick of turning this state of affairs to their apparent advantage. This kind of mother says to her eighteen-month-old lagging ten feet behind to investigate an interesting crack in the sidewalk, "If you don't walk faster, I'm going to go away and leave you here – bye-bye." It works every time. In a moment, the reluctant child has caught up, to the satisfaction of the mother, who takes no note of the child's evident anxiety. The mother has her wishes obeyed by exploiting the child's most pronounced fear at this age: abandonment. At eighteen months, if a child needs mother and merely loses sight of her it feels exactly as if he or she had lost her forever – she has all but ceased to exist. That is terrifying. At this age and much later, if a little child gets lost for even minutes, the sadness is unbearable. Abandonment to a child is tantamount to death.*

The fear of abandonment becomes a real fear once abandonment seems possible to the child. And it is precisely at this age, when the child has begun to walk and increase the physical

---

*Time, March 19, 1973, reports that when a psychiatrist asked the three-year-old child of Edith and Clifford Irving, who were both in prison, "When a baby is separated from its mother, the baby is lost, isn't he?" the little boy said, "No, the baby is dead."

separation from you, that the possibility of your leaving becomes real. That it will not happen is a fact that the child will not feel sure of for quite some time, and no child is willing to take a life-and-death gamble on it. All the child knows is that you and the child are clearly now physically separate beings and you therefore can be lost. If you actually threaten the loss, the reaction understandably is panic, not the instant obedience it appears to be.

Children whose psychological separation has not been completed and who have been deprived of their mothers become afraid of fear. Even a small amount of fear in them immediately intensifies to panic level and causes unbearable anxiety. Unable to control their fear, some become counterphobic — attempt to deny having fear by getting themselves into situations that test their ability to withstand anxiety.

A child unconsciously gives
you credit as an adult for being able to gauge
how much anxiety is tolerable
and to reduce it if it threatens to be excessive.

The common technique of saying "Bye-bye — I'm leaving you here" is damaging in that it attacks a child at an extremely vulnerable point. Ordinarily the child feels a thrust toward independence and moves confidently ahead as long as there is no great anxiety attached to independence. Development happens slowly enough for the child to get used to the changes involved. There are always a few small anxious moments, but they only help: they are usually just enough to encourage the child to move along at a pace that is neither too fast nor too slow. And then suddenly the child hears you threaten abandonment: "All right, I'm going to leave you." The threat sabotages the child's natural efforts toward psychological separation. All at once, separation becomes not the easy next step of development but one laden with danger, and the child rapidly regresses to a point where he or she feels safe again: clinging to you.

As a "good enough" parent you avoid this by being patient during the darting-away phase. You know that like all phases it eventually ends and meanwhile the child is responding to a developmental need. What enables you to be patient is empathy. When a little girl investigates the sidewalk, she is not dawdling. She is obviously delighting in her discovery of a part of the world that she has never seen before. She behaves as if she were from another planet: the world is novel. If you see her look up to reassure herself of your presence, you say, "Don't worry, I'm right here." She continues her investigation. There is a speckled stone to be examined and then carefully put back at the base of the tree. There are front steps to walk up and down, window displays to take delight in, dogs to be cautiously touched, and people to say "Hi!" to. She is starting what another psychoanalyst, named Phyllis Greenacre, calls a "love affair with the world."* You know that sooner or later the child will get bored with that fascinating crack in the sidewalk and will find that doorways and fire hydrants all too soon become dull and unremarkable.

One girl was heard to ask her mother why they had to hurry along when it was so much fun to stroll. "Because you're three and I'm thirty-three," the tired mother said impatiently. The little girl looked perplexed at this "explanation," then unhappy at the implied rejection.†

Similarly, until around the age of five or six it is quite beyond a child's intellectual capacity to understand the consequences of his or her own actions. Some authors advocate teaching a young child the logical consequences of his or her acts. But a young child is utterly incapable of logic, and it will be years before the concept of the consequences of one's acts becomes real. To allow the child to lag ten feet behind you and thus, as an object lesson, cause the child to be late for an anticipated treat only teaches the child not to rely on you. You are not a helpful adult but an untrustworthy one. The age at which children "dawdle" (it is dawdling only to adults) comes long before there is any sense of responsibility for one's acts. Through painful privation you can train a child to jump at your bidding, but training is not learning. And if you do train rather than teach, you can expect the child to resent in adulthood your manner of "upbringing."

If you are in a hurry to get back home before the plumber arrives to fix the leak in the bathroom, you *explain in advance*

*Phyllis Greenacre, "Considerations Regarding the Parent-Infant Relationship," *International Journal of Psychoanalysis,* 41 (1960): 571–84.
†A response of this sort is reminiscent of Ring Lardner's classic account of a father answering his son's question:
  "Are you lost daddy I arsked tenderly.
  Shut up he explained."

that you must get back, with no two ways about it, and then allow a moment or two, with perhaps a friendly reminder in the interval. This makes your child an individual, not someone who is merely ordered about. It usually works. If worse comes to worse, you could pick the child up in spite of loud protests — if you don't do that often. At least that would be preferable to threatening abandonment. Sometimes you really do have to maintain a schedule, a necessity that a child cannot understand until he or she is developmentally more advanced. But if time is critical, why not use a stroller?

The best and most common method of dealing with "dawdling" is to draw away from the child *gradually,* pause after a few feet, and say pleasantly, "Let's go — we have to get home." The child will gauge your increasing distance without much anxiety because you are moving away in a nonthreatening way and decide at some point to catch up with you. "Come on, I don't want to lose you" is a reminder that comes across as reassuring at the same time. Even better would be: "Don't worry, I won't go away and leave you," and after another moment: "We do have to get home."

After this darting-away behavior has been mastered and the child feels confident of being able to wander off a bit without being abandoned, a new phase begins — rapprochement: the child wants *actively* to be near you and have you share in his or her experiences.

For example, if during the second and third years you have begun reading books to your child, your child may one day sit on the floor with a favorite book in one hand and pat the floor with the other hand, *asking* you to sit and read. Thus the child signals *you* to diminish the distance between you. The child may be too big now to be held often. But that is compensated for by a new ability to do something about being close.

A phase like this sometimes seems to parents to be a regression. A child who has already gotten used to going away from mother and playing on his or her own, only occasionally looking up to make sure that she is still there, might at the age of two and a half begin to stay close to mother again. But there is a difference. Before, the child didn't want to be abandoned by her. And the wish for closeness was largely *physical:* to be picked up, for example. Now he or she chooses to be near her *emotionally.* The child wants her to share all the wonderful new experiences of life, falling much more deeply in love with her and soaking up as much closeness and warmth and love as possible.

There is at this time the danger of the mother's becoming impatient. Because of the child's lessening dependence on her she has begun to enjoy greater freedom of activity. The child's need for rapprochement might be resented by her unless she understands that it is a necessary phase before real independence is achieved.

If a mother pushes away her child or fails to respond to the principal emotional need of the period of rapprochement (the need for greater emotional closeness), the child will experience a reduction of self-esteem. Coming so soon after the great pleasure of the earlier, practicing period, the drop in self-esteem feels all the more severe to the child.

To be thus rejected by mother is a cause for mourning, except that young children are incapable of mourning. What would in an adult become mourning becomes for such a child depression instead, whose full force surfaces usually only in adolescence and adulthood.

It is not a coincidence that, as psychological separation proceeds over the next year or two, peek-a-boo becomes the game of choice. The child's pleasure in it derives from the help it provides in mastering anxiety over the disappearance of the other person. You may momentarily become lost to view but— what happiness!— *there* you are!

MASTERING ANXIETY

Throughout this whole period, one of the important developments is the baby's increasing mastery of anxiety. The great closeness and love between mother and child that characterize this period enable the child to build the inner strength to tolerate larger amounts of anxiety. What helps is mother's being there steadily and continuously. Nothing is more reassuring than her presence.*

*The British children who were evacuated from London for their safety during World War II suffered great anxieties because of being separated from their parents, whereas many of those who remained in London and lived through the nightly bombardments of the Battle of Britain, because they were at their parents' side throughout, showed little more than the usual anxieties of childhood. See *The Writings of Anna Freud,* Vol. III: *Infants Without Families: Reports on the Hampstead Nurseries,* New York, International Universities Press, 1973, especially "Annual Report (January, 1942): Summary of First Year's Work," pp. 142–211.

Anxiety and the mastery of it go through levels of development too (see table opposite). At the beginning of life the baby's dependence on mother is a life-and-death concern, and at that level the fear is of annihilation. As the baby slowly becomes aware of the mother (or mothering person) as a gratifier of needs, the fear becomes that of being abandoned by her and not having the needs met. When the baby becomes aware of mother as a real person who loves the baby, the fear becomes one of losing the needed love. Anxiety is always tied to a need.

Anxiety goes through further levels of change. Around the age of four, when children notice the sex difference, they begin to experience castration anxiety. After six, with the development of conscience (superego), prohibitions, values, and ideals are internalized, and the fear specific to that stage is that of loss of self-approval, or guilty conscience: superego anxiety.

Is there such a thing as normal anxiety? All these forms of anxiety are normal when they occur in their appropriate developmental stage and in manageable degree. They become abnormal if they continue beyond that stage or overwhelm the person by their intensity. But there is another form of anxiety, called "signal anxiety," and that eventually becomes *the* normal form of anxiety. With signal anxiety, the person is never overwhelmed by danger. The signal is a small dose of anxiety that mobilizes the person to deal with the danger.

PSYCHOLOGICAL BIRTH

The slow differentiation from mother, followed by the venturing away from her and then returning for an "emotional refueling," in its turn followed by the period of moving emotionally closer to mother — a two-and-a-half-year-long process of psychological separation — leads to psychological birth. Around the age of three the child feels reassured that the relationship with mother is constant and reliable. The child is now fully aware of being distinctly separate from mother and begins to move ahead in development as an individual.

ILLNESS AND THE FEAR OF ABANDONMENT

What happens if the ideal arrangement of mother's reassuring presence cannot be maintained? If during the two-and-a-half-year-long process of psychological separation there should

LEVELS OF ANXIETY

Anxiety	Developmental Stage	Age*
Fear of annihilation	The baby is totally dependent on mother (or mothering person).	0–8 months
Fear of abandonment	The baby perceives mother as a gratifier of needs.	8 months–3 years
Signal Anxiety	*The child, capable of being aware of a danger, experiences it in a small dose and acts to reduce it.*	*2 years on*
Fear of losing love	The child perceives mother as a real person who loves the baby.	1–6 years
Fear of castration	The child, noticing the sex difference, misinterprets female genitals.	4–6 years
Fear of conscience (superego)	The child internalizes prohibitions, values, and ideals and offers or withholds self-approval.	6 years on

*Ages are approximate: there is considerable overlap.

be an illness requiring physical separation, no matter whether it is the mother or the child to be hospitalized, the child experiences the separation as his or her worst fear come true: mother has been lost.

In recent years the medical profession has become more aware of the importance of psychology in overall medical wellbeing. Doctors have discovered that in convalescence a baby's or child's recuperative powers increase when anxiety is reduced. Therefore, to keep mother and child together is beneficial even medically. As a result, many hospitals nowadays permit and even encourage the mother to be hospitalized with her child. Young children like to be tucked in at night by the mother. If it is the baby or child who needs to be hospitalized, at least the psychological stress of hospitalization is limited to the physical ailment and its effects. The terrible fear of abandonment and the sorrow over losing mother are not added to it.

Anxiety is always tied to a need.

There was a time—quite recently too—when parents were not allowed to visit their hospitalized child because the child cried and protested at their leaving. Hospitals thought that the solution was to bar visits because when parents did not appear the child seemed calm. This "calmness" gradually became recognized as anxiety and depression. Therefore, if a hospital tells a mother she may neither stay with her child nor visit (there are still *many* such hospitals), she might consider choosing another hospital, if possible. If she can't stay with her child, she should visit as often and for as long as possible. Between visits she might call by phone if one is available and chat. Her presence and cheerfulness will allay the child's anxiety, help recuperation, and protect against psychological damage. Nothing a doctor could prescribe could accomplish more.

Many hospitals that have no sleeping facilities for mothers will nevertheless permit them to spend the night in a chair at the child's bedside, which will considerably lessen the child's fear. In England, one of the parents of all hospitalized children up to the age of six *must* room in with the child because of the beneficial effect his or her presence has on the child's health.

If there are other children in the family to be cared for, it might be less painful for them to be deprived of their mother for one or more days and nights than for the hospitalized child. They are at home, in familiar surroundings, and presumably have their father or a close relative to take care of them. They are not undergoing a severe illness or operation or similar experience. And, especially if they are older, they are less likely to experience the separation as a "loss of mother." (The younger ones would experience some degree of anxiety, which is unavoidable.) Therefore, although the separation may not be pleasant, it is easier for them to cope with, and the separation is less susceptible to misinterpretation.

If it is the mother and not the child who is to be hospitalized, it would be helpful to arrange to have the child visit her as often as possible. Most hospitals do not allow children to visit, but it is worth asking. There might be a restricted area where they are allowed to see each other briefly, even if it is somewhere else on the hospital grounds. Any visiting arrangement is better than none. And the mother might telephone her child as often as possible.

Under three years of age, a separation for *any* reason is difficult for a child. Therefore even if it is only a matter of taking the child to the doctor for an injection, it would be less upsetting if you remained at your child's side while the shot was being given. That way your child would not feel you have walked out on him or her at a time of need, and the experience would not seem quite so frightening.

CONVALESCENCE AND REGRESSION

A time of illness is never pleasurable for a child or an adult. After the suffering of the illness there is the monotony and boredom of convalescence and its forced passivity. Children usually hate it, and a parent does not have to fear that solicitude and attention during convalescence will make a child wish for or fake illness to get more attention and love. In those extremely rare instances where that does happen, the gain of love comes at such a high price in sickbed boredom that we can guess how little love and caring were experienced by the child before falling "ill." That, of course, is where the cause of the problem lies. If times of illness are the only times a baby or a child gets love, to pretend illness would be understandable.

During illness and convalescence everyone regresses, including babies and children. Even adults become more dependent again because they feel vulnerable and helpless, and the illness clouds their thinking and feeling. They find themselves going back to earlier times and modes of behavior, when their mother took care of them and made them feel comfortable and loved.

Regression caused by illness is no cause for concern. Meeting a child's emotional needs never spoils the child.

BABYSITTERS—SOME DIRECT ADVICE

Never leave a baby or a young child alone in a house – not even for two minutes – not even if the child is asleep – not even if "nothing has ever gone wrong before." If you must leave the house, either have someone come over or drop your child off with a neighbor or friend.

If you are going shopping, your baby would feel better being with you and would enjoy all the excitement of new sights and sounds. If you use a stroller, the baby will not be a bother to you: as fatigue comes, though there may be annoying moments, the baby, lulled by the passing sights and the motion of the stroller, sinks into a sleep as you shop.

If you want to go out for an evening and need to use a babysitter, on the first occasion you might have the sitter arrive a half hour or an hour in advance of when you plan to leave. That would give you an opportunity to appraise his or her capability and sense of responsibility and also evaluate the sitter as a person. You would feel safer knowing that the sitter is not someone who is going to spend the evening absorbed in conversation (or whatever) with a friend (sneaked over after you have gone), possibly becoming annoyed at your child for waking up and crying. Teenage girls who babysit tend to spend hours on the phone, ignoring the baby. Telling them that you will be calling up to see how things are acts as a deterrent.

A good sitter is someone who has a feeling for children. He or she should be prepared, if your child wakes up, to spend time talking or playing or getting the child back to sleep again. A loving, easygoing person is better than someone who knows the professionally "right" thing to do. Some sitters talk good theory but come across as distant or uncaring.

Tell the sitter what to do if your child should wake up, what your child's habits are, where you keep fresh diapers, and so on. This preparation will help make things function smoothly for your child during your absence. The absence alone, if your child should wake up, would be unpleasurable enough.

Having the sitter arrive early gives your child time to get acquainted while you are still there. Also, the child, by noticing your reactions to the sitter, learns that the sitter can be trusted. The somewhat older child — three or more years old — can become absorbed in play while you and the sitter are both present, and with that reassuring transition your leaving becomes easier to take. Once the baby becomes accustomed to the same sitter, that transition would not be needed on succeeding occasions. You could even explain ahead of time that you are going out and that, if your child should wake up in your absence, the familiar babysitter will be there.

Meeting a child's emotional
needs never spoils the child.

If you leave your child with a friend, preferably one who also has a child, it helps considerably if you both enjoy a short social visit before you leave. This helps the child to feel that your friend's house is a pleasant place to be, and consequently he or she will not miss you too much.

From the time the child is six months old or older and is approaching the period of stranger anxiety, it is important that he or she *not* be asleep when the sitter arrives and you leave. If the child should wake up after you have gone, your unexpected absence would be frightening. And the presence of someone else, especially a stranger, would make matters worse. An experience of this kind could lead to sleep disturbances and fear of the dark. Your child could equate sleeping and nighttime with losing you.

Similarly, if the sitter arrives and your child is awake, don't wait till your child is not looking to sneak out without saying you are leaving. That would be catastrophic. To the child it would feel like sudden and unbearable abandonment. In a circumstance of that kind the presence of the sitter would not be reassuring or calming but would arouse great anxiety about what might happen next, and this too could create fears and problems.

If the child is three or older, when you get home you might ask if he or she liked the sitter. An unhappy experience is a matter for concern. Any anxiety that your child experiences during your absence will make your succeeding absences problematic.

DIVORCE

One form of physical separation from one of the parents that is becoming increasingly common is divorce. Knowing what we do of a child's psychological needs, it is tempting to say flatly that divorce is undesirable, but like any blanket statement that would not be true. Sometimes divorce is the only tolerable course to take, preferable to maintaining a home in which the father and mother find it impossible to get along with each other and fight or forever bicker — or worse, rage below the surface — giving the child the impression that marriage is a relationship of hate rather than one of love and mutual respect. Sometimes children are abused in these battles, and in any case they never learn adequate marital or parental roles.

Can a divorce be arranged so as to cause the least possible harm to a child? Is there a "best" time for divorce — an age for a child to have reached before parents divorce?

Strictly speaking there is no good age for a divorce. It is important for every child's development to live with mother and father until full psychological maturity: postadolescence. (Psychological development continues beyond postadolescence, but that part of it often happens away from home and parents anyway.)

If the "best" time for a divorce can be a matter of choice, it would be somewhere *between* developmentally critical points. We cited an instance of this in another context: not abandoning the child to a grandmother (or new nurse) at the time of weaning. The same principle applies here. It would be best for parents not to divorce while the child is going through a separation crisis, for example, at the age of three. The reason for this is obvious. And generally it would be best if the divorce came sometime after the age of five or six, after the time of what analysts call the oedipal crisis, because during that crisis both parents are needed for the successful resolution of important unconscious trends. The child needs to express love for both parents and to feel love from both.

Generally speaking, the later the separation, the better off the child. If the parents are separated in the child's fifth year and the mother assumes full responsibility, at least the little boy or girl will have had the experience of seeing what father is like and how he is different from mother. The child will have had father as an aid in psychologically separating from mother and as someone to identify with and strive to emulate. The father will have become a real person to see and hear so that the child could have trimmed the inevitable overidealization of him. If the parents had separated when the child was six months old, the child would have missed out on these important aspects of development.

After a divorce, if the child can see father at least once a week it would help greatly. ("A father who comes once a week and hugs you and takes you for a walk in the park and asks you about your report card is better than a father who never comes at all."*) To a child, the disappearance of a parent feels the same as rejection by that parent. Therefore, the father's presence is itself important to the child. He can be seen and heard and touched and reacted to. If the child becomes angry at father because of some momentary frustration, the child's anger is not so powerful as to "destroy" him. Thoughts can't kill, as the child thinks. Father is *there,* alive. Anger is an emotion, not a lethal weapon. Completely fatherless upbringings are freighted with unconscious problems of precisely this kind.

The child will sustain the least damage if the divorced parents act as positively toward each other as possible, because the child's feelings of loyalty to both will not be too severely strained. Where the strain is great and there is much anxiety, the child ceases to feel warmly toward either. The budding young feelings of love become crippled because love itself is experienced as too stressful.

Divorced parents can maintain a positive relationship with each other by making it clear to the child that although father may not have been a very good husband, he *is* a good father, and the same for mother. By distinguishing between the roles of spouse and parent, you tell your child the truth, you preserve and protect *both* parents, and you don't fall into the trap of extolling your ex-spouse's virtues to the point where your child one day wonders why, then, you ever got a divorce: he or she apparently *wasn't* a marvel. But a woman *can* be an

*Joseph Goldstein, Anna Freud, and Albert J. Solnit, *Beyond the Best Interests of the Child,* New York, Free Press, 1973.

unsatisfactory wife and at the same time a "good enough" mother, and the father who finds it intolerable to live with such a woman might acknowledge to his child (if it is true) that she is nevertheless a mother worthy of respect and love. If that is *not* true, silence would be better than criticism. Criticism would only place the child in the position of being Mommy's (or Daddy's) protector, and that is psychologically hard for the child. As an emotional burden, it would be developmentally beyond his or her abilities.

Parents should be careful to emphasize, and more than once, that they did not get divorced because of the child. *The child is in no way responsible for the divorce.* This is important because children tend to think that somehow they *were* the cause of the divorce and feel guilty as well as sad and brokenhearted, or they tend to feel that they could somehow bring mother and father together again.

A mother should be careful not to say "Daddy left us." A child would feel personally deserted by father if the divorce were presented in that light. Even in those cases where that is strictly true, the mother might nevertheless place the matter where it psychologically belongs: because of problems involving *them,* mother and father decided to separate. "But Daddy still loves you and always will."

Anger is an emotion,
not a lethal weapon.

It is important to a child to have two visible, touchable parents. A boy grows to be a man by becoming like his father, and a girl becomes a woman by identifying with her mother. A girl sees how a man — a special man of some importance to her — behaves, and she learns to appreciate his different ways. A boy watches his mother and learns how this special woman, who has been so constant in his life, likes to do things. If the divorce is the bitter kind and one parent, filled with revenge and hatred, takes it out on the child by depriving him or her of contact with the other parent, these important developments never take place and problems arise. A boy who grows up without a father risks developing a feminine orientation. The opposite case — a girl growing up without her mother — is rare because until recently courts have almost always awarded the child or children to the mother.

Mature parents don't get carried away by such infantile emotions as revenge and hatred aroused by something so irrelevant to a child's development as the lateness of an alimony check. Parents who are concerned with their child's wellbeing don't involve him or her in real or imagined skirmishes between themselves and don't use the child to spy on each other or try to get the child to side with one or the other. Fathers don't disappoint the child by failing to keep dates or by breaking promises, to get even with their wives. They don't refuse to see their child altogether to avoid the pain of being at the mercy of their ex-wives' manipulations. The mother who told her little boy, "You are the only way I have of hurting Daddy" did psychological damage to the boy, not to her ex-husband. It may have been an impulsive remark on her part but it left a scar, as became clear in a series of anxiety dreams that he began having of female monsters. Ironically, her revenge backfired: her son developed negative feelings toward *her,* which promptly became buried because of their threatening nature. The point is that whatever the reasoning or motivation, it is cruel to involve a child in a divorce. This mother was merely stating explicitly what other mothers convey in ways that are all the more destructive for their subtlety. The trouble is that many people who get divorced were not mature enough for marriage and are therefore not mature enough for the problems created by divorce. They simply act out their problems to the detriment of their children.

11

Speech

How can I tell what I think till
I see what I say?

E. M. FORSTER

Thus far we have been discussing chiefly the baby's evolving motor skills — crawling, walking, bringing food to the mouth — and how they are related to emotional development. Other equally important achievements, however, belong to this same period — the second year — including the uniquely human phenomenon, speech.

VOCALIZATION

Speech begins as vocalization. Between the time that he or she lallates (says "la-la-la-") and the time true speech is learned, the baby vocalizes — issues piercing yells and shrill demands. Vocalization is self-expression, not true language: language is intentional communication.

In the second half of the first year, the baby makes sounds that are experienced as pleasurable to the lips, tongue, palate, and throat, squealing with delight, saying a meaningless "uh-h-h," and occasionally issuing a gleeful screech out of the sheer joy of living. These vocalizations are among the most difficult events of infancy for parents to get used to. After a long, tiring day you finally put the baby to bed, enjoy an all-too-brief evening to yourselves, go to sleep exhausted — and are suddenly awakened by sharp, insistent squeals coming from the crib even though it is still dark outside and the clock says

5:45. It is an understatement to say that not getting a full night's rest after a long day of keeping up with a toddler feels unfair. But empathy comes to your aid: you realize that without language it is the baby who has the more difficult time of it, not you. A preverbal child's only means of getting needs satisfied is by making curt, insistent sounds. The sounds are not meant to annoy you or make your life miserable. The baby makes the sounds in response to needs or discomfort and to the anxious feeling that his or her needs will not be understood or met.

HOW SPEECH DEVELOPS

From these sounds speech develops. To use our model for growth (physical maturing, psychological development, and the enviroment coming together): the mouth and throat muscles mature (strengthened by sucking), and as you talk to the baby, the baby feels a wish to communicate with you.

A child's urge to communicate is a powerful force. The baby goes through periods of practicing specific sounds. For days the baby might say "ah!"—either a short, staccato "ah!" or a long-drawn-out "aaah." For a while it might be "*ee*!" Linguists say that *ah, ee,* and *oo* are "primary vowels," common to most languages and learned early in life.* They are learned earlier than the consonants, of which *m* and *n* usually appear first, *r* and *l* later, and the *th* sound one of the last because it is relatively difficult to say.

Toward the end of the first year the baby clucks, coos, gurgles, hums, and bawls, trying out a range of sounds so wide that many of them will never be needed in speaking English. (They are, of course, used in other languages, such as Tagalog, Swahili, German, Japanese, Hawaiian, Chinese, French, and Swedish.)

Babies actually learn languages twice. First, language is a privately devised code that you soon learn to understand from context. "Nah-*NEE*!" for example, may be an early attempt at saying "Mama," but it might also mean, "Pay attention because I want something," "Give me what I need," "More!" and so on. "*EEEE*!" might mean "I'm unhappy," "I'm anxious," "Don't you *dare* displease me!" and so on. In the course of the second year this private language gives way to the language of

*Adrian Akmajian, oral communication.

the particular culture as the baby learns "real" words, or the common code.

Slowly, out of love for you and to get needs satisfied more efficiently, the baby begins to mimic you and, by the end of the first year, learns simple words like "Mama" or "Dada" just by hearing you repeat them. (Don't be surprised if "Dada" comes out first even if Mama did most of the nurturing.)

Whether it's Mama or Dada, the name will be an all-purpose sound with global meanings. "Mama" could mean, depending on inflection and circumstances, "I'm happy," "I'm sad," "I want you, Mother [or even *Father*]," "I hate you, Mother [or Father]," "Stop," "Continue," and so on.

By the beginning of the second year the child learns words like "bye" and "hi." "Bye" is a highly compressed code word to a baby. It could mean "I want to go out," "I want to shut you out," "Get lost!" "I don't like you," "Good-bye."

Then come the names of familiar things: "dog," "cat," "table," "flower," "light," although the two-syllable words take longer to master. "Moon," once a child is used to saying it, might be pronounced "MOOOONNnn!" A child delights in saying it because it is a pleasurable sound to make and the moon a fascinating sight.

By the age of fourteen months, the child is building a vocabulary at the rapid rate of several words a week. By eighteen months comes the refinement of two-word combinations, forming primitive sentences. Adjectives and adverbs are coupled with nouns. "Nicky more" means that the child wants more of what he just had or more of some new and exciting experience. "Rachel nice" or "Mena good" are self-explanatory —and charming. The word "I" is acquired later: by the age of two years and ten months the child uses it correctly and often. The use of the word "I" implies much emotional growth.

It is a temptation for adults to use baby talk with a child once they have heard the cute way the child has of pronouncing certain words. But the child is not talking baby talk. He or she is trying to imitate you. If you talk like your child you slow learning and introduce confusion. If you find your child's mispronunciations irresistibly cute ("brekdis" for "breakfast"), repeat them not to your child but later, to your wife or husband or the grandparents.

In another year or two your child will delight you with spontaneously made-up words. One three-year-old boy enjoyed his mother's cooking so much he told her she was a good "fooder." He knew the word "cook" but "fooder" more nearly expressed the depth of his feelings. Between two and three, children begin to talk so much that it is clear that they have been storing up ideas and feelings for many months, awaiting only the vocabulary to express them.

SPEECH AS SEMANTIC COMMUNICATION

Etymologically, "infant" means "not talking." Therefore, infancy is literally left behind once the child can use words to convey meaning to another person rather than merely to create a mood or a feeling. A baby's first attempts at speech are reproductions of the music of our voice. Babies learn inflections earlier than they learn words. "There is a certain age at which a child looks at you in all earnestness and delivers a long, pleased speech in all the true inflections of spoken English, but with not one recognizable syllable. There is no way you can tell the child that if language had been a melody, he had mastered it and done well, but that since it has in fact a sense, he had botched it utterly."*

Where before "speech" was first only vocalization and then a crude communication, in its verbally advancing form it becomes a way of *spanning the space* between parent and child. Language begins to replace bodily closeness. And as physical contact diminishes, emotional ties increase in measure, which is a truly impressive and quite human development. Touch gives us sensations. Feelings bring us closer — and words express feelings.

Thomas Mann once said, "The word, even the most contradictory word, preserves contact." Speech is a higher form of contact because it is more symbolic and sophisticated than touching. And more advanced functioning always brings subtler pleasures.

There are many paradoxes in growth, human psychology being as complex as it is. Speech, which brings us closer together, at the same time emphasizes how separate we are from each other. Earlier, feelings and needs were "understood." The baby felt that he or she and mother shared in a union that made communication unnecessary. In fact, there was a much cozier "communication" in muteness. But now words emphasize that parent and child are separate. Speech,

*Annie Dillard, *Pilgrim at Tinker Creek*, New York, Harper's Magazine Press, 1974, p. 106.

therefore, makes a considerable contribution to psychological separation.

This separation is further stressed when the child learns proper names. Having a special name, "Ralph," makes the child feel like a unique being. You are Mommy and Daddy. He is Ralph. He is someone else, not you. Nor is he his friend Marcus.

This psychological separateness can be undone if, for example, you habitually anticipate your child's every wish. That would be like being able to read his or her mind. It is preferable for a child to ask for something and then get it — to verbalize needs.

Feelings bring us closer—
and words express feelings.

Explanations, however simple, now become possible, and this opens the way to a great spurt of growth. Earlier, to demonstrate clearly that you were not leaving the baby's side, you tried as much as possible to stay in view. Now you can leave the room after *explaining* that you will return in a moment. When you do return promptly the child sees that your words have reliable meaning. In addition to teaching the child something about truth and reality, the reliability of your promises helps make your next short absence easier to take. With the dosage slowly increased over time, physical parting can become more frequent and last longer without arousing anxiety.

Speech helps in dealing with anxiety in other ways. Around the beginning of the second year there are verbal indications that the baby is aware of your importance for survival and happiness. For example, one fourteen-month-old girl who had learned the word would say "Hi!" whenever her mother frowned or sounded annoyed. It was as if the girl were afraid that she was the cause of the frown or annoyance. The "Hi!" expressed a small but unmistakable degree of anxiety as she attempted to elicit a reassuring response from her mother.

COMMUNICATION

If we bear in mind that a child is learning things for the first time and assumes nothing, we see that every communication has two parts: a speaker and a listener, the message and the response. To a child a communication is definitely completed only when it is acknowledged. A child needs to know that you are aware that he or she has spoken. If you don't respond, the child will repeat the statement until you do. "Froggy!" the child will say and wait for you to reply, even if it's only "I see" or "Oh, froggy." Communication is reassuring to a child. One mother, in response to a statement of her little boy, said to him, "Uh-huh," to which he replied, "No, Mommy, say *words*."

A parent who is not altogether empathically attuned to a child might become annoyed with a repeated statement, finally acknowledging it with, "All *right,* I heard you the first time!" This angry response shocks and confuses the child: "If you heard me the first time, why didn't you acknowledge it and not have me repeat myself?" the child might wonder.

Communication is an immensely useful detour. Until a baby acquires speech, feelings are largely expressed directly through acting. If a baby doesn't want something you offer, he or she might take it from you and fling it away. That is a preverbal baby's way of refusing what you give – or getting rid of you. It also means "I'm angry at you and hate you." The gradual substitution of words for actions makes for richer psychological and social development. Words may not be as direct as action but they accomplish incomparably more. Without language a baby can only feel. With language a baby can *say* what he or she feels, and by saying it, know it.

By expressing feelings, speech increases self-knowledge. As the child learns new words, thinking expands its range through the use of those words. Words deepen relations with others by making communication more subtle. And in a circular way, the expression of increasingly subtle gradations of feelings enhances self-awareness. The child who articulates feelings comes to know that he or she *has* those feelings.

Words are more practical and efficient than actions. A baby merely cries when hungry, but a little child can be precise about hunger: "Cookie!" "Juice!" The child no longer responds only to inner stimuli but, being verbal, responds ever more specifically to the environment and is thus drawn out into the world.

At the age of fifteen months a baby might try to destroy you by angrily hurling an alphabet block at you (missing you by five yards), but at the age of three years he or she might tell you that Mommy or Daddy is "no *good!*" – a tremendous advance. Such outrageous generalizations will eventually seem unconvincing even to the child, who will modify them to something closer to the truth.

What will make this modification much more possible is precisely the child's verbalization of the feelings in the first place. Once taken out of the realm of the unconscious and connected to words, what were formerly nonverbal fantasies and feelings now become susceptible to change. They can be judged and matched against a sense of what is real, then corrected, modified, refined.

"NO"

In the period of acquiring language as communication, the child comes across a word that he or she will hear with considerable frequency for several years. The word impresses itself on the child so much and contributes so greatly to further development that Spitz assigns it the same importance he gives to the smiling response at three months and the stranger anxiety at eight months: the word "no."

Words are more practical and efficient than actions.

When you communicate to a child through language, the first meanings you convey are commands or prohibitions. You want the child to do or not do something. A child first learning to walk can get into trouble—the child may pick up a fork or knife left within reach by a momentarily distracted parent or walk over to an electrical outlet and play with the wiring. Suddenly you have to bridge the distance between yourself and the child immediately, and the way that comes automatically to you is speech. You shout, "No!" and perhaps vigorously shake your head.

The "No!" comes to the child as something immensely interesting yet mystifying. The child has literally never before seen you behave this way and is intrigued by the sudden change that has come over you. Until this point you have certainly been a fascinating person, but now you take on an unsuspected dimension: the child doesn't know what you mean and studies your face. Is your yelling the word connected with something the child was doing? To test this hypothesis the child repeats the action — reaches for the wire to the floor lamp. And you yell "No!" again. Now the child feels more certain that there is a connection but still doesn't understand why you are reacting — and reaches for the wire again.

Although in moments like this you are tempted to think that the child is deliberately defying you, to the child this is a learning experience. The child is conducting the experiment of trying to ascertain, through repetition, what cause-and-effect relation there is, if any, between his or her actions and your reaction. What are you communicating? Why are you communicating it? Does it have to do with reaching for the wire? What does the *sound* "No!" mean? (To the child it is not yet a word.)

The child looks at you again and makes the same move as before. If you shout the same loud "No!" the child is apt to be delighted because it is becoming clear that there *is* a connection between the child's action and your reaction.

Also it is great sport to control your behavior. It gives the child a sense of power: "I can perform actions in the world in response to which things happen." This sense of power fits in with the child's feelings of omnipotence. Anything that underscores a feeling of omnipotence feels "right" to a child.

THE FIRST ABSTRACT CONCEPT IN LIFE

Once the meaning and effect of "no" have been understood, the child begins to use the word, and that, as Spitz says, becomes "the first abstract concept formed in the mind of the child." "No" is not the name of anything, nor does it point to any object. It is a complete abstraction. With the word "no" the child becomes capable of negation and refusal.

Also the child identifies with mother and father even more now in their new image as powerful, commanding, prohibiting persons — *because* they are powerful: the child wants to feel such strength and power too.

"NO" AND SEPARATENESS

Whenever we acquire something that delights us we tend to overdo it for a while. This is what happens when a young child learns the word "no." The overdoing it is very much like an older child's learning what a hammer is for: from that moment on, until the novelty wears off, it seems that everything in the environment could benefit by a good, solid hammering. A child thinks he or she is being just like the parents by going around saying "No!" to everything. The greatest enjoyment comes from saying it to the parents, from "frustrating the frustrater." The word "no" has magic powers: a simple monosyllable uttered by the child and—how amazing!—the behavior of adults is altered.

As the mood strikes, therefore, the child says "no" no matter what he or she may feel. In fact, sometimes "no" is used to mean the opposite. There is a brief phase in the middle of the second year when parents are puzzled by this apparently contradictory behavior. They say to their child, "Would you like a piece of candy?" fully expecting the obvious answer, yet with all the contrariness in the world the child comes back with "No!" *and then reaches for the candy and takes it.* What does it mean?

With the word "no" the child becomes capable of negation and refusal.

One thing is obvious: the child doesn't mean "no" but "yes." But how can "no" mean "yes"? Translating the "no," we might get this: "You offer me candy, which you know I like and want. However, I say 'no' to you to make it clear that I don't want the candy *because* you are offering it: I want it independently of your offer. In this way I assert my independence from you. At the same time I succeed in sounding loud and forceful, like you, which alone gives me pleasure because it makes me feel big and very much your equal."

"NO" IS POSITIVE

It is clear that the word "no," though a negative, is a positive acquisition. In fact, the child's understanding of the concept "no" is what leads to an understanding of "yes." As Spitz points out,* there cannot be a "yes" without a "no." One defines the

*René A. Spitz, *No and Yes,* New York, International Universities Press, 1957.

other. If a person is capable of saying "no"—rejecting—then "yes"—acceptance—is also a real choice. If events happen because the person is *in*capable of saying "no" to them, they are not the result of a decision ("yes") but merely a yielding.*

When your child begins to shout "No!" at you, take it as a confirmation that you are doing a good job. Your baby's "No!" is one of those surface indications that great internal organization is silently going on, thanks to your "good enough" parenting.

"YES," "NO," AND MORALITY

Through "no" and "yes" the child begins to acquire an awareness that some actions are bad and some good. The words become more educational than their simplicity suggests. If the child does something right, you smile and say, "Yes." If the child does something wrong, you frown and say, "No." This is moral suasion at its simplest level.

Because the child can now speak, moral education begins to be possible. Speech, aided by your facial expressions, reveals what *you* consider good or bad. It suggests to the child attitudes to have and provides a basis for evaluation and judgment. Because your child loves you and has by now a fairly good understanding of how much you are needed for survival, he or she is quite willing to accept your values, which will remain unexamined until later, when thought becomes more advanced.

PLAYING WITH SPEECH

Once words have reliable meanings, those meanings can be played with. If a three-year-old girl knows that she is definitely a girl and you playfully tell her that she is a tomato, she will burst into delighted laughter at your humor and perhaps call you a pancake.

At around three and four years old the child might make spontaneous attempts at primitive verse: "Nickels, pickles,

*One adult outcome of this problem from the second year is "the girl who can't say 'no.'" Although she seems to be saying "yes," she is not choosing her lovers. She would become capable of choice only if she could sometimes say "no" too.

giggles!" "Kittens and mittens!" "Giggle, gorgle, gaggle, gog—tim, tam, *tum*." From this to literature is a small step.

CONTRARINESS AND INDEPENDENCE

At an early age, a difference of opinion may be only a matter of the child's doing something his or her way, however fumbling or inefficient that way may be. Not being altogether familiar with gravity yet, the child may want to place a ball on an incline and have it stay there. If in a contrary mood, the child will brush aside any suggestion or help you might offer. It doesn't matter if what the child is attempting won't work. You allow it. This tells the child that there is your way and there is also his or her way, and that you are therefore indeed two separate beings. The difference in opinion emphasizes independence by permitting the child to make a few errors of judgment and then make corrections. And, of course, you welcome and foster any move toward psychological separation (*always* allowing it to come from the child). Everyone has the inalienable right to be wrong. Some of a child's choices may be poor ones but at least they are independent choices, and that is what is important.

One universal form of contrariness is to defy a command before complying. For example, you might say to your son, "Matthew, no, no, don't touch," as you take the empty coffee mug away from his hand. To Matthew that is an irresistible invitation: it becomes almost impossible *not* to touch the mug now. So, looking at you, he pointedly lifts it up again and puts it down.

What should you do? Nothing. What is important is that your message got through. You know that once he satisfies his need to assert his autonomy and independence by defying your order he won't feel the need to touch the cup again. He attains his purpose and you attain yours. That one last "no"—in this case delivered in an action rather than a word—enables the child to save face.

If you fight the contrariness, Matthew might become even more contrary and make contrariness a habit, which would interfere with his development and also make life difficult for you. There will be times in life when contrariness could be especially trying, as when you are teaching the child to use the toilet. But remembering that these expressions of contrariness are growth-promoting may help you to ignore them, especially if you also bear in mind that the need for contrariness will exhaust itself with increasing development.

TEMPER TANTRUMS

Temper tantrums may begin around the age of eighteen months. More often than not a tantrum is brought on by fatigue and triggered by a frustration. As we have seen, the frustration can be the result of a discrepancy between the child's wish and an unyielding reality. The child still can't express all frustration by means of words and so resorts to actions — becomes explosively preverbal. Hence the tantrum.

At first tantrums resemble a sit-down strike. The child gets furious with you as the frustrater and deliberately plops down and refuses to budge except to flail and scream or pound the rug with fists and kicking feet.

Don't necessarily give in to tantrums, but do comfort.

Part of what the child feels in this rage is a great though momentary hatred of you: reason is temporarily overwhelmed by the turbulence of some not-so-pint-sized emotions. Their expression is unpleasant enough for you, but they are terrifying to the child. The tantrum is a stormy release, and a child would like nothing more than to be stopped. Contradictory though this may sound, the child also wants *not* to stop or be stopped but wants you to appreciate the fury and understand the reason for it — namely, your "cruelty." It may be hard but try not to retaliate (or laugh): let it blow over.

If you allow the tantrum to go on and on, the child begins to feel anxious because of the unsuspected intensity of so great an outpouring of feeling. A child tends to think that he or she is immensely powerful (due, of course, to feelings of omnipotence) and so is afraid that his or her rage might actually destroy you and the world. In fact, you *are* being destroyed — in the child's feelings. And worse, the *child* is also being destroyed at the same time. As long as a child has not psychologically separated from you, to destroy you is to destroy the self.

If you react in alarm, that convinces the child that the terrible power he or she imagines having is objectively real and dangerous. But if, on the contrary, you react calmly, you reassure the child that he or she may *feel* destructive but really is not.

WHAT TO DO ABOUT TANTRUMS

To yell back or hit would make matters worse. If things don't just blow over after a moment or two of tantrum behavior, try to hold the child's flailing arms gently or calmly hug the tearful, angry body to you, speaking in a quiet voice. This soothing outward control leads to a good feeling inside. The child may go on crying and feeling enraged for a while longer, but some of the more intense feelings will subside because of your reassurance that you have control over the situation and that you want to help. The original feeling of frustration will diminish with your show of concern. As the rage subsides, the child realizes you have not been destroyed nor the world annihilated by the tidal wave of feelings, and that too feels good.

After the tantrum is over you might tell your child you know how things must sometimes feel, but no matter what, you will always love him or her. The child feels bad enough as it is. Showing that you care accomplishes two purposes: it demonstrates that there is no need for the child to feel anxious that you might retaliate, and your love tames a bit more the still raw aggressive feelings that occasionally come pouring out.

If the tantrum is an attempt to get you to do something, don't necessarily give in on the point but do nevertheless comfort. If you give in, tantrums might become the method of choice for getting things from you. On the other hand, to comfort does *not* mean you have given in. It soothes feelings. In fact, it makes your stand easier for the child to take.

If your child says angrily at your attempt at comforting, "Go 'way! Leave me alone!" respect the wish. That too saves face and smoothes over feelings.

In the second or third year every child is apt to have a tantrum at one time or another. A tantrum merely indicates that a frustration has become too much to bear. But tantrums do not occur often if the child's emotional needs have been met optimally and if frustrations have not been permitted to build too much.

12

Parenting and Liberation

I am always on the side of the revolutionists, because there never was a revolution unless there were some oppressive and intolerable conditions against which to revolt.

MARK TWAIN

Thus far, although we have talked of "parenting," much of our discussion has centered specifically on the mother, with only occasional references to the father. In the contemporary climate of opinion regarding the sexes and their "roles," this imbalance requires comment. There is much talk today about "sex-role stereotyping," "culturally induced sex discrimination," and similar problems. The issues merit consideration.

SUGGESTIONS OF THE WOMEN'S MOVEMENT

For whose benefit should parenting be done, the parents' or the child's? The answer is: both—and why this is so is the subject of this chapter. The Women's Movement—a term that refers to all women who speak for the cause of equality of the sexes as well as to a growing body of feminist literature— offers a variety of proposals for new ways of parenting. Central to all these proposals is the concept that mothers and fathers should share equally in childrearing.

Biologically, of course, the mother's part in childbearing and birth is primary.* But once the baby is born, it is suggested that the father take his turn in mothering activities. He should not merely change an occasional diaper but actually feed,

*Those couples who choose prepared childbirth, however, involve the father during the last months of pregnancy and delivery.

bathe the baby, rock the baby to sleep in his arms, and undertake all other aspects of care and nurture. This program, it is claimed, will enable the mother to return to work when the baby is as young as three months old. An alternative proposal that is sometimes suggested is parttime employment for both parents. The husband should be permitted by his employer to work half a week and to stay home the other half to be a parent, relieving the mother to go to her job for half-weeks at a time, just as her husband does.

It is not necessarily implicit in this view that mothering is disagreeable and that men should therefore be made to suffer it too. But many women who become mothers feel shut off from life. Some assume that mothering for more than the first few months is a "new and subtle form of antifeminism" promoted by men and therefore to be resisted as much as possible.*

Let's consider these proposals in the light of what we have learned so far about the psychology of infancy and early childhood. Suppose the mother returns to her job when her baby is three months old. We recall that it is at three months that a baby responds to the configuration of a human face by smiling. The baby has now grown comfortably accustomed to human beings, though still regarding them only as friendly, need-gratifying "faces." And we also recall that at three months the face that elicits the smile can be anyone's: to a baby any person can be the need gratifier.

This fact would seem to lend support to the Movement's claim that any or all of several people (father, mother, surrogates, nurse, relatives, or neighbors) could be "the mothering person." Since no baby knows who the real mother is, the baby will not discriminate among all the faces.

The simplicity of this claim would be appealing if it did not overlook certain psychological facts. By eight months the baby recognizes not just a face but a *specific* face. The baby has seen this one face more than any other and has become attached to it, feeling anxious, tense, or uneasy if he or she "loses" that face by being given over to the care of someone else. This highly critical bit of development indicates that the "face" has gradually become more of a person. The face is no longer only a signal that the baby's needs are about to be gratified but is now

*Margaret Mead, "Some Theoretical Considerations on the Problem of Mother-Child Separation," *American Journal of Orthopsychiatry,* 24 (1954): 471–83. (Quoted in Barbara Seaman, *Free and Female,* New York, Coward, McCann, and Geoghegan, 1972.)

Mother (and in second rank Father, and after that family, then stranger). People have just begun to be real.

This development can encounter problems if the mothering person does not remain constant for at least the first nine months. If by the fourth or fifth month the baby has only just begun to recognize mother, the baby who spends most of the time with surrogates will tend not to see the mother as anyone special — in fact, could tend not to see *anyone* as special. The baby's relations with others, an area of functioning of the utmost importance, can be adversely affected.

"Eighth-month anxiety" marks the very beginning of human relations. Yet, as crucial as this development is, it is not clearly noticeable in the behavior of an eight-month-old baby and can escape notice, especially if the mother is often absent and the care of the baby changes hands. But the difficulties that stem from critical points of normal development, such as eighth-month anxiety, can create the deepest psychological problems of all because of their inaccessibility to consciousness.*

Few people are aware that, after the first three or four months, babies care *deeply* to have their mothers at their side

---

*Anna Freud, in *Infants Without Families*, after acknowledging that babies of low-income households who were *not* breastfed developed better from birth to five months in the Hampstead Nursery, says that they suffered by being at the nursery during the second half of the first year. They were less lively, less social, less responsive to people entering or leaving the room, and less able to differentiate among the changing personalities of the personnel. They also had less ability to imitate and exhibited slower responses to an adult's changing facial expression or voice. "The comparative backwardness of the residential baby at this stage is due to comparative unfulfillment of his emotional needs." In the first five months of life, the emotional interplay between child and adult occurs exclusively during feeding, bathing, and changing, and in this regard the care at the nursery matched conditions at home. But between "5 and 12 months, emotional interplay, and the intellectual stimulation which results from it, is more or less distributed over all the waking hours of the child's day. Consequently, the nursery child, who receives individual attention only when he is fed, bathed, or changed, is at a disadvantage. The amount of further individual attention — play hour, outings in pram, baby gymnastics etc. — which can be given to a child depends on the staffing of the nursery and other routine arrangements. *Attention of this kind has of course to be given by a mother substitute to whom the child is attached. It is valueless when offered by visitors, strangers, or occasional "voluntary workers."* [Emphasis added.]

"On the whole we can say that in the second half of the residential child's first year the loss in emotional satisfaction outweighs the gain in bodily care." (Anna Freud and Dorothy Burlingham, *Infants Without Families: The Case For and Against Residential Nurseries*, in *The Writings of Anna Freud*, Volume III, 1939–1945, New York, International Universities Press, 1973, Part II, pp. 544-46. See also "Report 43," *ibid.*, Part I, pp. 436–51, especially "Reactions of Bitterness and Disappointment After Separation from a Substitute Mother" and "Conflicting Allegiances.")

most of the time. The companionship of mother is the delight of their life — just as it is with a foal who *enjoys* staying close to its mother. Leaving babies with someone else, even a familiar friend, if that happens more than infrequently, makes them anxious. When the baby's spectrum of emotions widens, the baby becomes resentful of mother as well. Although babies are incapable of verbalizing, they do experience strong emotional ties, including angry ones.

When a person attains adulthood all relations with others, and especially with a mate, will be modeled unconsciously on precisely such events as this first outflow of love and the manner in which it was met. If the love met with discontinuity or inconsistency, the identical pattern may well be reestablished in adulthood, leading to shallowness of love, promiscuity, or an inability to make a commitment to a mate—all of which can be disguised as "sexual freedom" and "alternatives to the stereotype of the monogamous, nuclear family lifestyle." It would be ironic if the concern of women today over the relations between men and women should itself become the cause of a weakening in the feelings of love between women and their mates in the future.

Babies care *deeply*
to have their mothers at their
side most of the time.

Multiple mothering runs such a risk. The mother who returns to her job when her baby is three months old may not be aware that she is depriving the baby of some portion of a profound human right, the right to enjoy deepening ties with one special person, which leads to healthy psychological growth. If this "special person" becomes two or three persons, the baby's feelings are spread thin, which weakens the ties of love. And it is libidinal ties with others that bring any satisfaction in life, whether the ties are personal, marital, societal, professional, or occupational. The better the quality of one's relations with others, the better one's life. Care is indicated, therefore, to make sure that the early development of constancy and depth in human relations, which goes on silently and below the surface, is not unwittingly undermined.

THE DANGER OF SPLITTING PEOPLE

We spoke earlier of a baby's tendency to "split" mother in two, a "good" mother and a "bad" one, and of the way in which this erroneous view gets corrected as the child gradually recognizes that the "bad" and the "good" mother are in fact the same person and (at least typically) is more helpful and loving than frustrating. We can see how this universal tendency might become defeated if a child is offered more than one mother. Multiple mothering could play into the infantile fantasy that one mother is "good" and another "bad," thus reinforcing, not healing, the split. (The real mother would be the "bad" one because of her absence.) The child's view of people would then fail to move to a greater understanding of them as whole and therefore real persons, capable of good and bad. The child would continue to see others as *either* gratifiers *or* frustraters of needs — as partial people. "Those who gratify me are good. Those who frustrate me are bad." Frustrations, so critically important in promoting growth, would also thereby lose their value.

THE PROBLEM OF SURROGATES

The issue is complex. The great majority of working mothers are far from callous toward their newborn. They love their child and sincerely believe they are doing the right thing by taking care of the baby for the first three months and only then returning to their career. (On most jobs in the United States, women who do not return to work at the end of three months are dismissed for cause — although some mothers would go back to work at that time anyway.) Not being informed otherwise, they go on the assumption that what is chiefly important is their personally feeding the baby and giving loving care for the first three months. They have not had it explained to them that the warm, intimate closeness they have so carefully established is, from the baby's point of view, incomprehensibly broken off. They have not had it explained that the baby needs them for the first three years. The smooth continuity of the baby's first relationship in life is abruptly ended, and the satisfaction of needs is partially cut off.

Women of the wealthiest families have long enjoyed some of the freedoms that the Women's Movement today advocates for all women. Typically, when a baby is born to a family of means, a nurse is engaged to relieve the mother. Because some nurses care only for infants under six months and others only for those who are older, generally when the baby is six months old a new nurse — a new face — is engaged to replace the first, leaving the baby to puzzle over the disappearance of the face he or she had grown fond of. As for the mother, the baby sees her for a part of each day, but so much less continuously than the nurse that the baby might regard her as an interesting stranger, not a special person. In any event, she appears and disappears too unreliably to form a deep attachment to. She is not that wonderful, need-gratifying face that the baby gazes at so fondly, the face that feeds, holds, and loves — the temporary nurse's.

When the baby is six months old, some of these parents go on a world cruise to "rest and recuperate" and thus irreparably shatter any chance that the baby might develop feelings of emotional continuity. In a further compounding of the problem, after a year with the second nurse the baby is placed in the charge of a governess. The baby, attempting to become accustomed to a succession of surrogates, has difficulty learning to distinguish his or her *psychological* parents.

A child does not grow up automatically loving the biological parents because of some mystic tie. There is only one set of real parents to a baby: the psychological parents. A child learns about biology and origins only long after the ties of love have been formed with whomever he or she looks on as mother and father. This is dramatically — in fact, tragically — illustrated by those unfortunate occasions when an adopted child is legally reclaimed by the biological parents after years of living with adoptive parents. To the child, that is nothing less than being cruelly handed away to strangers. The reaction of the child is unspeakable depression and grief, generally followed by hatred for the biological parents, the strangers who separated the child from the "real" parents, and anger at the psychological parents, the family who failed to rescue.

Using this model of childrearing — though in genuine ignorance of infant psychology — some feminist writers advocate multiple mothering. Moreover, they argue that it offers a means of avoiding overattachment to the mother. But multiple mothering can have exactly the opposite effect: if it is done when the child is less than three years old it can lead to anxious clinging — superattachment — and also to depression.

So fragile are emotional attachments in early life that

external stability is required for them to develop strongly.* If a child's first attempts at love should not meet with success, the next attempts would acquire urgency, demanding immediate gratification. Subsequent attempts would deteriorate into a ceaseless demand, until the search for love passed beyond the possibility of satisfaction—remaining, in fact, a *need* for another, not love. All subsequent relationships of "love," especially those in adulthood, would inevitably suffer.

It should not be surprising, therefore, to learn that many wealthy parents, who pride themselves on giving their offspring "the best advantages in life," have children who suffer from emotional problems. The wealthy seldom *appear* to have emotional problems: the problems are covered over by the pursuit of pleasure, and, as protection against social envy, their manner of living is hidden from public view. But it takes little insight to understand that to go from one diversion (or holiday) to another is only one of the ways to fight off an underlying depression. And it is an especially striking behavior pattern of the wealthy that a shallowness of feelings leading to casual infidelity is so widespread a phenomenon that it passes as a mark of aristocracy.

This emotional deprivation—the deprivation of profound libidinal ties with one principal mothering person—although cutting deep, leaves few surface clues, if any. Children are extremely resilient and their misery is quickly covered over. Their high degree of adaptability enables them to accept the inevitable, and an irrepressible buoyancy keeps them going. Their need for love persuades them to placate the parents. It is only later that problems appear. As adults they might, for example, have trouble experiencing great tenderness toward another and only go through the motions. Or their love for their parents might gradually weaken and become *pro forma*. When babies and young children feel abandoned by their parents to a succession of surrogates, their subsequent attachments tend to be distrustful and transitory.

Parents' greatest gift to their children is a loving home. All else counts for less. Parents who love each other and their children give them the truly best advantages in life. Authors who suggest that the odds are stacked against ghetto children do not understand that these odds are often only material ones. (Other deprivations—social, economic, political, and educa-

*It is quite possibly the universal recognition of this psychological fact that accounts for the origin and great durability of the nuclear family.

tional — have importance later, however.) They do not understand that children below school age are scarcely aware of material hardships, which is why the children of the poor can be as happy as the children of the rich. There is neither the need nor the desire for money in early childhood, only for love, a few toys, and the pleasant and dependable presence of parents.

Margaret Mead, the much respected anthropologist, in an "intensive study of parental care among the natives of Bali and Samoa," found that "babies are cared for by any member of the family, including the father, grandmother, and small brothers and sisters, and apparently the emotions get no initial focus on the parents. They may even suckle from a number of different women." But, except for the "different women" who suckle them, these persons are no more than the extended family, a boon that past generations enjoyed even in this country. "Father, grandmother, and small brothers and sisters" are not day-care personnel, babysitters, nurses, or other caretaking adults who merely come and go in the child's life. Moreover, some factors are left unaccounted for by Dr. Mead. For example, several women might suckle a baby, but the mother may be the principal nurse. Also, an anthropologist's concern might overlook the psychological importance of timing. At what age does the baby encounter the suckling by different women? At one month? Three months? Six months? A year? The experience would have different significance at different ages, depending on the quality of preceding experiences, with particular reference to stranger anxiety. Multiple suckling at the age of one year following twelve months of satisfying constancy would have an effect different from that of multiple suckling from three months onward by a succession of surrogates.

Children are extremely resilient,
and their misery is quickly covered over.
It is only later that problems appear.

Anthropologists, who are not expected to study unconscious psychological phenomena, by training tend to see problems as they take societal expression. Accordingly, Dr. Mead says that these children are "adjusted." But analysts know how "adjustments" can hide unconscious conflicts. Dr. Margaret A. Ribble takes exception to Dr. Mead. In such children, she claims, "emotional ties are never soundly built up . . . emotional and social relationships throughout life remain insecure."* Although to the author's knowledge the children of Bali and Samoa have not been psychologically studied as adults, one wonders what such studies would teach us.

IS THE BABY A PASSIVE ORGANISM TO BE TRAINED?

Because they are not psychologically based, the approaches to parenting discussed above assume that babies do not have innate developmental thrusts or needs involving the continuing presence of one mothering person. But we have seen that they do. In marked similarity to Victorian parents, some parents of today tend to think of a baby as a miniature adult whose needs in upbringing can be adequately met by societal programs. Their view seems to be that, since babies and children adapt more or less readily to any lifestyle, parenting can be arranged to suit the career and the personal goals and needs of adults. But, as we have seen, infants have specific psychological needs that emerge according to an inner timetable, and those needs have begun to be understood.

UNMARRIED-BY-CHOICE MOTHERS

In today's permissive atmosphere, a growing number of women feel that marriage need not be a prerequisite for motherhood. For a variety of reasons, some decide to become parents while remaining single, describing themselves as "unmarried by choice."

But this choice might hide an emotional problem. Such a woman might wish to become a mother out of unconscious feelings of loneliness or might despair of coping with a long-term commitment to a man—a problem not restricted to unmarried women. A woman who feels this way might expect a child to give her the love she has stopped expecting—or wanting—from adults. Sadly, however, the attempt is foredoomed. A baby is born needing the very love and closeness that the mother might need and hope to receive. She would have to give of herself, not get, at least not sufficiently, and that might make her feel even more alone and unloved.

*Margaret A. Ribble, *The Rights of Infants,* New York, Signet, 1973, p. 109.

If her reason for husbandless parenting were not loneliness, she would nevertheless be placing a burden on the child by attempting to have the child supply *her* needs, rather than the other way around. A child brought up in such circumstances would have an extra obstacle in life. Beyond that, the child might suffer from the absence of one parent: if the child is male, problems could arise in identification, including sexual identification. If the child is female, the sex drive could be deflected from its natural outcome in heterosexuality. Besides, girls also need an adult male to identify with. Also good psychological separation may be hindered where there are not two parents, because the child may tend to develop overly strong attachment to the remaining parent.

The foregoing comments apply to homosexual parenting also, except that in this case the child's sexual identity would in all likelihood be confused because the parent's own sexual preference would serve as a model.

Parents' greatest gift to
their children is a loving home.

It is quite important for a child to have two parents, an adult of each sex. Otherwise the developmental stages of the fourth through the sixth year—the resolution of oedipal feelings, problems of identification, and so on—become greatly complicated. In addition, a child would feel too different from others, lacking something, once he or she learns about mothers and fathers. A child would feel this deficiency not because of any cultural indoctrination but for innate reasons.

THE WORKING MOTHER

All working mothers know that the choices confronting them often turn out to be a variety of evils, *any* of which seems inevitably to involve personal sacrifice, complications in lifestyle, and much guilt.

Granted, because psychological separation is not achieved till the age of three, a child's emotional development is best fostered if he or she is cared for by both parents in those years. But what if that is not possible? What if work is a necessity for both parents? What if a mother is faced with the task of childrearing alone and at the same time must hold a job?

According to the Department of Labor, in 1972 more than 40 percent of the women in the United States worked, and of these more than 5 million were mothers with children under six. This fact alone suggests how urgent is the need for day care.

It is of course true that the best possible day care is offered by the extended family, where that is available. Sitters often turn out to be temporary, leaving after a year or less, and even while they last they seldom feel the deep love for the child that a grandmother does. In our society, however, families usually live apart, and extended families in close proximity are a rarity. This accounts for the increasing use of day-care persons and facilities.

The best day-care person is one who approximates the family relation: someone who will continue indefinitely in the role of caretaker. This would allow the child to build deepening ties with one person and not suffer a confusing succession of caretakers. Similarly, the best day-care arrangement is a center to which the child is sent until its services are no longer needed. Although its employees might leave, the place, the arrangement, provides *some* constancy.

Some mothers, however, feel considerable ambivalence toward a permanent, fulltime day-care person. Out of jealousy, they begin to compete with her, fearing that the child will form a closer bond of love with the caretaker than with them. This possibility causes real anguish, and many a mother is tempted to hire different persons so that she will remain the only constant figure in the child's life. But psychologically one person is preferable to a succession of persons, for reasons that we have seen.

Day care is less problematic once the child has reached the age of three because by then, if all has gone well, he or she has achieved psychological separation and can tolerate spending time away from mother. But that situation does not always obtain. What can be done if there is a need for day care before the child is three? Is there a special way of handling the matter?

If the child is under three, the mother should introduce him or her and the day-care person to each other, and *the three of them together* should spend time talking and visiting during a transitional period of a week. In that time, as a first step the mother might leave and return in five minutes, in a practice run, then do the same for fifteen minutes, then later for an hour. If a week proves not to be enough, the transition should be extended until the child feels little anxiety.

Once the routine has been established and mother is working, on returning from work she might try to be extra warm and loving and *spend much time with the child*. The mother may be exhausted from an especially bad day at work. Still, it is important to minimize the effects of the child's feeling of abandonment by her, a feeling that is inevitable in some degree. Her caring helps smooth things out.

Care provided at home is easier on the child because of the familiar surroundings. If the child is to be left at a center, a longer transitional period is required before the mother starts her work. The younger the child, the less certain the feeling he or she has of ever seeing mother return again—until she reappears. This would be especially true of the first few separations.

If geographical circumstances permit, it would help if she could get away from her job during the day—during lunch hour, for example. Leaving the child in the morning and again after lunch would make the child cry and feel sad both times at first, but after a few days he or she would feel that things aren't so bad because mother sounds cheerful and happy and offers kisses and tells stories.

That day-care centers and leaving the child to others are a psychological strain on mother and child is undeniable. A child left at a day-care center needs sensitive treatment, with extra sympathy for his or her needs. For this reason it would be wise for a mother to observe the working of the day-care center and its staff, just as she would any institutional arrangement— later the child's school, for example. On her return from work, she might ask her child how the day went. The child may need her protection against callous treatment, inadvertent negligence, or the meanness of another child, which she may want to report.

Many day-care centers are committed to meeting the needs of working mothers and have a trained staff of professionals who do a conscientious job. But a mother should not assume that all centers are like this. Not all day-care staffs are necessarily competent or understanding of a child's needs. Many staff members are not parents and might lack her knowledge of childrearing, learned from many months of experience. They might not be as patient with her child as she is. And though they may be friendly, a child might experience them as distant and uncaring. Some day-care centers hire high school students, who sometimes work only for the money and in individual instances have been known to dislike children. Some day-care centers are run like collectives: what is everybody's responsibility often ends by being nobody's responsibility. Some day-care centers are illegal – at the present count, approximately 100 in New York City alone.

Sometimes it is parents who cause problems in day-care centers. Fortunately, truly inept and uncaring parents are few, and to discuss those whose childrearing methods are poor is not to imply that all or even most working parents are this way. But it might be worth commenting on mishandled day care if only as an object lesson.

Some harried mothers, who are unhappy over their life circumstances and feel unusually guilty toward their child, have been observed to drop their child off and rush away, leaving the little boy or girl in tears. Some of these parents feel too distraught or too pressed for time to deal with this situation. Some, unable to get away because the child chases after them and tearfully implores them to stay, feel so frustrated that they slap the child in anger before leaving. Although these parents might feel remorseful later, a child treated in this way, feeling inconsolably miserable, may spend the entire day clinging desperately to a toy thrust by the mother at the child before leaving and only repeating "Mommy" when spoken to. In such cases day care is emotional starvation and disaster, not the helpful tool it is intended or hoped to be.

What if the child of a working mother falls ill? At such a time, all substitute care should be temporarily suspended. The mother (or father) should stay home until the child feels better.

If a child must be raised with the help of a day-care person, what of stranger anxiety, psychological separation, and the other important events of development that we have discussed? Being prepatterned and innate, these developments take place regardless of external circumstances, but naturally they reveal the influence of those circumstances. However, mothers or parents who have no recourse but to work accept the risk of some problems and try to work them out subsequently.

Not all working mothers work because of financial need, and

some of those who hold a fulltime job purely for the sake of self-fulfillment sometimes tend to feel more guilty about it. Their choice to pursue a career is not an easy one, and it takes time for them to resolve emotional conflicts. It takes time also for their baby to adapt to the chosen lifestyle. Many contemporary mothers are questioning traditional values and the roles of men and women in society and are opting for careers.

Although many women – and men – are still fighting for the cause of women's rights, signs of a reaction from within the ranks of women are already appearing. A few mothers have begun to question the value of the dual role of mother and career woman after having had direct experience in the business or professional world, but this has been mainly true of women who have found little fulfillment in their career. Some are discouraged when they realize the extra expenses involved in holding down a job: the need for more clothes, lunches out, commutation, prepared foods to save cooking time, additional laundry, and – the biggest expense of all – the sitter or day-care person. Unless the mother is able to earn an unusually large salary, she may find that between the cost of the sitter and the other expenses she is likely to net very little. Add to this her daily concern over her child's development and what might be happening to their relationship and it is not surprising that some women have begun to reconsider the fulfillment in being a bank clerk in charge of safe deposit boxes or worrying over whether the detergent commercials are moving the product.

THE QUALITY OF MOTHERING

There is a kernel of truth in the assertion that the quality of mothering is more important than the quantity, that _how_ a mother spends her time with her baby has more importance for the child's development than the mere number of hours. The difficulty is that in human relations quality and quantity are not always clearly distinguishable. One pediatrician-mother who combined fulltime work with parttime parenting complained that the quality-quantity issue is based on the convenience of adults, not the baby's needs.*

To a baby, quantity _is_ quality. (It is to adults too.) A baby is neither developed nor social enough to know how to enjoy the

*Dr. Sally E. Shaywitz, "Is Mommy Necessary?" _New York Times Magazine,_ March 4, 1973, pp. 50–53.

good "quality" of a mother's brief presence between her return home from work and the child's bedtime. Dr. Sally Shaywitz describes her joy on seeing her infant son's hands fluttering toward her when she dashed home from her office to be with him for a while during the day and her sorrow on noticing the abrupt stop of his happy gurgling sounds when he suddenly understood that she was about to leave again. It was quite apparent to her that quality alone was not enough for him — nor for her and *her* needs. In fact, it was heartbreaking for both.

To a baby, quantity *is* quality.

Dont let time pass before you realize

She describes how she missed her son's first smile: the housekeeper informed her of it. Later the housekeeper reported that he had spoken his first word. It soon became clear that it was the housekeeper and not the mother who was experiencing all the exciting events of infancy, those once-in-a-lifetime occasions a parent ordinarily enjoys so much and later cherishes in memory. And as if that were not sad enough, after a time the housekeeper began to feel proprietary toward the baby and seemed to be putting up with the intrusions of the mother.

As for the baby, he looked unhappy and seemed to be bewildered by an upbringing based on "quality" mothering. Dr. Shaywitz says: "I learned that while it is true . . . that the quality rather than the quantity of mothering is of paramount importance, nevertheless *a mother must be there all the time in order to be there at those unpredictable times when it really matters.* When the quality of her mothering will really count."

She comments further: "One morning, attending a lecture by a psychoanalyst on the vital importance of early interaction between mother and child, a medical student asked, 'But how does my baby know I'm his mother? I'm away all day. He sees me only fleetingly in the morning and for a couple of hours at night. Won't his vital interaction be with my housekeeper — and not with me? How is my child to know who is more important to him?'

"The lecturer's answer was, 'Of course, in such a case the child's psychological development would necessarily deviate from that of a child whose mother was with him all the time.' His implication was that the deviation would be for the worse, not the better."

Dr. Shaywitz concluded, therefore, not only that the quality of mothering does not replace quantity, but also that typically both mother and child suffer unhappiness in their developing relations if mother is away most of the day in the first three to five years of life.

KIBBUTZIM AND COMMUNES

Can kibbutzim and communes replace the nuclear family? Many contemporary approaches to childrearing seem to share the belief that people are uniquely or preponderantly the product of cultural indoctrination—that their behavior, being determined by social attitudes, can be altered by altering these attitudes and the society that produced them. Passing over its sociological aspect, such a view ignores the fundamental role of the inner timetable we have been discussing in this book, the *psychology* of development. From the beginning of time, whatever the social, political, or cultural circumstances, each baby has gone through the same stages of growth. To be workable a technique of childrearing must be based on the psychobiological givens—on the satisfaction of innate needs—of infants and parents. Any technique that attempts to meet the needs of one at the expense of the other rather than satisfying both, aside from being unnatural, would ultimately be unworkable. The reason that so many childrearing methods have been tried and discarded over the centuries, and perhaps especially in recent decades, is precisely that they have tended to go against human psychology in their pursuit of one-sided goals, whether to champion the cause of babies, of parents, of working mothers, or whatever.

That much is obvious—at least, so it is hoped. But less obvious to many adults is that a child's psychological needs are more critical than an adult's because the needs are far more rapidly evolving ones. Each need appears at a specific stage in development, and each builds on the satisfaction of the needs belonging to the preceding stage. For development to continue to advance, therefore, the timing of each satisfaction assumes importance. In contrast, an adult's needs are never so critical: the more basic psychological stages have already been gone through, and timing is less important. An emotionally adult person's satisfactions can be postponed to a much greater extent than a child's. Furthermore, although a child's needs can *generally* be met at the expense of an adult's with little or no harm to the latter, to meet an adult's needs at the expense of a child's would create problems in the child.

For childrearing to have a successful outcome, therefore, it must be based squarely on psychological givens, not societal programs. To return to our question: can kibbutzim and communes replace the nuclear family? Let us answer by asking a question. Are kibbutzim and communes based on psychological givens, meeting innate needs of infants and parents as we now understand those needs, or are they arrangements based on the societal needs of only the parents?

Psychologists doubt that substitutes for parents are ultimately satisfying or beneficial to psychological growth. The love between parents and children, based on the profoundest of ties, is probably unmatched in even the warmest camps and centers. Although we seldom view it in these terms, a child is a father's and mother's narcissistic extension of self (in this connection, analysts use the term "narcissism" in a positive sense), and it is this peculiar psychological fact that makes parents care so much about their children—this and their sense of responsibility toward a new life. One proof of the nature of this love is the striking fact that parents always feel less toward the children of others than their own, even though they may love, enjoy, and want to protect those others. In this way nature protects *all* children (generally speaking): each parent takes special care of his or her own because it is pleasurable to do so.

On the children's side, they feel that they *belong* to someone. That feeling too satisfies an innate need, and when it is not sufficiently satisfied — when children are cared for in groups — their emotional development takes a shallower course.

Observers report that in the Soviet Union and Israel the children raised in collectives and kibbutzim seem aloof in their relations with strangers and display a strong sense of duty and great conformity to group standards—and their loyalty is to the state. They tend not to form deep attachments in general, nor do they function effectively when away from their group.* Parents in other countries of the world might ask themselves if

*Bruno Bettelheim, *The Children of the Dream*, New York, Macmillan, 1969, especially Ch. 5, "Results of Kibbutz Education."

this is how they would like their children to be. Observers of those raised in kibbutzim correlate the generally middling level of intelligence of the children with the lack of close family love and stimulation.*

For childrearing to have a
successful outcome, it must be based
squarely on psychological givens,
not societal programs.

Psychologically there is reason to think that in contrast with the various forms of state collectives, voluntary communes might be preferable because at least there children can live with their parents in the early years and enjoy the developmental benefits that that arrangement offers both. And the others of the commune, forming an unofficial extended family, become a built-in source of reliable auxiliary, not substitute, care.

CAREERS AND MOTHERHOOD

Is there no solution, then, to the problem of how a woman can enjoy being both a mother and a person? Is it possible to be a working mother without being an uncaring parent—and

*This discussion is far from exhaustive. To cite only one of many factors to be considered:

"The experiences of the children brought up in the communal setting of the kibbutzim in Israel suggest that the constant presence of a single mothering figure (the ideal of our conception of the nuclear family) is not as essential to healthy development of the child as we have been led to believe. Within the well-defined social organization of the group nursery designed especially for the life of the kibbutz, children do prosper, even though they spend most of the day apart from their parents. Nevertheless, we should not draw unwarranted conclusions from these special conditions. Success in the case of the kibbutzim probably rests on the fact that the social context of the nursery is an integral part of the kibbutz society as a whole, not an idiosyncratic pattern of child rearing adopted by some individual families. The experience with children of the kibbutz cannot simply be lifted out of its context and applied in other, alien circumstances. In our society here in the United States, for instance, prolonged separation from her infant may be psychologically harmful for a mother because it may interfere with the development of her maternal intimacy with the child. As the person designated by our society to be the child's primary caretaker, she needs this sense of intimacy in its fullest development. Physical contact in the early months is just as important for the mother as for the child, because it helps to seal the bond that establishes the two as a mother-infant couple." (The Boston Children's Medical Center, *Pregnancy, Birth, and the Newborn Baby*, New York, Delacorte Press/Seymour Lawrence, 1972, p. 251.)

labeled as such by society? The life of a working mother is unquestionably difficult, and the additional worries over her child's psychological problems only weigh her down more. But knowing what these problems are might help in dealing with them and in lessening their impact.

Women, working or otherwise, need respect as persons perhaps more than they need anything else. At bottom, this is the Women's Movement's greatest concern, not just equal pay and equal job opportunity. The pressures of a heavily sexist society demand that women stay home and be mothers — or suffer guilt. But at the same time, the economic realities insist that women go to work and be providers — and do so within a sexually exploitative, double-standard society at that. A third important element in this cultural predicament is that their inner drives and resources create the same need for self-fulfillment that men have — through career opportunities limited only by individual abilities or wishes.

What a woman wants is what any human being wants, a life of fulfillment as a person, not just as a parent. To be merely a parent is confining and inhuman because no one is *just* a parent. To seek fulfillment as a person means to be able to pursue one's goals, many of which may be unrelated to parenting. But more than that, it means having choice: the right to *choose* to be a mother and homemaker rather than be forced into the role, to *choose* to be a career person rather than have to fight for the right, to *choose* to do both at different times or even at the same time — in short, to have a significant say in one's destiny. Self-fulfillment gives birth to self-respect, and self-respect brings with it the respect of others. The cause of mutual, universal respect will be greatly aided when certain forms of work and character traits cease being regarded as "male" or "female" but come to be defined as human.

What can working mothers do? If the mother needs the money or feels it is important for her wellbeing to resume a career when her baby is only a few months or a year old — rather than wait until the baby is at least three years old and has achieved psychological separation — it might be preferable for her *not* to breastfeed at the outset but start the baby off on a bottle. When she returns to her job and leaves her baby with someone else, there would be one less fundamental change for the baby to adapt to. If she hires a caretaking adult, it would be preferable to find someone who can start with the newborn and remain for at least the first three years and perhaps beyond. The same is true of a day-care center.

Just as breastfeeding is *not* psychologically the best feeding method if the mother has feelings against it, to go against one's drives in an attempt to do "the correct" or "the best" parenting is *not* in the best interests of a child. If staying at home to be a mother makes a woman bitter and miserable and going to work makes her a happier mother, she really ought to go to work. There would be psychological risks involved, but she might elect to take them.

Early in the chapter we mentioned an alternate suggestion made by some members of the Movement, that both parents should work parttime and share the parenting. This is clearly a matter of personal choice. Some parents may prefer this alternative, even knowing that there might be rough spots along the way. But spending as much time as possible with the child and offering much love can smooth out many of the roughnesses. What is essential to bear in mind is simple: *any* lifestyle is a good one for childrearing if the child's emotional needs are met in a "good enough" way.

To be merely a parent is confining and inhuman because no one is *just* a parent.

Some suggest that society is capable of adapting to the changing view of sex roles. Certainly some changes would be psychologically beneficial. For example, parttime work arrangements, which in many businesses are practical though they remain untried, would help parents and child. Or employers might allow mothers flexible hours so that they can work and tend to their families. They might be allowed to go home once or twice during the day if they live nearby or, if they commute, to visit their child during long coffee breaks in a professionally supervised play group for preschoolers in or near the building where they work. Other suggestions include family-centered maternity care, full-pay maternity and paternity leaves without mandatory dates for leaving and returning, new career opportunities provided by redefining jobs, shorter work days and work weeks, federally funded day-care centers of good quality to eliminate some of the current "parking lots for children," and government "salaries" for mothers who are alone and poor but who would rather raise their children themselves than work in an office or factory. Those proposals are important to the country, not just to the cause of women. Their proponents argue that the cost to society would be less than the costs of delinquency, mental health problems, and the human unhappiness that we currently bear.

13

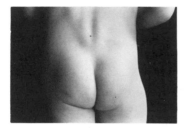

Toileting

Take not the first refusal ill;
Though now she won't, anon she
will.

THOMAS D'URFEY

Having paused to consider some contemporary proposals on mothering and fathering, let us continue our discussion with the understanding that today most early parenting is done by women, with fathers in a secondary role. Whether these role distinctions will continue indefinitely no one knows, but for the time being the matter is a social issue, not a psychological one.

Let us move ahead to the second and third years, to the period in which the child is taught to use the toilet. Contrary to the impression created by many authorities, toileting can be easy for both child and parents if the child is not forced to start too early and if there have been no previous developmental problems straining the relations between them.

Parents become understandably impatient with diaper changing: it is a bore and an unpleasant mess. They are so eager for the baby to grow old enough to use the toilet that they welcome any authority who tells them that toileting can begin at twelve or fifteen months. Some make the attempt only to find that toileting proceeds with poor results and is prolonged over a period of a year or more. In this case they often feel the fault is their baby's, not in the advice.

As always, patience is best—not rushing the child and not reacting with annoyance during diaper changes. (If you can afford disposable diapers, patience comes easier.) Though the child may seem distracted during a diaper change, he or she is reading you at every moment, so that if you were to make a face, the child would feel hurt. And because children at first do not distinguish between themselves and the products of their body, they think you are making a face at them—that you dislike them for doing something wrong. Being patient implies being cheerful as well, saying loving things to your child as you dispose of the diaper and wash off the baby's bottom. At all times, a baby or very young child is only doing what is natural and loves you very much. Your offer of praise makes sense to him or her.

AT WHAT AGE CAN A CHILD USE THE TOILET?

To be truly effective, learning cannot be hurried. The period of teaching a child to use the toilet is a lengthy one and at times seems a nuisance, but it does not have to be a problem. Much of the annoyance and trouble parents so often complain of is due to their doing things incorrectly. They attempt to force-train their child, so that toileting becomes a contest of wills, and that leads to conflict and mutual unhappiness. The phrase "toilet training" might itself be what is at fault. "Training" is not what is needed. Toileting is a *learning* experience.

On the parents' side—always—is nature: the inner timetable. There is no way of speeding up physical maturation. And learning to use the toilet depends first of all on the development of specific muscles. Therefore, toileting can be accomplished only at a certain age and not before. Studies made by psychologists show that babies who are given early training and those who are not trained at all end by learning to use the toilet at approximately the same age—*two and a half years old.* Only at that age is the body completely able to exercise control from within.

According to the developmental timetable, the maturation of a child's muscles synchronizes with certain functions. Muscles controlling hand-to-mouth coordination, for example, mature early, and walking and leg muscles become capable of their task around the end of the first year. But the muscles that exert control over bowel and urethral movements, the sphincters, develop later. Just as a very young child does not yet have the muscle control to throw or catch, he or she does not have control over the anal and urethral sphincter muscles before the middle of the third year.

Early signs of sphincter control sometimes appear during the second half of the second year. "Signs," however, are not control: they mean only that the muscles are maturing. They are not yet equal to the task.

In the first two years of life the sources of physical pleasure are few. Primarily the child enjoys putting things into the mouth, and in the second year a new pleasure makes itself felt, the rectal sensations accompanying bowel movements. There is pleasure in both holding on to movements and letting go. The child clings to these pleasures tenaciously. The willingness to give them up comes only after they have reached a peak of pleasure. The child who enjoys sufficient pleasure in elimination experiences a lessening of anal interests and curiosity. Only the full satisfaction of a pleasure reduces the need—and the search—for that pleasure. Once satisfaction has been achieved, a new feeling always asserts itself that older pleasures can be left behind in favor of newer, untried ones—about which more will be said in a moment.

Toileting can be accomplished only
at a certain age—*two and a half years old.*

LEARNING TO USE THE TOILET VERSUS CONDITIONING

Some parents claim to have trained their baby fully by the age of one year, but this "training" must be distinguished from learning to use the toilet: it is out-and-out conditioning—like putting an animal through its paces. The mother recognizes the signs that the baby is about to have a bowel movement and propels him or her at full speed to the potty—making one wonder, in fact, if it is the baby or the mother who is being conditioned. She admonishes the uncomprehending baby to do it on the potty from now on, at an age when the baby doesn't know what "it" is. Or she sits the baby on the potty for half hours at a time in solitary confinement, until the baby happens to have a bowel movement or produces one to ransom escape. But true learning is more than training. Genuine control is internally achieved, not externally imposed.

CONDITIONING ATTEMPTS AND FEELINGS
OF INADEQUACY

Force-training a baby to use the toilet asks him or her to do something that is not physically possible. But because it is mother or father who is asking, the baby might feel it *should* be possible to have sphincter control — adults must know what they are doing. When it becomes clear that it is not possible to achieve control by an act of will, the baby might conclude that he or she, through some personal deficiency, is unequal to the task.

What complicates matters and makes that misinterpretation possible is that force-training occurs before there is any language comprehension. One of the advantages of postponing the teaching of toileting until a more appropriate age is that communication becomes an aid. Conditioning a child between the ages of one and two years is handicapped by the child's limited vocabulary, which makes it difficult for the child to understand parents' true intention in teaching toileting. The child knows only that the parents are making demands and expressing disapproval, sometimes even anger.

When this misunderstanding is spread over a period of months, the child draws a false but sweeping conclusion: in some peculiar way he or she is inadequate, ineffective, incapable of accomplishment or success. One outcome of these unconscious feelings is the self-evaluation that appears in adulthood: "Other people don't seem to have problems, but I need to strive for perfection to become as good as they are. And even then, I will not succeed." These negative feelings sabotage the child's growing self-image and contribute to the formation of a harsh and judgmental conscience (superego). Psychologists have long recognized that much personal unhappiness in many men and women who feel relentlessly driven in life can be traced to faulty toileting.

THE FLUSHING MECHANISM

A two-year-old who has slowly become aware that adults use the toilet from time to time becomes intrigued by what they do there, and by nothing so much as the flushing mechanism. When you pull down on the handle there is a sudden roar of cascading water. The child wants to do that too, but he or she is timid at first. A flushing bowl looks and sounds like a waterfall close up, and small children are afraid they might fall in and be carried away. Fascination and boldness overcome their apprehension, however, and they give it a try—and are delighted. They want to repeat the experience again and again, just as they would a new game.

In letting your child play with the flushing mechanism, you make sure only that the handle is not broken by an inept grab by explaining that he or she should pull straight down. Getting used to flushing will come in handy once the child has learned to use the toilet.

READINESS TO USE THE TOILET

Toward the end of the first year and all during the second, you become familiar enough with your child to know when he or she is about to have a bowel movement or has just had one. You notice those moments when noisy activity suddenly becomes suspended and the child stares into space: a bowel movement is in process.

> Genuine control is internally achieved, not externally imposed.

Beginning when your child is eighteen months old, you might occasionally—but not in any nagging, persistent way— use these opportunities to encourage the child's awareness of the bowel movements. Preferably this should not be done *while* the child's bowels are being moved, because in those moments the child would be distracted. If there is about to be a movement, which you have learned to recognize by a sudden quiet, you might ask, "Would you like to go to the bathroom and do it the way big people do?" You might expect complete indifference to your suggestion. Don't let that disturb you. What matters is that you made the connection between bowel movements and having them in the toilet. That's how toileting starts.

Over the next weeks and months, if you notice that your child has had a movement, you might ask if the full diaper feels comfortable. By the end of the second year a child does begin to feel discomfort when the diapers are full, and sometimes the dried feces chafe the child's bottom.

Soon the child may even begin reporting to you when the diapers are only wet, and sometimes in overzealousness he or she might report the passing of gas as a bowel movement — you check the diaper only to find it empty. But the reporting reveals the beginnings of an awareness — the awareness that you encouraged — that bowel movements and urinating are of common interest to you.

Equally important, the child's concern over anal and urethral activities is a clear sign that he or she is beginning to wish for independence in toileting. The child has begun to dislike diaper changes more than ever and shows an increasing readiness for some other way. The child is willing to learn to have bowel movements in the toilet because *it is your way of doing things and your child wants to be like you.* When toileting happens in the third year, and therefore coincides with the innate thrust toward psychological separation and independence, it takes a course that is natural and easy — for child and parent.

We recognize here our model for growth: physical maturing, psychological development, and the environment synchronizing. The sphincters are maturing, the child wants to be both independent and more adult, and you encourage without pressuring.

It might be best to start toileting with a child-sized seat placed over the adult seat rather than with a potty. This eliminates the need to teach toileting in two phases, with the child sitting first on the potty chair and later on the toilet seat. If you explain that it might be fun to sit on the toilet seat when the child feels the approach of a bowel movement, he or she might ask to be placed on the seat immediately to try it out. But you can expect the child to continue to eliminate anywhere at any time for several more months.

Habits don't change easily. To punish, embarrass, criticize, or show impatience would have unfortunate psychological repercussions. Patience is especially needed when the child develops urethral control. Long after they have learned to use the toilet for bowel movements, most children continue to wet themselves, not just at night but during the day as well. It usually takes longer for them to want to achieve urethral control than bowel control.*

*With some children, however, the order is reversed. Perhaps especially in childrearing, blanket statements and overgeneralizations should not be heeded uncritically.

There is another element that contributes its share to growth. Like most learning, learning to use the toilet is accomplished primarily through the child's identification with the parents. Setting an example is always better than training. A twenty-four-month-old child understands what you do in the bathroom and begins to want to do the same.

A child who loves you is not a rejecting but a cooperative person. Where there are no problems, children are eager to please. And doing things out of choice is always more growth-promoting than doing them in response to force. When children see that you are pleased at their learning to use the toilet, they take further pleasure in feeling that you and they get along well together. Toileting also gives them a sense of mastery — another pleasure.

Yet an additional incentive to controlling bowel movements is that holding back for a moment or two increases the sensations in the rectum. Withholding briefly in order to eliminate in the toilet thus becomes associated with pleasure, and whatever becomes associated with pleasure becomes easier to do and wished for.

ONE DAY IT HAPPENS

Once fully aware of toileting, the child might be tempted to try it one day, at first in a practice run. For example, some children walk into the bathroom, sit on the seat fully dressed, and have a bowel movement in fantasy. Some ask to have their clothing removed — only to peer into the bowl. Some stride into the bathroom, station themselves at the toilet bowl in a businesslike way, move their bowels in their diapers, and stroll out again. These approximations become gradually refined until one day the child asks you to remove the diapers and provide help in getting up onto the seat, and to your astonishment and delight has a bowel movement in the toilet, just as you have been suggesting.

However much you may have longed for this event, its appearance does not mean that the learning is over. The first (or second or third) time should not be made the occasion for an abrupt change. As always, a transition is required, during which the need for diapers continues, especially at night. The temptation to rush matters because of a demonstrated ability is difficult to resist. But after having waited this long, you try not to mind those few additional weeks, at the end of which the ability will be consolidated once and for all.

THE CONCERN OVER BODY PRODUCTS

After the child has learned to move the bowels in the toilet, the child shifts his or her concern to the feces and their fate. One little boy commented unhappily on their disappearance when he saw them flushed away. Next time his mother offered to let the feces sit in the bowl for a while, assuring him that if she decided to flush she would inform him. At the next bowel movement, when his mother let him see the feces lying at the bottom of the bowl, he went away satisfied – but returned in a moment to check. They were still there.

When he remembered later, he looked again, and this time his mother suggested flushing them away. To this there was a strong reaction. Why not keep them? The toilet bowl might, in fact, be a good storage place.

His mother explained that there would always be more bowel movements, a possibility that had not occurred to the boy. He mulled it over: if they got rid of his "kaka," as he called it, there would always be more to come. He decided to accept his mother's suggestion and he did so with trust: never in his experience had she suggested anything that had turned out bad. He felt moved, however, to lay down a condition that only made her smile: *he* should do the flushing.

It was clear from his earnestness that he had been looking forward to flushing "for real." Keeping a careful eye on the contents of the bowl, he pulled down the handle and, with the interest of a scientist, watched his "kaka" swirl away and disappear. By way of reinforcement, his mother waved her hand and said, "Bye-bye – there'll be more later," and he delightfully repeated after her: "Bye-bye. Bye-bye, kaka."

A TRANSITION—FOR CONSOLIDATION

Until he consolidated his ability to use the toilet, his mother kept him in diapers for another two or three months. He still moved his bowels in his diaper at night and occasionally, though with decreasing frequency, in the daytime too. She accepted these occurrences as normal and transitional and made no comment. Not only did she never criticize, she made it a point to praise him at those times when he used the toilet.

Motivated by the praise, more and more often he went to the bathroom and experimented with the new achievement that was making him feel grown up.

Then a new development appeared. One day he emerged from the bathroom and informed his mother that his kaka looked "teeny." She inspected the bowl at his request and said, "Big kakas are good, and teeny teeny kakas are good too." That sounded reassuring: size and quantity were unimportant. (As for the mother, she knew that whatever was inside would eventually come out.) A day or two later, as she went past the bathroom, she heard a soft chanting inside: "Big kakas are good, and teeny teeny ones are good. *Both* are good. Big kakas are good, and teeny teeny ones are good. *Both* are good." Peeking in she saw him balanced contentedly at the edge of the toilet seat, at ease with himself and life.

USING BATHROOM TISSUES

Most parents find it best to teach self-wiping from the moment the child has learned to use the toilet. Because children generally tend to be interested in this activity too, you will in all likelihood encounter no resistance. They may wipe clumsily and poorly at first, but doing it at all is so much progress that you won't mind. You will be giving a bath soon, and besides, at this point what is important is not great cleanliness — for the first three years a baby's bottom is never clean for long anyway — but consolidating the new ability.

ANAL PLEASURES AND ARRESTED DEVELOPMENT

The casual approach is best in teaching children how to wipe themselves. The risk of parental overconcern is that it may eroticize toilet functions. At this stage of development the child's pleasures are principally oral and anal ones. Genital pleasures are only incipient. As oral pleasures were in the first year, anal pleasures are the sex life of the second and third years. The child who feels that anal functions have importance for you rather than for the child could invest emotional interest in the activities themselves. To the child, toileting could, in fact, unconsciously become a seduction scene, with the parents "taking pleasure" in the child's body.

If parents take too great an interest in the child's body in one of its areas of pleasurable functioning, this could have two adverse effects. One is that the built-in taboo against incest would unconsciously be threatened. And the (genital) sexual drive, which reaches a first stage of maturity between four and six years of age, might attach itself too strongly to anal functions rather than the specifically genital one.

It would be unrealistic to expect to teach toileting without *any* trouble. There will be moments of impatience at the child's inability to achieve control quickly. You might even feel angry at the thought that the child might have had a bowel movement on purpose, especially when it happens just after a diaper change, although in calmer moments you are sure that that is not true.

There might actually come a time, however, when the child, feeling annoyed with you, in fact does deliberately wait to get off the toilet seat before having a bowel movement. Or perhaps you have just had a difference of opinion, and the child, feeling frustrated, angrily refuses to have a movement. But these are temporary setbacks and quite normal.

THE ANAL PERIOD AND CHARACTER TRAITS

Only those parents who force-train their child find toileting a difficult period. The more they insist on the training, the more their child asserts a new-felt power over them — refusal. The child glories in this power all the more if the training takes place, as it so often does, during the no-saying period of the middle of the second year — another reason not to rush toileting. A child cannot eliminate at will, but once the sphincter muscles have matured he or she can easily withhold, and might adopt withholding — and controlling — as a policy. Power is one of the most important feelings that develop during the anal stage, and control is a form of power.

The normal contrariness of this age added to the wish to withhold and control produce the character trait of stubbornness. To a child who was once schedule-fed — that is, to a child who endured feeding as a frustrating, withholding experience — the temptation not to learn toileting is strong.

The character trait of miserliness is a reaction to the loss of the body's most tangible product: feces. A child's view of feces is different from that of an adult: feces are a part of the body — a part of the "I" — and therefore have value and importance. A child feels disturbed by the ease with which this part of the "I" detaches itself from the body and becomes lost. That is why the child wants to save and hoard the feces, not flush them away. Parents who disregard these important feelings about the "loss" of the feces, and especially those who force-train at an early age, cause the child to want all the more to hold back or store up. In this impulse, miserliness finds its unconscious roots.

The character trait of compulsive orderliness is formed by the child's reaction to full diapers and their smells. In overcompensation, the child eventually develops a need to be excessively neat and clean, as if to deny the earlier pleasure in messiness, and in obedience to a strict training.

Stubbornness, miserliness, and compulsive orderliness are undesirable character traits because they are excessively reactive. They confine development and shackle spontaneity. Along with a sense of inadequacy, these personality deformations are the characterological residues of attempts to teach toileting too early, too insistently, too strictly, or with too little regard for the child's feelings. The natural way is always more relaxed — and easier.

Temporary setbacks are quite normal.

BOWEL MOVEMENTS AND DISGUST

As we have suggested, far from being ashamed of bowel movements, a child feels extremely possessive toward the products of the body and holds them in high esteem. Bowel movements give sensual pleasure to the membrane of the rectum, and feces look as though they would be fun to play with, warm and squishable. The child might pick some up to bring to you proudly, the way he or she might offer a favorite toy, and look to you for appreciation as if to say, "This is something I want you to have."

For an adult it is sometimes difficult not to react with disgust. Children don't have the same notions of cleanliness or disgust that adults do. These feelings are acquired only gradually. To a child anything pleasurable is good, even playing with feces. (If you think of feces as very close to mud or clay in color, texture, and consistency, it's not difficult to imagine the tactile pleasure a child gets from playing with them.) At this age body products have no more offensive smell to a child than they do to an animal, and in degree of socialization a child is still not far removed from an animal.

At the age of two and a half or three, a child often explores his or her body just as in the past, except that sitting on the toilet seat exposes parts of the body that are ordinarily covered. In the course of exploration the child might insert a finger into the rectum, to learn how the inside of it feels and try to understand the part of the body that produces the pleasant sensations accompanying bowel movements. The finger, on some of these occasions, might encounter feces, and the child tries to help the feces to emerge. A natural curiosity leads to examination of the fingertip: the child pursues the study of the feces with the principal investigative means available at this age — the oral — by putting the finger into the mouth.

A father who one day happened on this scene winced inwardly but showed no reaction. But it was not the kind of behavior he wanted to encourage, and he felt that his watching entirely without comment might be construed as approval. Wishing to convey neither approval nor disapproval, thinking fast he asked in a matter-of-fact voice, "How does it taste?" The little boy said, "Good," to which the father replied, "Some like it, but others don't. Big people don't — I personally don't care for it," and shrugged his shoulders and walked away.

If this father had forcibly stopped his son's playing with feces the boy might have continued out of stubbornness or defiance. If, on the other hand, he had encouraged him the child might have lingered over the play as a socially acceptable activity and again might have prolonged his interest in it. But by adopting a neutral stance, the father let the child's curiosity exhaust itself. At the end of a few weeks the anal experimentations spontaneously stopped.

TOILETING: A DIFFICULT TIME FOR PARENTS

Toilet education is an especially trying time if you are unusually neat. But it might help to remind yourself that the baby is going through a phase and that all phases end. Development will be aided if you can subordinate your need for neatness and cleanliness to the child's transitional pleasures in messiness. These pleasures have their share in growth. Later you can assert your wish for cleanliness as a standard for your child to adopt, and at that more appropriate time it will be accepted by the child without incomprehension or resistance.

It might also be helpful to remember that development is all of a piece. Parents who schedule-feed a baby and thereby frustrate him or her run the risk of having a protracted and wearying toileting experience.

To parents of two or more children, it is tempting to rush the toileting of the youngest to get once and for all beyond the messy stage. Such parents may have spent literally years living among smelly diapers, puddles, and accidents on the floor. But the messiness has been the parents' experience of life during the past few years, *not each new baby's*. Each child has to go through developmental phases one at a time, just as the brothers and sisters did who came before.

A NEW LEVEL OF PERSONALITY DEVELOPMENT

As the child's learning to use the toilet becomes an accomplished fact, the pleasure of direct instinctual gratification — holding onto the feces and playing with elimination — gradually yields to substitutive forms that offer even greater pleasure. Yielding to substitutive forms happens because the instinctual pleasure of eliminating has been sufficiently gratified. The child feels an inner push to move ahead in development. New feelings and a new stage of growth assert themselves once optimum pleasure has been achieved for a given stage.

As a substitutive pleasure, the child is now permitted to mess up a part of the house or apartment set aside for that purpose, an innovation he or she takes to with great enjoyment because it comes along at an opportune time. In a special area of the home that is all his or hers, the child has the right to scribble on large sheets of paper tacked to the wall (or sometimes directly on an unpainted wall), draw with pencils or crayons, paint with watercolors or fingers, or play with modeling clay or Play-Doh. If the child is given a small part of the house to mess up — an arrangement young children find reasonable — the child will respect the neatness of the rest of the house, or will try to.

"Indirect" or substitutive forms of pleasure are greater because they involve more of the child's being. The pleasure of playing with feces gratifies chiefly instinct, but substitutive forms of the same pleasure involve more levels of functioning, some complex: coordination, judgment, thought, aesthetic sense, and so on. The more of ourselves we involve in a project, the more we enjoy ourselves.

Part of the pleasure comes purely from the functioning itself. Just as a baby enjoys "using" the body for crying and kicking, the child enjoys using more of his or her whole being. "That which is used develops. That which is unused atrophies," Hippocrates said two thousand years ago, and that certainly applies to psychology and art. The child experiences more of the self when involved in painting than in bowel movements. Painting, therefore, affords more pleasure.

PARENTS NEED TO BE UNDERSTANDING

With development, unhurried progress is smooth progress — slow change is lasting change. It takes time to become accustomed to new ideas and ways of doing things. And as you congratulate a child on each bit of progress, learning is reinforced. If a child walks into the bathroom, stands at the toilet bowl, but has a movement in his or her diaper, the mother might offer praise for doing the right thing — doing it in the bathroom. She might hint that next time the child might try doing it in the toilet with the diaper off — knowing full well that "next time" means "eventually."

New feelings and a new stage
of growth assert themselves once
optimum pleasure has been
achieved for a given stage.

You would do well to turn a deaf ear to reports about the little girl down the block who learned to use the toilet at eighteen months. She may or may not have, depending on definitions (probably not), and besides, competition with *her* mother is irrelevant to the healthy development of *your* child. A deaf ear should also be turned to old wives' tales about regularity in bowel movements. On some days there will be several movements and on other days *none.* Both are normal.

THE ACCEPTANCE OF PROHIBITIONS

What induces a child to accept a prohibition of unrestricted instinctual pleasure, in this case the pleasurable sensations in the rectum? The child is not yet a reasonable creature who can deliberate rationally the pros and cons of your request to learn toileting and understand the practicality or social desirability of moving bowels in the toilet. But a child *is* a creature with feelings, and feelings provide the impetus in all development: a little girl or boy accepts a parent's prohibitions out of love. A pleasure is given up in order to receive a greater pleasure — your love. What helps too is the child's ability to tolerate delay in instinctual gratification, learned earlier and now further pressed into service.

Learning to use the toilet is the second major frustration of an instinct. The first was weaning — giving up sucking as a means of getting food. If the feeding was sufficiently gratifying and the important ability to tolerate delay has developed well enough, the toilet phase becomes easier to manage precisely because of the child's degree of emotional advance.

If problems arose in the feeding stage and the baby did not develop patience and trust, at two or even two and a half he or she would resist suggestions about learning to use the toilet. The frustrated child becomes a frustrater.

GROWING BEYOND ANALITY

Toileting is one of the turning points of early life. A child learning to use the toilet learns to relinquish an instinctual pleasure at someone else's request. The child no longer gives in to any passing impulse but learns that growing up and entering the world of adults entail body control and the acceptance of restrictions on unrestrained pleasurable activities.

The unfettered gratification of an instinct is a great deal to give up. But although it sounds negative to speak of "giving up the unfettered gratification of an instinct," the child experiences it positively. Using the toilet may diminish pleasure by placing restraints on instinct, but it gives the child a sense of responsibility for actions, which in turn promotes further psychological development. And as the child learns more self-control, the need for external controls diminishes.

The new degree of self-control serves to promote many unconscious trends, not the least of which is the later, highly important development of conscience — the inner sense of what is right and, equally important, what is wrong. Conscience, in one of its aspects, is internalized control.

Learning to use the toilet is an important step also because it is the first opportunity a child has for giving or refusing. Because you have waited until the child is the appropriate age and therefore have language communication to help you, the child has a good understanding of what you want and is in a position to choose to cooperate — or not, if there is stubbornness. The child has a tremendous amount of say over bowel movements: nothing *you* do can make the child's bowels move. But where there are no problems — no past or current deprivations or ungratified earlier needs — a child always cooperates and does not need to engage you in a power struggle.

THE TRANSFORMATION OF AN INSTINCT

Like any instinctual pleasure that has once been enjoyed, the impulse to derive gratification from the activity of moving the bowels continues indefinitely. But some of the impulse undergoes transformation. New pleasures appear, superior pleasures that derive from feelings of power (mastery), control, and neatness. The child, being a better organized person, becomes culturally more advanced. In the realm of personal aesthetics, for example, there now appear some early glimmerings of an interest in dress and appearance — even cleanliness, a *little* bit. In the realm of achievements, the child feels a pleasure in being able to get things done — feels productive and creative.

BEDWETTING

Bedwetting (enuresis) is a problem only if it persists much beyond the age of four. Very often the recommendations offered by books on childrearing are not helpful: not giving the child fluids before bedtime, seeing to it that the child goes to the bathroom before going to bed, or carrying the child to the bathroom for a "draining" in the middle of the night (even though sound asleep). These recommendations treat the symptom and ignore the cause.

The cause of bedwetting is anxiety and hostility. Sometimes children feel angry at their parents but are afraid to show their feelings openly or verbally. Or they feel unloved by their parents (both or one of whom might be domineering) because of excessive punishments or an excessively high standard of behavior demanded of them.

Some children feel unsure of their parents' love after the

birth of a brother or sister, and they feel tempted to emulate the rival by regressing to the bedwetting stage, theorizing that perhaps in that way they too will be loved just as the baby is. This type of bedwetting, though, is transitory.

A child might unconsciously use bedwetting to express the most important feature of personality, spontaneity. The spontaneity would not have to take the form of bedwetting, however, if the child felt that other forms of expression were permitted.

BEDWETTING AND SEXUAL TENSION

A child eroticizes play very easily. If a parent plays with the child before bedtime in a physically stimulating way — a rough game, pretending to be wild animals — he or she might wet the bed out of exuberance. Viewed in this light, discharging urine during sleep out of erotic excitement is remarkably similar to the eventual adult expression of sex — orgasm. This form of bedwetting, however, is usually an isolated occurrence, not the chronic kind.

ENEMAS

Enemas and suppositories should be avoided. Unless there is something seriously wrong, which is extremely rare, children do not get constipated except possibly during illness, and for that a laxative, *if prescribed by a doctor*, is sufficient. Whatever is there will come out. There is no need to be concerned about "regularity," quantity, or frequency. On some days, there will be *no* bowel movements, and that is normal. Parents who are concerned over these matters might consider whether they are expressing anal concerns of their own.

THE HARMFULNESS OF ENEMAS

Enemas hurt physically and they also do incalculable psychological harm. To a very young child an enema feels like a violation, and it is: an enema is a form of rape.

And besides, what if a child is temporarily constipated because of an unconscious need — perhaps anger at the parents — that might cause the child to withhold a bowel movement? An enema would ignore the underlying anger. At the same time the enema would undermine the child's growing sense of independence and inviolability of self. Turning development back to an earlier, passive mode by forcing the child to yield, and in a particularly submissive stance at that, would defeat whatever has already been accomplished toward independence.

ENEMAS ARE EROTIC

To complicate matters even more, enemas are also erotic. Although an enema is disagreeable and painful, it can produce pleasurable sensations in the rectum. To accompany that pleasure a child might construct the unconscious (or conscious) fantasy of being loved by the parents *because* he or she submits to bodily penetration by them, a fantasy that receives confirmation when the enema works and the parents are pleased.

If an enema is performed by a father on his son, as sometimes happens, the problem is intensified by the obvious homosexual implications. In all cases the parent-child relation becomes greatly eroticized, and the child, who seeks pleasure much more directly than adults, might unconsciously be tempted to become constipated to repeat the associated pleasures and receive attention and a show of concern. And as if all the foregoing were not problematic enough, not only does the use of enemas eroticize the child's relations with the parents, it eroticizes anal functioning itself, causing arrest in psychological development, which then moves forward to the genital phase with some difficulty and reduced strength.

14

The Early Expression of Sex

There's more enterprise in going naked.

YEATS

We have suggested that the child learns toileting by identifying with the parents. Once the child knows what parents do, he or she tries to do the same. But here a question might be raised: should a parent use the toilet while the child watches?

NUDITY AND CHILDREN

A mother might let her little girl watch her use the bathroom to see how toilet functions are performed. The girl, through identification, would do things mother's way, and that would facilitate toilet education. But what about a boy? Watching mother on the toilet seat with her clothing disarranged could have more of an erotic effect on him than he could deal with, and his way way of urinating is not like hers. In theory, then, it would be a better way of learning for the little boy to see his father use the toilet. But because of the male position in urinating, the father might seem to be exposing himself to his son, and what about that? Depending on the layout of the bathroom, the father might be able to stand in such a way as not to offer a frontal view, and do this without being obvious.

FAMILY NUDITY

The question of family nudity is a matter of personal preference. But nudity between parent and child *seems* to have a less than desirable effect on the child, at least in our culture, where nudity is not universal. Those who are for nudity say that a child growing up with no mystery surrounding anatomy will have fewer psychological problems in adulthood. Those who are against nudity say that the "mystery" surrounding anatomy disappears sooner or later, and family nudity does not reduce problems because psychological problems are not caused by clothing.

It is true that the practice of wearing clothing in even the most uncomfortable weather subtly conveys the attitude that portions of the anatomy are to be hidden because they are shameful. In this sense it is conceivable that a child in whose household nudity is practiced may grow up with fewer problems about exposure. But it is also true that children play harmlessly together in the nude ("harmlessly," it should be added, as long as they are with peers, not in a mixed group including older children), expose themselves in erotic games like hospital or doctor and nurse, and examine each other when adults are not present. It is not long before all children know how male and female genitals look.

Nevertheless, for a child, viewing adult genitals is a quite different experience from viewing the genitals of another child. A little boy seeing his father's penis unconsciously compares his own unfavorably. His father's greater size — in body and genitals — only confirms any negative feelings the boy might have about himself. He doesn't reason that with time he too will grow large and powerful. Although misconceptions can be corrected, children very often don't voice their anxieties or misconceptions. Once a boy thinks of himself as inferior, it becomes hard for him to assess himself realistically later. The emotion-laden, distorted evaluation of the early years tends unconsciously to persist. Further, when he is a bit older, around four or five, he might unconsciously covet his father's "powerful" genital because the larger penis may account for mother's preference of father over the boy. Maybe *that's* why the boy can't be her husband. Maybe that's why she only smiles when he suggests marrying her some day. It is in these subtle ways that a boy invests the penis with an interest beyond all reason and overvalues it.

For a boy to see his mother nude would arouse erotic feelings in him that he is not equipped to deal with. She is not a child or playmate but someone he already has strong love for. A boy's love for his mother and a girl's love for her father are sexually tinged from the start and need no further eroticization. And incestuous feelings, however unconscious they may remain, create considerable guilt feelings, however unconscious *they* may remain.

A girl reacts differently to parental nudity. Her mother — the parent she compares herself with and identifies with more — at least is like her in that neither of them *apparently* has genitals. (Because girls' genitals are inside the body and not visible, girls and boys believe that females lack genitals.) When children sexually examine girls, the play focuses on their bottoms. In contrast, her father's penis and testicles seem to her frightening appendages. But they don't just threaten her — unconsciously they also arouse her sexually. The excitation might be too much for a girl to cope with for the same reason that it might be too much for a boy to see his mother nude: the degree of sexual excitation is developmentally premature, and whatever is developmentally premature is traumatic. In addition, seeing the way her father urinates makes a girl want to try to do the same — only to suffer disappointing results and damaged self-feelings.

PENIS ENVY

Another difficulty for a little girl is that unconsciously she feels castrated, as if she (and her mother) once had a penis and lost it. If both her father and little boys have one, and if boys' bodies and girls' bodies appear alike in all other respects, it would seem natural for the girl and her mother to have a penis as well.

This preoccupation is easily observable by anyone watching children playing together in the nude. The bodies of little boys and girls sometimes appear identical with the exception of a single feature, which by its difference attracts all the more attention. Girls can be observed glancing with furtive interest at boys' genitals, and it's not surprising: in the early years especially, every child wants whatever any other child has. This wish for a penis becomes intensified when a little girl sees how much fun boys have in urinating standing up and making the stream go high, low, or wiggly. In spite of herself she is impressed as she watches a little boy direct his gargantuan stream — all things are relative — at a lone ant hurrying homeward through a sudden downpour. (The wish for omnipotence is inexhaustible in its guises.)

It is an easy and common misunderstanding of anatomy. Three- or four-year-old children do not yet know of reproduction and therefore have no reason to make sexual distinctions. This misunderstanding of anatomy and the concomitant frustrated wish for sameness can unfortunately lead a girl to have feelings of inferiority and a desire later on to derogate men, if she has been made unhappy by them, by devaluing the penis. The misunderstanding also becomes a fertile soil for self-criticism and feelings of inadequacy resulting from body image. In addition — and more important than is commonly thought — it becomes a source of unconscious resentment toward mother for having brought her into the world incomplete. A girl might in fact feel disappointed in her mother at this implied rejection of her: "My mother gave birth to me before I was finished" is a sad but common fantasy in childhood. In today's more permissive atmosphere, adolescent girls and women who examine their genitals with the aid of a mirror almost always react to the experience with a heightened sense of wellbeing. It is as if their adult perception of their genitals corrects the negative view developed much earlier, when they compared themselves with boys. They see that they are in fact complete.

A boy's love for his mother and a girl's love for her father are sexually tinged from the start and need no further eroticization.

The envy of males is also generally misunderstood. The difficulty in dealing with the concept of penis envy is that those who try to deny its existence tend to look for esoteric meanings in the unconscious, overlooking the simple fact that at some point children realize that there is a sex difference and that those who appear to have "less" of a body feel slighted. We know that many men come to envy women their breasts and their ability to bear children — "breast envy" and "womb envy" — for similar reasons: *they* feel slighted. In fact, analysts have long known that women too have breast envy, which the Women's Movement's more confessional (and psychologically invaluable) literature abundantly confirms. To say that women have penis envy and men breast or womb envy has never been intended as criticism but as a statement of objective fact.

What often escapes notice is that in adulthood penis envy takes *substitutive* form. Penis envy is to be understood metaphorically. Few women are so one-track-minded as to continue to want an actual penis or—except perhaps in ill-kept public facilities or on camping trips—seriously cherish a desire to urinate standing up. Most are quite content with the pleasures afforded by their clitoris and vagina. But many women do envy men what their maleness ensures them in our society: better occupational positions, greater worldly success and recognition, and more professional opportunities.

This is not to say that the claims of the Women's Movement for equity should be viewed negatively as penis envy. Rather they constitute a legitimate demand for equal treatment, human fulfillment, and respect.

BOYS ENVY GIRLS TOO

Before there is any awareness of the process of reproduction, boys and girls both want to produce babies. Boys have to be informed that they cannot. Nevertheless they enjoy playing with dolls and want to push strollers around "just like Mommy." They sometimes even go through a period of trying on girls' or women's clothing. They are still finding out who and what they are. These natural, normal events show clearly that sexual identity is only slowly formed and is not completed until some time after the age of five or six. The notion of unisex, therefore, does have a basis in fact, but not, as its proponents claim, in adulthood: it belongs to early childhood, before the discovery of sex difference.

THE IMPORTANCE OF SEXUAL DISTINCTIONS

It would be misleading to generalize from the early behavior of children either in support or in criticism of adult behavior. Human development is a continuum of shifting subphases. The significance of a given pattern of behavior depends on the age at which it occurs. *Before* the discovery of sex difference, boys and girls have more in common than they will ever again have. *After* the discovery of sex difference, their sexual identity becomes surer and their development begins to diverge. The divergence arises not out of cultural conditioning but out of innate factors — hormones, glands, and chromosomes.

These differences are not merely physical, as is sometimes argued — although even if that were true, we know that physical differences are the basis of differing psychological responses. The endocrine system is, as it were, a link between the physical and the psychological. Therefore, it is an exaggeration to say that all psychological differences between males and females have been artificially maintained over millennia purely through cultural conditioning.* Rather, the reverse would be true. Any attempt to obliterate male-female psychological differences would require strenuous and permanent cultural conditioning. And to do so would exact an exorbitant price: the attempt would run counter to the endocrine glands, counter to what we are born with—glands whose functioning steers our lives, however deflating it may be to our vanity to acknowledge the power "mere" glands have over us.

Penis envy is to be
understood metaphorically.

It is the discovery of sex difference, not cultural conditioning, that initially sets off the psychological change in children and makes them either "boys" or "girls." Once sexual identity begins to take hold, therefore, children should be provided with clear sexual models to follow — with the natural differences of those models kept clear. If a child is encouraged to perceive little if any difference between mother and father or is told that their roles are interchangeable and are not some old "stereotypes," sexual identity blurs. There is a contemporary attempt to promote an undifferentiated sexual identity

*"Our own personal observations, as well as the literature we have read, indicate that for the most part boys behave in masculine and girls behave in feminine ways because of the way their bodies are structured. Admittedly, society expects certain things of girls and certain other things of boys, but it is our feeling that society came to expect the things it did because of the way people behaved in the first place. It seems probable that if for the most part boys had not behaved boyishly and girls had not behaved girlishly, society would have developed different expectations." (Louise Bates Ames and Joan Ames Chase, *Don't Push Your Preschooler,* New York, Harper and Row, 1974, p. 60.)

("gender blur"). But unisex is a regression in ways that we understand. It tries to undo the important step forward achieved by the realization of sex difference. More openly, it tries to deny anatomy as well. If such attempts were to succeed, a child on hearing that boys and girls are not so different from each other could find in this a "corroboration" of a universal unconscious fantasy and one that is considerably at variance with reality—namely, that there is only one sex: the male sex. Unconsciously both little girls and boys feel that everyone is or is supposed to be born with a penis. Up until the discovery of sex difference, mother is assumed to have a penis. Many girls believe they were deprived of their penis because of a misdeed or because their mother made them "incomplete" or "unfinished." Analytic findings in thousands of women who were raised in different social and cultural settings corroborate this, as do the sexual theories voiced by little girls.

The conclusions encouraged by this blurring of sexual difference would be unfortunate. To the child's mind, if there is only one sex and males have a penis, females *must* have a penis, against the evidence of the senses.*

Where men and women are thought of as not just equal but the same, problems of sexual choice ensue, and these introduce difficulties into the child's development. No one can feel happy and fulfilled who also wonders: "Am I male or female? Or somehow both? Whom am I attracted to? Does it matter?" One possible outcome of this is homosexuality.

The contemporary insistence on equality sounds a disquieting psychological note. Women's demand that men share *identically* in the tasks of childrearing might be a not so disguised demand for sameness, not equality—a demand for the obliteration of sex difference. However similar men and women may be in some respects, they are nevertheless quite different in others. Legal, moral, and social forms of equality alter neither the physical nor the psychological differences between men and women. That men and women have different musculature, different sexual organs, different voices, and a different way of moving and walking is obvious. More: women have different mineral needs because of their differing body chemistry, and, being constitutionally hardier than men, have

---

*Some forms of pathology have this unconscious fantasy at their core: fetishism and transvestism, for example. Unconsciously the fetish is taken to be the woman's penis. This reassures the fetishist that women are not castrated—and therefore he won't be. (There is no record of a female fetishist.) The transvestite, by dressing as a woman, denies that women have no penis.

a lower mortality rate from the fetal stage to old age. Men and women differ in every cell of their bodies and in their chromosomes, endocrinal secretions, and hormones. These genetic and glandular differences influence the functioning of the brain and the central nervous system of the fetus and newborn, producing effects that are carried forward in the psychological functioning of adult men and women.

Many girls believe they were deprived of a penis because of a misdeed or because their mother made them "incomplete" or "unfinished."

And not just in their sexual organization. The difference between male and female sexual organization, impossible to deny, is freely conceded, but it is conceded as if that difference were unique and therefore must be gotten out of the way before getting down to cases. In fact it is only one among many psychological differences. But even the sexual organization, with its special glandular secretions, makes for reflected *behavioral* differences, because though we may be talking of cells and glands and muscle fibers, these underlie psychological responses. Different glands stimulate different emotions. The pituitary gland secretes prolactin in the mother's breast, which stimulates maternal *feelings,* not just milk. And in intercourse the female's allowing or *wishing* penetration by the male is not purely a physical matter but is psychological as well. Or, to choose the tritest of everyday examples, when it comes to eye contact few women, even in the contemporary climate of permissive sexuality, attempt what men routinely do. Men still have the sexual prerogative of openly looking a woman up and down, wherever they happen to be, whereas women don't feel they can risk the reverse behavior, because it takes much less than eye contact to effect a psychophysiological change in men—to arouse them sexually. This aggressive behavior by men has not been imposed on humans by cultural conditioning. In fact, so natural and basic is the psychology of this behavior that it is a cross-species phenomenon observable among the higher mammals.*

---

*Clifford J. Jolly, "The Seed-Eaters: A New Model of Hominid Differentiation Based on a Baboon Analogy," *Man* (1970), pp. 5 ff.

To obliterate distinctions would create problems for a growing person, who is not aware of the historical or sociological sex-role issues of contemporary adults (which are moreover the adults' concerns and not the child's). Unisex among adults is a dangerous fiction. According to modern genetics, a person is chromosomally either a male or a female. Each person needs to know, by the time adulthood has been reached, that he is a man or she is a woman and not some combination of the two that has hitherto escaped notice. Men and women are not interchangeable. Some roles arise out of *natural* feelings based on sex (gender) difference. That is real. And any attempt to deliberately blur reality must be resisted if one's hold on reality is not to be lost, with all the dangers to mental functioning that that implies.

Sexual identity and behavior are largely preprogramed and work in accordance with a physiological substrate. By the time children reach the age of five or six, most boys, if left alone in a room full of toys, will reach for the trains and trucks and most girls will reach for the dolls and ribbons. Is this purely because of cultural conditioning? The boy who formerly wanted to have a baby now prefers to fly a plane. But although a girl may also want to fly a plane, she still wants to have a baby. In contrast, the girl who formerly wanted to play with a racing car now prefers to play house. But although a boy may also want to play house, he would prefer to play with a racing car. Each wish, each shading of emphasis, is appropriate to its phase of development. To encourage boys to continue to play with dolls and girls with fire engines — that, in fact, would be to condition them to adopt roles.*

Even among the "liberated" children of kibbutzim, where upbringing in the early years is sexually undifferentiated, "girls are more integrative (helpful, affectionate, co-operative) than boys, and boys more disintegrative. In all groups boys engage in more acts of conflict than girls, and in all but one group the boys engage in more acts of aggression than girls."†

Sometimes even for a while after sexual identity has begun to take hold, children under six seem not to make the sharp

*According to David C. Taylor and Christopher Ormsted, in "Ontogenic Analysis of Sex Ratios in Disease," girls display greater ability in tests of verbal intelligence and boys in nonverbal, and boys learn to talk and read later than girls. Christopher Ormsted and David C. Taylor, *Gender Differences: Their Ontogeny and Significance,* London, Churchill Livingstone, 1972, p. 224.
†M. Spiro, *Children of the Kibbutz,* Cambridge, Mass., Harvard University Press, 1958, pp. 247–48.

distinction between "toys for boys" and "toys for girls" that adults do. This doesn't necessarily mean that adults are biased and only children retain an innocence about sex-role differences. It only means that the views of adults differ from those of children—usually in being more subtly perceptive and knowing. A boy of six wants to play with a miniature kitchen not because there are no differences between males and females but because he likes squirting the water from the faucet in the little sink: that fits in with the unconscious phallic preoccupations appropriate to his age. For similar reasons a girl might enjoy playing with a flashlight, as an expression of a phallic fantasy, or with a dump truck, as an expression of a birth fantasy, both appropriate to her age.

Eventually an innate feeling asserts itself quite independently of cultural conditioning, and former needs and interests give way to new needs and interests. Perhaps the most important point this book hopes to convey is that *human beings are perpetually in process.* Needs evolve according to inner change. What is normal behavior at age four is no longer quite so normal at age eight and is abnormal at age eighteen. If a few boys like to play with dolls at four, it would be a psychologically unwarranted conclusion that *therefore* boys and men *naturally* like to do so-called female things but are prevented from doing so by a cultural conditioning that intervenes. So sweeping a generalization is without foundation.

Unisex is a dangerous fiction.

Some say that girls are trained purely through cultural bias to play a feminine role. But that too seems an exaggeration. It is certainly true that little girls like to hammer and fix things with their father or mother or play with trains just like boys, but it is also true that they *instinctively* like to mother—hold and feed the kitten in a way that some mothers describe as "uncanny" in its naturalness—and true too that, unlike boys (with rare exceptions), they like to put on makeup the way Mommy does and be seductive with Daddy. Nor is this seductiveness culturally conditioned. Rather, it derives from an innate thrust originating in the endocrinal and hormonal substrate and given impetus by identification with one aspect of mother — mother as the sensuous woman. It is an aspect of themselves that almost all women intrinsically enjoy. It would seem sensible to suggest, therefore, that the psychological differences between men and women should be accepted and that society should make use of what is by nature in men and women and not deny or fight it.

SEXUAL MATTERS AND MISUNDERSTANDING

Psychologically speaking, direct observation of parental nudity is not particularly helpful to a child. Answering the child's questions on anatomy forthrightly and within the limits of the child's understanding could satisfy curiosity more effectively, with the added benefit of encouraging psychological growth in the specifically human way, verbally.

Besides, babies and children are not entitled to sexual intimacy with parents. They *are* only children. They will have their own sexual intimacy when they grow up, to which their parents will not be privy.

In contrast, verbal "nudity" between parents and child is psychologically beneficial. Body parts should be referred to with candor by their proper names: vagina, clitoris, penis, pubic hair, breasts, rectum, anus. For a parent never to refer to these parts of the body in this way implies unmistakably that the parts, hidden by not being named, are shameful and dirty and, by extension, that people are creatures of shame and evil.

This behavior seems to be especially true of masturbation. Not mentioning it conveys the message that it is a shameful act whose existence is to be denied. Some adults are disturbed by the mere mention of the word "masturbation." But the harm in masturbation stems not from the act but from the anxiety that may become attached to it. Guilt, not masturbation, does the harm.

Sexual matters are easily misunderstood. A child's view of events is not the same as an adult's. The view evolves, and with it an understanding of the significance of the events. That is why it is definitely not recommended that parental intercourse be witnessed by children. They are not "too young to understand." (In fact, it is somewhat harmful to children to witness or hear parental intercourse even at a later age.) Viewed by a child of six, intercourse is a frightening struggle and arouses in him or her a wish to protect the mother from the incomprehensible brutality of the father, who looks as if he were hitting, crushing, or suffocating her. Sometimes the child sees the father as the one being engulfed and destroyed by the mother. (Similar misinterpretations occur when parental intercourse is only heard and not seen.) But by ten or eleven, the significance of the act changes. Now boys or girls might be shocked that their parents engage in so "animal" an act, and at the same time they might find the parents' intercourse intensely stimulating sexually. At both ages the feelings would arise out of a distorted sense of what is happening. An adult would understand, of course, that what is happening is quite simple and natural: the parents are merely enjoying sex.

For this reason, analysts consider it inadvisable for parents to share their bedroom with a child, even an infant. Unless you can't afford it, each child would be better off with a private room from the start. The analyses of many adults indicate that witnessing or hearing parental intercourse, distortedly understood, had a disturbing effect. The disturbance can date even from earliest infancy.

Body parts should be referred to with candor by their proper names.

Similarly, if a boy of one year sees an older sister nude, it has no effect on him — not consciously. But seeing his sister nude when he was five might arouse castration anxiety in him by making him wonder what happened to her penis, or whether she was born without one. It's the same anxiety — and the same implied derogation of females — because it emphasizes the *absence* of a penis, overlooking the *presence* of a vagina. Unless sex is explained and openly discussed the discovery of the vagina usually comes late, sometimes as late as adolescence. The lateness of this discovery does not seem very important, but its repercussions are far-reaching, even to occupational prejudice.

One of the few statements about the sex drive that can be made with any certainty is that it never needs encouragement. The drive is powerful and lifelong. It develops and changes in its own way and in its own good time. If anything, its remaining latent during long periods of growth is more beneficial to the individual, because the later the appearance of the drive in childhood and adolescence—within limits—the better equipped the child or adolescent is to deal with its concomitant psychological effects.

CASTRATION ANXIETY

Beginning around the age of three or four, boys universally experience an unconscious fear of castration. Although the fear is built in,* external events arouse it, and one of these events is the discovery of sex difference. The fear stems from the perception that girls do not have a penis (without the understanding that they do have a vagina). To a boy this means that he could lose his penis "also." The boy almost invariably feels (unconsciously) that it is his father who will castrate him, partly out of a general rivalry but chiefly in punishment of the boy's sexual urges toward his mother.

At first psychoanalysts believed that girls are better off than boys in that, not having had a penis, they don't fear losing it. But later it was suggested that girls have one more complication in development than boys do: although boys and girls originally love mother more than father, to boys the mother is at least a heterosexual choice, whereas girls must shift their love from mother to father to attain heterosexuality.

Consciously or not, all girls theorize that they once had or should have a penis. Some hope that a penis will grow one day. Some fantasize that they in fact do have one but it is inside them—a wishful theory that comes remarkably close to one truth about their genitals while altogether missing the longed-for "truth." But by and large a girl's interests shift as she accepts her body as it is, all the more so as she slowly learns from early childhood on about reproduction and her crucial role in it, and especially in the late teen years, when she begins to enjoy intercourse.

From the age of three to five, the time Freud labeled the "phallic stage" because boys are (relatively) so preoccupied with their penis and girls with the sensations in their clitoris, the fear of castration spreads to more than just a concern over the genitals. Around this time and somewhat beyond, children show unusual apprehension over cuts and bruises. And not just on themselves: a scratch on *your* hand interests them as much. How did you get it? Did you bleed a lot? Does it hurt? *Is it going to be all right?*

*Here too anatomy is destiny.

From there, the concern spreads to objects as well. The boy whose anxiety made him fondle his penis continually through his pants pocket would not permit anyone to watch him remove his underpants and developed a horror over things breaking. If a plate broke or an object was taken apart his anxiety was intense. He once saw a fishing pole disassembled for the first time and asked anxiously, "Can you put it back together again?"

Because this is the age of genital play and a time when boys and girls are especially sensitive to threats of bodily damage, a tonsillectomy — indeed, all surgery — should be avoided whenever possible. Doctors are coming around to the opinion that except when they are absolutely necessary, tonsillectomies do more harm than good (tonsils are lymph nodes and help fight infections). In any case, to perform one when a boy or girl is anywhere from three to six would be to arouse a high degree of castration anxiety. To the unconscious mind, castration and tonsillectomy are equivalent: a portion of the anatomy is surgically removed. To a boy this could mean that the loss of his penis is a possibility too. To a girl it could mean that "one more" part of her body is taken away. The integrity of the body (one's *self*) is violated — one's being is diminished.

If a tonsillectomy is necessary but can be postponed, that would be advisable. Everything we have just said about it would still be true later on, but with age comes greater understanding and, equally important, less misunderstanding.

If a boy was not circumcised at birth, then *don't* have the operation performed later in childhood. Perhaps more than any other kind of operation, a circumcision would be psychologically equivalent to castration. (If *he* decides on it as an adult, that would be another matter.)

MASTURBATION

Anal and genital pleasures are easily confused because they overlap considerably in development. The confusion is also partly due to anatomy: boys and girls at the age of three and four typically think that a girl's anus is her genital organ, and it is years before that error is altogether cleared up. Little boys urinate through the part of their body that also affords them the sexual pleasure of masturbation (without, at this age, ejaculation) and therefore might think of urination as a sexual pleasure. This lumping together of the two functions requires much sorting out.

During elimination, body parts are more exposed than usual, and the exposure lends itself to exploration while on the toilet seat and inevitably to genital fondling. Boys do this more often than girls because their genitals are more accessible. But little girls discover that when they put their hands between their legs, as they sometimes do automatically when they become aware of a pressing need to urinate, they feel pleasant sensations. After that they sometimes snuggle their hands between their legs to lessen anxiety—or just to feel good.

Adult genitality does not suddenly appear in full bloom one day. Babies go through preliminary sexual phases. Feeding, in the oral phase, definitely had its highly enjoyable erotic component, and later came the anal erotic pleasures. Masturbation can be understood, therefore, as the next step in a series. The primacy of pleasure zones shifts from one part of the body to another in accompaniment with the physical maturing of the body. When children masturbate (fondle themselves) from the third year on, this expression of their erotic feelings is appropriate to their age and level of development.

In its development, the sexual drive undergoes a major change. It begins as a *self*-involvement (originally playing with the mouth, then the anus, then the genitals), then advances to an involvement with *others.* This same shift occurs in all functioning. At the start of life the "self"-involvement is extreme: the baby exists alone and only slowly perceives that there are others, then begins building ties to those others.

Around the age of three, and for the next year or two, little boys get erections frequently and as an expression of their involvement with others like to exhibit themselves. The boy juts out his penis as far as he can and shows it off. One boy was overheard to remark to a girlfriend, who was visibly bowled over by the phenomenon, that he was "driving his penis." "Driving it?" she asked incredulously. "Yes, like a car." On another occasion this same boy held a ball against his erect penis and said, "Ready, aim, *FIRE!*" He hurled the ball from his penis as far as he could, saying to himself with satisfaction, "A long one," revealing his wishful view of the size and power of his penis in an unwitting parody of emission.

Because these early sexual pleasures are so easily aroused in connection with toileting and bathing, washing a child's bottom and genitals should be treated casually during a bath. Besides, the skin of young children is soft enough not to need special care in washing.

A mother is sometimes tempted to play with her little boy's penis while drying him after a bath. It seems innocent to give a playful dab with the towel or chuck it with a finger, especially when the little boy laughs delightedly and asks — or looks expectantly — for more. Unfortunately, however, this may lead to unconscious incestuous fixation. Once enjoyed, a pleasure is not easily given up.

SELF-STIMULATION AND SELF-COMFORT

The tendency to seek genital self-stimulation is not a phase restricted to adolescence, as people used to think. Except for the first few months, it is a lifelong phenomenon.

The genital area is a highly pleasurable one because it is rich in nerve endings. Once this source of pleasurable sensation is discovered, at the age of three or earlier, a small child gives it up only intermittently until latency, which begins some time after the age of five, during which sexual pleasures remain dormant. Interest in it returns again in adolescence, after which it eventually gives way to the greater pleasure of sexual relations with another person. Even then, in moments of regression or enforced abstinence, masturbation offers a mode of discharge, affording self-comfort and relief.

Ordinarily most people regard self-stimulation as a limited pleasure because it is not emotionally satisfying. In sex there is an emotional orgasm as well as a physical one, and the emotional orgasm is lacking in masturbation. If masturbation is permitted in a noncondemnatory atmosphere in adolescence, it soon feels inadequate and even dull. Dissatisfaction with the "loneliness" of masturbation increases one's sense of the value of another person. Except where there is an emotional problem, the love of oneself never offers the deep pleasures that the love of another does.

That is not true in the earliest years, however, when a baby finds physical satisfaction partly from the mother and partly from his or her own body. Where there is insufficient pleasure from the mother, the child turns to autoerotic pleasures: thumbsucking, rocking, head knocking, and genital self-stimulation. This is especially true if the child has been deprived of mother for periods of time, has lost mother (either totally or emotionally), has been weaned too early or too abruptly, or has had excessive prohibitions placed on natural impulses.*

Masturbation is a sensitive and complex experience. It appears more prominently from puberty onward because it is then that specifically sexual glandular secretions are continuously produced. In one form or another, *some* periodic discharge becomes necessary and, of course, normal.

When a little boy aged three or four fondles his genitals with pleasure, it may be that he is simultaneously having unconscious fantasies of loving his mother. At that age masturbation is the only manner of expressing erotic love that he is capable of. (*All* love is erotically tinged, consciously or unconsciously. "Pure" love exists only in the minds of puritans.) Therefore, if the boy's mother, anxious at the sight of his masturbating, were to criticize him for it, she would in effect be spurning him, which would disturb his relationship to her and perhaps even blunt his feelings of love in general. Feelings of love, especially at so young an age, are tender and fragile. It is the same with a girl and her feelings for her father, except that she is apt to feel an edge of rivalry and not just rejection if her mother interferes with her masturbation.

The tendency to seek genital
self-stimulation is a lifelong phenomenon.

Self-stimulation is one form of expressing love. Prohibiting it, therefore, has the effect of introducing a disturbance into the natural development of *all* feelings of tenderness and affection. The erotic love of oneself and the erotic love of others are the same drive at different levels of development — and with considerable fluidity between levels. The acceptance or condemnation of one level becomes, consciously or unconsciously, the acceptance or condemnation of the drive altogether.

*Anna Freud, *Infants Without Families,* in *The Writings of Anna Freud, Vol. III, 1939–1945,* New York, International Universities Press, 1973, pp. 605–6.

MASTURBATION AND INDEPENDENCE

Most authors of books on childhood make it a point to speak approvingly of masturbation in moral rather than psychological terms, saying or implying that there is "nothing wrong with it." This no doubt is a reaction to a puritanical past. But to view masturbation morally is to view it in negative terms. There is a *positive* psychological reason for masturbation, one that partially accounts for the prominence of its appearance at certain phases of development. Masturbation is performed alone and privately. Parents and others do not have to know about it, which in itself has positive value: children learn that when they stimulate their genitals *they can provide themselves with pleasure.* They are not compelled to depend on someone's being there to reduce tensions or anxiety for them. They can actively take over for themselves.

This privacy, if respected by parents, emphasizes a child's feeling of separateness and promotes a growing autonomy. (Thumbsucking is an earlier form of self-afforded pleasure, building toward independence.) Masturbation reinforces psychological separation: the need for sex, the powerful instinctual drive, can be satisfied without outside aid. Being alone while masturbating, even if it means at times feeling actually lonely, enchances the sense of self because it compels a child to feel what he or she is. If a child were not to masturbate at all, it might very well mean that something had gone wrong in psychological separation. The child would feel incomplete, incapable of doing things for him- or herself. Gratification would necessarily depend on the outside, on another person.

WHAT TO DO ABOUT MASTURBATION

Why, therefore, do anything about masturbation? Neutrality is the best course, neither encouraging nor discouraging it. If you encourage masturbation, these early impulses could become exaggerated and lead to fixation in development. But because masturbation is an expression of an instinctual force, if you disapprove of it, it will find a secret, guilt-laden outlet, again leading to fixation. Shame and self-loathing, both extremely destructive emotions, would also be aroused. Secretiveness and shame give rise to lifelong feelings that sex is dirty, crippling the normal expression of the sex drive and leading to poor sexual functioning and unhappiness. To disapprove of masturbation is to call sex bad. Is it? To make threats against a child for masturbating arouses castration anxiety. Does that help?

As we have seen again and again, development runs its course in miniphases. Each phase lasts only a while and plays itself out when there is optimum gratification. We can be sure that it is the same with masturbation.

Some authorities suggest offering a favorite toy as a distraction to a masturbating child. But after you have done that a few times the child catches on to the trick and gets your unspoken message that masturbation makes *you* anxious, and soon he or she feels anxious too.

The more honest contemporary literature — to say nothing of surveys — is making it clear that adults, married or otherwise, masturbate out of need. Why should children be forbidden it? Is it to teach them "good" habits? If that approach really worked, after generations of "moral" indoctrination, no contemporary adult would ever masturbate — an absurdity. The subject has been so thoroughly suppressed for so long that it is still the case that many find it difficult to imagine that their adult friends as well as their elders masturbate with greater or lesser frequency.

Masturbation reinforces
psychological separation: the need
for sex, the powerful instinctual drive,
can be satisfied without outside aid.

Neutrality means not bending over backward either, which is sometimes a temptation. One mother overcompensated for her puritanical upbringing by carrying matters to an extreme. She told her teenage son that any time he felt like masturbating he should feel free to tell her so and then go to his room and do it. As she well knew, but was reluctant to acknowledge, this created a highly charged incestuous atmosphere between them (satisfying a need of hers), to say nothing of attempting to rob the boy of his growing sense of autonomy by tearing down any privacy in the act.

Overpermissive mothers tend to bend over backward and encourage masturbation, sometimes even telling a child to do so openly. We might, however, contrast this with the way one "good enough" mother handled it. One warm summer day her little boy, just under three, pushed his erect penis against her leg with a happy look of affection and pleasure all over his face. She didn't say "No!" which would have had the effect of rejecting the obvious love for her that he was feeling. He would have felt incomprehensibly criticized for a natural expression of an instinct. On the other hand, she didn't just stay where she was and let the play go on, which would have had the effect of encouraging further eroticism. Instead she casually adopted a neutral course by pretending after a brief interval that a pot on the stove needed looking after. In a moment he became distracted, and the episode ended as naturally as it had started.

15

Learning and the Increasing Hold on Reality

One real world is enough.

SANTAYANA

Starting sometime before the age of three and continuing thereafter, your child relies on you to clarify perceptions of the real world, to distinguish between what is real and possible and what is not real and impossible. To a child of this age almost anything *seems* possible. Magic and reality are as one. What is merely imagined becomes real. That is why anxiety dreams—those dreams that are popularly misnamed "nightmares"*—are so unusually terrifying to a very small child: the distinction between dream and waking reality is hazy. It requires your explanation for a child to know that he or she was dreaming. You explain that dreams are pictures we see "inside our head" when we are asleep. Sometimes those pictures don't seem to make any sense, and once in a while they might even be scary, but then we wake up and they go away.

The need to distinguish between the real and the imagined is never altogether outgrown. We spend our lives distinguishing between ourselves and others, the proof being the ease with which we attribute to strangers feelings that belong to us—the notion that they are thinking critically of us, for example.

In gradually distinguishing between the real and the imag-

*Nightmares are harrowing experiences during sleep, not dreams, and extremely few people ever have them. Most readers of this book have never had one and never will.

ined we follow a tenuous course at best. Good development can all too easily be undone. Some adults, to discipline a child, claim to be able to read the child's thoughts by looking into his or her eyes. A child would of course believe this. Paranoia sometimes is rooted in common, innocent-seeming events of this kind. The falsehood that mother is able to read the child's thoughts tears down the good work that he or she has so far accomplished toward differentiating the self from her.

A child is still learning that we live in a cause-and-effect world. If a child disobeys your command to come to your side and a moment later trips and falls, you would be making a serious mistake if you said, "You see? You fell because you didn't come when I called." The child would understand that literally, even though it is of course not true. With this kind of treatment it would not be surprising if such a child grew up with faulty reasoning ability.

A similar hazard in this period is the doctor who "reassures" the child, "You won't feel the shot," or that tearing off the bandages "won't hurt a bit," and thus damages both a sense of reality and trust. The truth is always better: "You *will* feel the needle a little, but the feeling will last only a couple of seconds." "It *will* hurt to tear this bandage off, but it might hurt more to remove it slowly." Children do appreciate the truth.

YOU INTERPRET REALITY

A child needs your help in acquiring a better understanding of reality. You organize the world, assigning to all the daily events a sense and a value. When you say, "Oh look, what a *friendly* dog," the child sees not just the dog but the essential friendliness of domesticated animals. If you say, "These flowers are beautiful and smell so sweet," you begin a lasting aesthetic appreciation of nature. Your statements assign names to things and describe them to the child, who is a new arrival in life, and at the same time suggest attitudes to adopt toward the world as something interesting and exciting.

In interpreting the real everday world you also help organize a child's self-image by the same means. "You are a boy. Your sister is a girl." However obvious that is to adults, at the age of two and a half years it is a thought-provoking bit of knowledge. "You're an intelligent girl and can do so many things" becomes a feedback to self-image. Children learn from parents who they are, what they are like, and whether they are good or bad. Of course they are all good, but they don't always feel that way within themselves unless you reassure them. They need you to corroborate objectively what is real.

There are dangers inherent in their depending on you for feedback. Overgeneralizations like "You're *always* slow!" and "You *never* do things right!" tear down a child's good self-images. They are untruths. No one is always slow. Everyone does things right sometimes.

The worst danger is that your statements might become unconsciously accepted as suggestions for the child to carry out. "You *never* do things right!" actually helps to form a person who ends by seldom doing things right. Your statement is taken not as an opinion but as the truth, as a final judgment: that's the way the child *is*. So the child grows into your expectation of him or her. "You are Mama's good little boy" becomes a prescription for behavior. The boy might spend the rest of his life living up to Mother's pathetically limited expectations, thus emotionally crippling himself. "You're a bad girl and always will be one!" is a condemnation that keeps on working unconsciously so that on reaching womanhood the girl, if further demoralized over the years, might act on the parental "suggestion" and lead a life that fulfills the unhappy prophecy. This propensity can be turned the other way to great advantage by instead emphasizing whatever is praiseworthy. "You really are a wonderful person — I'm sure you're going to have a fine life when you grow up" becomes a better prophecy to fulfill.

A positive self-image helps build a strong sense of identity, a matter of special importance to children of minority, racial, ethnic, and religious groups. It is a function of parental protection to fight bias with the truth. To be a Puerto Rican, Oriental, Chicano, Jewish, black, or white child is to be a fine human being. To be Catholic, Protestant, Moslem, Hindu, or atheist is to exercise freedom of belief. Every person on earth has his or her beliefs, and each person's beliefs merit absolute respect. No background is an inferior background to have — although some might be culturally handicapping, which would be a cause for concern, not contempt. No human being was, is, or ever will be superior to any other human being except in special abilities (such as IQ, for example), which, however, are not a license for looking down on others. No matter what the child's origins or upbringing, each child is an invaluable and unique person with a right to life, love, and fulfillment.

As further protection you might point out that unfortunately there are many millions of prejudiced people in the world who think they *are* superior to their fellows because of skin color, national origin, or religious beliefs. Although we may pity them because we know that their sense of superiority is merely a mask hiding deep fears, it is wise for the minority child to be prepared to encounter their hatred and discrimination. To teach, as most school systems do, explicitly or implicitly, that the world is a fundamentally kind and rational place to live, that people have an essential goodness that always wins out over evil, is to teach what history repeatedly shows to be a lie, and it sets up an innocent child for more than a few shocks and disillusioning experiences. It would be truer protection and a greater psychological service to the child to say that people should learn to behave better with each other than they do but that in fact they behave irrationally and callously much of the time. The child might emulate what is good in them and learn to deal with the rest.

"You are Mama's good little boy"
becomes a prescription for behavior,
a living up to Mother's
pathetically limited expectations.

SANTA CLAUS AND THE TRUTH

What about Santa Claus and reality? If you tell your child that Santa is real and then say that he is not real, you don't inspire confidence in your word, and suddenly the trust that has been built up over the years is seriously eroded.

To a child Christmas is so intensely invested with anticipated joy and pleasure and Santa is believed in with such religious fervor that for some the disillusionment at suddenly learning the truth makes reality seem a terrible "cheat and a disappointment." Children actually fight off the reality and persist in believing the myth for another year or two until they are forced to yield under peer pressure. But they yield unhappily.

Should you, then, deprive your child of the pleasure of jolly old Santa? Not at all. Some parents tell their child from the start that there is no Santa. They explain that it is *fun* to make believe that we get Christmas presents from a fat, rosy-cheeked old man who lives at the icy North Pole and travels through the sky in a sleigh drawn by reindeer and then slides down chimneys to put pretty packages in everyone's living room. This tells the child the truth yet preserves the fairy tale. It doesn't destroy the pleasure of the myth any more than the pleasure is destroyed when you tell a child about the "good fairy," who is a pretend person, or the bad witch in "Hansel and Gretel" and how she finally gets baked in the oven, which you explain is "just a fairy tale."

Besides, the real pleasure for children at Christmas comes not from Santa—who can be a frightening figure, as you discover when you sit your child on his lap in a department store—but from the presents. And it doesn't matter to children who *gives* presents just as long as they *get* presents. When it comes to gifts, children are practical first and last and show no false modesty or hypocrisy about taking.

IS LYING BAD?

If acknowledging what is truthful and real is good, is lying bad? Lying is bad if it is deliberately used to deceive. That kind of lying destroys belief and trust between people.

But a useful and valid distinction should be made. Although bad lies fool people or hurt their feelings, there are other lies that are spoken out of politeness and are in fact intended to protect people's feelings—good lies, or half truths. This needs to be explained to a child.

There are also self-protective lies, and these are innocent enough to ignore. For example, four-year-old Maria accidentally dropped a ceramic bowl, which smashed into a hundred pieces. Her mother rushed to the scene to see what had happened and unthinkingly asked, "Did *you* break that?" Maria assumed a plausible "Who me?" expression and said, "Oh no, Donna broke it," at which the mother couldn't help smiling. Donna happened to be away at the time.

LYING AS A GAME

Once language is acquired, making communication possible,

spurious communication becomes possible too. Some lies are innocent fibs offered in fun. In fact, a child might try twisting meanings to their opposites to see if you *can* be fooled, like playing games with words to experiment with reality, about which there is still much to be learned.

A child is only delighted if you believe something he or she knows is not true. It is a funny bit of knowledge to discover that you, an adult, can be tricked. But because your child loves you, the attempt will be made only once or twice just to see that it works. After that it loses its excitement. Children are guileless. No child has a need to *really* lie if you have been honest, have not made him or her feel that there are things to hide, and have not withheld your love. A child has no need to lie unless you lie or convey the impression that an honest expression of feelings is unwelcome to you.

Some children lie because their parents suppress information (lie) about sex. Children are quick to perceive this, and their lying is a repayment in kind. Some parents try to make their children suppress their sexual impulses — no thumbsucking, no anal pleasures, no masturbation. This conveys to children that some feelings are to be kept hidden, and this tendency to hide feelings slowly spreads. In addition, it becomes a pleasure to lie to parents — to hurt them in revenge.

LYING AS A MOVE TOWARD INDEPENDENCE

Suppose that there have been openness and honesty between you, and your child feels no need to hide things but does something you don't like and then lies about it. If it is an isolated lie and you feel there is no danger of its becoming a habit, you might let it pass without comment for a positive reason: a child who tells a fib learns an extremely valuable lesson — namely, that you have no way of knowing what goes on inside him or her without being told.

A child is still not sure of this. The child may still have a vague notion that you as an adult have perfect knowledge of what goes on in his or her mind. Fooling you with a fib makes it clear in a simple and dramatic way that you and the child are two distinctly different persons.

This type of lying, because it is in the service of psychological separation, tells you you have been doing a good job. Development is proceeding satisfactorily.

IDEALIZATION

Although all through the third, fourth, and fifth years your child is learning what is real, the perception of you continues to be quite unrealistic. Your child idealizes both parents, frankly adoring you and overestimating your strength, your intelligence, your abilities, and even your looks. In another two or three years, if there have been no great problems between parents and child, to a little boy his mother becomes a womanly ideal of competence, grace, character, and beauty. To a little girl her father will seem the best man in the world, compared with whom all others pale or have faults and shortcomings.

This idealization is a highly important development. A child grows up wanting to be not just like you but like the idealized view of you, wanting to see you as a less imperfect model than you are so that he or she can identify with the *improvement* over you and grow into the model. And within limits this is extraordinarily beneficial to the child — and to the world. He or she aspires to be better than the persons in the immediate environment — us, with all our shortcomings. It is in ways like this that advances are effected in human events.

> Fooling you with a fib makes it clear in a simple and dramatic way that you and the child are two distinctly different persons.

Naturally, as the child grows older, this idealized view of you slowly becomes tempered by reality. Your child begins to see your limitations. It may sound contradictory, but that is a desirable development too. It is good because alongside the continuing feelings of idealization there is a growing awareness that you are only human. If this awareness does not happen too soon or too abruptly, which would result in a too deep disappointment in you and a collapse of ideals, it helps to make the child feel that you are not paragons living life on a high and unattainable plane. He or she won't despair of ever meeting a mate someday to take your place. Your child begins to perceive you in an idealized view that is somewhat corrected by reality. It is a gradual and necessary disillusionment fostering growth.

CONSTANCY AND SEPARATION

Just as we never fully distinguish between ourselves and others, we never fully complete psychological separation. The process continues throughout our lives. The separation we have been speaking of at the age of three is a first round. The sense of separateness that a child develops leads to his or her psychological *individuality*. In adolescence there is an even greater movement toward psychological separation, and it is with the success of that attempt that the person begins to attain true and lasting independence.

What makes separation possible is that you become "constant" in your child's feelings. From the age of three on, the child becomes able to separate from you for longer and longer periods because of the realization that you exist even when he or she doesn't need you. A child has to learn that you are a real person and that you exist by and for yourself, not just as a gratifier of needs. Back when you were merely (to the child) a need gratifier you had no other reason for existence. In fact you did not really exist *except* when you were gratifying needs, the way a waiter in a restaurant exists for you only when you order a meal. Indeed, it doesn't matter to you who waits on your table as long as the food is served and your needs are met.

Slowly, over time, the child has come to a truer recognition, that you have a separate existence. Even when the child doesn't need you for anything, he or she realizes that you are a real person with an existence independent of the child's needs. You are valued even when *not* needed — a state of emotional advance that will benefit later relationships with friends or a mate.

If the child knows you can be relied on, your disappearance from view does not arouse anxiety. *You continue in your existence.* The importance of this is that when the time comes to enter your child in a nursery school or kindergarten, he or she will not have trouble parting from you on that crucial first day. The first day of school is the acid test of how well separation has been accomplished. If psychological development has proceeded well, it will be possible to leave your child in the care of the teacher, with the child feeling confident that you will return later in the day. In fact, there might even be some sense of accomplishment on your child's part if your leaving can be tolerated easily.

What happens when psychological separation from mother

does not succeed? "Unseparated" persons are the ones who can't do things on their own. They seem always to require the presence of another for them not to feel helpless or incapable or for them to get things done. They are wives who are dependent and held down not necessarily by a male-dominated society but by their own psychological difficulties – they in fact welcome passively being cared for. Or they are husbands who are threatened by any thrust toward independence by women, because that to them is unconsciously tantamount to losing the mother or mothers that they are always looking for. Or they are the ones who drop out of society in their early adulthood for questionable reasons, at that critical moment when for the first time in their development they are finally in a position to move out on their own into a life of independence and individuality.

INTERNALIZATION

Your child's ability to tolerate without anxiety being dropped off at school (or nursery school) on the first day is one of those developments that tell you that all your care has paid off. What makes it possible for the child to get through the first day is *internalization.* Through internalization your child in effect *has* you inside, carries you around in an unconscious mental representation – the personal version of you. If this mental representation (a composite of a great many pictures and impressions of you) has been slowly built up and stored away in memory so that your child feels confident of your emotional availability and your existence even though you are out of sight – if you are internally constant – then he or she will not experience stress on being separated from you for these longer and longer stretches of time.

PRESCHOOL ANXIETY

A child who becomes anxious at being left at the nursery school needs more time to internalize you and separate from you. Psychological separation is not complete. It is for this reason that it is never very wise to take a child to nursery school when he or she is only two years old: developmentally the child is not ready. Some time after three is safer. Unless it is absolutely necessary, the use of day-care centers or fulltime sitters is not advisable before the child is three.

It would be best not to insist, pressure, or try the sink-or-swim technique of just dropping your child off and running. Separation is a psychological weaning and like weaning must be done gradually if problems are to be avoided. If necessary, accustom the child to your going away by staying on a while at the school for the first few days, gradually tapering off your stay until by the end of a week or two your absence can be tolerated.

Once a child becomes accustomed to nursery school, the new surroundings help development by providing exciting and different stimulation. This is particularly true of city children, who are often cramped in the small space of their apartment or room. In nursery school, children learn better how to play with other children (especially true of an only child), and also they have access to many different toys.

MATURE PARENTS *ALLOW* PSYCHOLOGICAL SEPARATION

Implicit in all we have been saying is the parents' ability to *allow* psychological separation. What makes this possible is your having experienced fulfillment from your child through all the phases since birth. Also you feel mature enough to tolerate your child's increased psychological independence. As natural as this process seems, some parents find it difficult to let go, to permit independence in their child. They encourage dependence to meet their own unconscious needs. But if you yourself have had good early development and achieved psychological separation at the appropriate time in *your* life, you will not cling now. You feel no difficulty in accepting the inevitable development of your child into an individual person who begins to do more and more things in response to innate forces.

SEPARATION AND DEATH

According to a French proverb, "To part is to die a little." It may seem odd to link death with separation. But to a very young child they can be psychologically identical. When separation is premature or sudden the child experiences it as abandonment. To a child, abandonment feels like death.

A child, with typical egocentric reasoning, experiences a parent's death (or forced physical separation) as *intentional* abandonment. It is as if in a desperate attempt to live in an ordered world, a child imputes to adults motives that adults don't have, to try to make some sense out of events. Adults don't die: they deliberately go away from the child.

This accounts for a child's uneasiness at the idea of death — however fuzzy that idea might be. It is not death that is terrifying but the thought of being abandoned, left utterly alone.

DEATH

Around the fourth year, a child's vision of life begins to expand, and emerging questions reflect an awareness of the greater world outside the home and parents. The child's curiosity and imagination become powerful instruments for learning. No longer satisfied that things are, the child now wants to know *why* they are, *how* they came to be that way, and what *other* things there are in life.

Separation is a psychological weaning and like weaning must be done gradually if problems are to be avoided.

When thinking has advanced to a certain point, the child comes unexpectedly to the realization that individual life has a beginning. (The realization comes sooner if there is the birth of a sibling.) That interesting thought is not a disturbing one because all it means is that the child is here and so are you, a reassuring state of affairs. But the companion realization is that possibly life has an end, and that thought introduces a vague anxiety. The anxiety is only vague because death is not yet real. There is life, life has an end, and that end is called death. As adults we know that it is in fact the reality of death that gives increased value to life — quite a positive view to take and one that enables us to function well for as long as we live. But "life," "nature," and "time" still do not make sense to a young child because these concepts — as we adults tend to forget — are abstractions.

A child's asking questions about death is not an indication of morbidity, therefore, but an avidity to understand more. What would it be like if there were no life? Once it starts, why does life have to end? What if there were no death? What *is* life? Where do we come from? What happens after death? The curious part of all this is how close the very young child comes to the central and perennial questions of philosophy and theology. With many people, one of the eventual expressions of a longing for immortality and omnipotence is a religious conviction in which their own limitations are recognized once and for all, and the unconsciously wished-for omnipotence is attributed to a supreme being who confers immortality on all.

The child's questioning the inevitability of death and feeling sad at your affirmation that it *is* inevitable are an indication that the child has developed an awareness of the pleasure of living — and an awareness that there is a future. The sadness also stems, however, from another source: if the child must someday die, that is one more blow to the infantile feelings of omnipotence.

But even with these questions and answers death does not become real. The child tries to understand it in the only terms possible: death is a going away. That is how the unconscious views it (there is no death to the unconscious), and the child's best thinking is still similar to the peculiarities of unconscious mental functioning. (In dreams, death is very often represented by a trip or a voyage.) But this going away places us back again on familiar ground: death means losing you.

To a child, abandonment
feels like death.

The fear is of your loss whether the child thinks of his or her own death or yours. You may feel gratified when your child expresses the wish that you will never die, but what the child is unconsciously saying is that your death would make the child anxious at being abandoned. Separation anxiety also leads to the fear of death, the ultimate separation. The French poet Lamartine beautifully expressed the fear and desolation of an intolerable separation: "Only one single person is lacking — and the entire world feels empty."

THE DEATH OF A PARENT

If one parent should die when the child is very young, the child will worry that the other parent too might be lost. To counter this anxiety it would be helpful to reassure the child that the surviving parent will take care of him- or herself and will always be there.

It would be a mistake to discourage or minimize a child's grief at the death of a parent. A parent is irreplaceable, and that should be acknowledged: *no* one can takè the place of a dead parent, ever. This might even be openly expressed — the truth is always reassuring. Not much of the grief will show on the surface, but all of it is important to feel. Mourning is the most natural response to death, and the child should be allowed to feel every bit of the sadness that is there. The child's feelings should not be covered over, which would only prolong them. Mourning comes to an end sooner when it is more deeply felt, and it does need time for all of it to be worked through.

Death is a going away.
That is how the unconscious views it.

If it is the father who dies, leaving a son behind, it is quite unwise for a mother to say to the boy, "Now *you'll* be Mommy's protector and take care of me." The intention is to compliment the boy and make him feel grown up. But its unconscious effect is to increase the boy's anxiety: to all his feelings of sadness and anger at his father's loss he now adds guilt at replacing his father. Besides, it burdens him that he, a child, needs to protect or care for the mother, who is an adult, when he still needs it to be the other way around. Such an attempt would deprive the boy of his childhood. In a case of this kind it is up to the mother to assume the father's role and reassure the boy that she is quite capable of caring for and protecting both of them.

If a mother dies leaving a daughter behind, the father might be extra careful to avoid any intimacy with the girl — true of mothers and sons too. He can remain quite warm and loving toward her while keeping their relationship of father and daughter clearly understood. Anything that preserves strong lines of identity reassures. To eroticize this relationship — a subtle, unconscious tendency that would have to be guarded against — would create problems for the girl.

The death of a parent makes a child unconsciously angry at being abandoned by that parent. Always reassure the child that the parent did not abandon or stop loving the family but that death comes to all, to some sooner than others — *though the child still has many years left to live.* Death has no hidden significance: it just happens. Everything that lives dies.

Sometimes a child feels guilty because he or she wishes in anger that the parent would die, and then unexpectedly, the parent does die. If the child shows signs of guilt or brooding, it would be immensely reassuring to explain that the parent's death was *not* the child's fault. Death is not the "fault" of anyone nor is it caused by people. People die from illness, age, or natural causes.

Should your child attend a funeral? At any age under approximately seven, death is not real, but even so there is no harm in having a child attend a funeral. The dread of death felt by some might have been lessened if it had been a part of their experience rather than hidden. Death is a natural event. Nothing is gained by sheltering a child from grief, which is a part of life.

ANSWERING QUESTIONS ABOUT DEATH

If you answer questions about death, it would be better *not* to compare it with sleep. Parents sometimes attempt this because they feel it makes death less threatening. But it could make bedtime and sleeping into a feared experience, the child unconsciously equating going to bed with dying.

If your child asks when *you* are going to die, it might be helpful to know that the question usually means, "Are you ever going to leave me?" This too calls for reassurance. You might reply that you will not die for years and *years* — asserting this strongly. Obviously, it is impossible to say exactly how many more years you will live, but, assuming you are a new parent, quite possibly forty or fifty (to a child that's astronomical) and maybe even more. To the child's unstated question, "Will you abandon me?" your answer means, "No, I will never abandon you."

Around the fourth year and a little beyond, a child asks many questions that seem unrelated to death but symbolically have the same meaning as the more obvious questions. "What

would happen if the house blew away? *Could* it blow away?"
The unspoken question is, "Would *you* go away and let my life
end?" The child of this age feels a need for permanence and
reliability. Some variant questions are more transparent:
"How many orphans are there in the world? Do some children
get born without mommies and daddies?" Sometimes the
question is subtle enough to elude any immediate connection
with death, like "What would happen if the sun didn't come
up?" The subtext is again concern over reliability and the
permanence of life. So too are questions like "What if I didn't
have any eyes or ears and mouth?" In all cases any reassuring
answer will do, especially if spoken cheerfully and confidently.

THE CHILD AND SELFHOOD

Childhood is advanced enough now for us to talk of a child's
selfhood. The child has already achieved a *self,* a sense of
identity. What was once a newborn with innate potential
interacting with an environment has begun to be a person.

The child's feeling of self carries into all the spheres of life.
For example, even at the age of four, five, or six, children are
more aware of themselves as persons and therefore more
aware of their clothing and surroundings. They don't talk
about it much (it mostly doesn't occur to them to talk about it),
but both boys and girls have feelings about what they have on
and whether it is attractive, appropriate, or embarrassing—
what *others* think of it. One five-year-old boy surprised his
parents by telling a playmate who was visiting that the
handsome lobby of the building he lived in usually had drapes
and couches but that they were away for their annual clean-
ing. Clearly he wanted his friend to know he lived in an
attractive building whose appearance was better than the way
it happened to be that day. This same boy at six expressed
pleasure at seeing his father dressed in a blazer. Feeling good
to have a father who dressed well, he went to his room and
emerged wearing *his* good jacket and smiled warmly when
someone remarked on what a fine appearance father and son
made.

We might conclude from events of this kind that children by
the age of six are not too young to be consulted about the
clothing to be bought for them. It would be premature to give
them a totally free hand, but their wishes should be listened to
and reliably followed up to a point. Their vote in these matters

can begin to take on increasing weight. That makes them feel even more like persons.

THE CHILD'S GROWING INTEREST IN TELEVISION

As a part of this newly developing sense of self, a child begins to have likes and dislikes, enjoying looking at books and reading stories, although perhaps feeling indifferent as yet about music. (Generally, music appreciation seems to be a later development.) But what if, as is so common, a child of four or older seems to prefer TV to reading? This disturbs many parents, who are afraid that watching TV might impoverish a growing child's imagination or impair a budding ability to think. They are afraid that the child might become habituated to being passively entertained.

What matters, however, is degree. A certain amount of television watching actually stimulates the imagination and provides it with images and thoughts for later use. Whether the programs are about children's stories or everyday happenings in the real world, they teach a child about life and all the things in it, more than the child would experience in the relatively circumscribed world of family life.

But in the matter of degree, how much is too much? Children like structure in their life. As long as you behave reasonably, children like guidelines within which they can feel free — bounds invariably strengthen and develop the self — although this doesn't mean that they won't complain a bit at first. For example, TV may not interfere with naptime. In the evening, bedtime and (later) homework take priority over TV. A child easily becomes accustomed to any regime you impose — and will also follow the example of *your* TV viewing and involvement in other activities. It might be comforting to know that in a few years' time, with some children the TV viewing goes the way it does with some adults: the child will end by getting bored with whole blocks of programs, viewing shows selectively.

What about the violence on TV — cops and robbers, cowboys, and the like? If children watch these programs, will they grow up to be violent adults? The answer is if they do, it will not be because of TV viewing. All children go through the primitive stages of the human race, enamored of guns and weapons and "Bang-bang! You're dead!" There is no intrinsic harm in any of this. The stage becomes outgrown the same way that children spontaneously outgrow their cruelty to insects and eventually get bored with the murders and poisonings of the Brothers Grimm and Hans Christian Andersen. Boys and girls who play at being cops and robbers, gun molls, and soldiers grow up to be advertising account executives, computer programers, and doctors.

Violence in children has a different source. If you slap or beat a child or speak harshly as a *habitual* way of behaving, that would engender in the child feelings of hatred and rage. *These* can lead to crime. Criminals are not necessarily those who watched too many TV programs or read too many murder mysteries but those who were treated brutally and at the same time were deprived of love. There were violent crimes in the world before the appearance of TV, murder stories, or horror movies.

This is not to deny that there are occasionally TV dramas, and movies too, that treat brutality and violence with a casualness designed to shock. Parents can selectively prohibit those programs that explicitly show gore and violence. But the biggest source of violence on TV is the nightly newscasts— mass murders and grave sites, horrible mutilations, cruelty to children, stabbings, arson, suicide, war, guerrilla bombings in heavily populated urban settings—a deadly list of brutality and barbarism that is the typical fare of news programs that many adults watch avidly. Curiously enough, children don't show much interest in these programs.

Most parents don't need to be advised to encourage children to watch shows that are entertaining or instructive. In many cities there are excellent programs for children, from "Sesame Street" to "Wonderama." Parental selectivity helps to build in the child a growing value system, the capstone of which ultimately is that peaceful pursuits are more enjoyable.

There is a tribe of Indians in a remote part of Mexico famed for its complete lack of violence. Of particular significance is the fact that no member of the tribe *ever* inflicts pain on a baby or child to produce "good" behavior. Hitting and spanking and all hurtful punishments are strictly avoided. Instead the children are offered love and affection, and as they grow to adulthood they live in peace and harmony with each other.

EDUCATION

Learning is an ongoing, perpetual event. It doesn't begin in school. It begins at the breast. It begins with the first breaths of life and the taking in of nourishment. It continues in those early months with the baby's clumsy attempts at self feeding, the knee-bends in your lap, kicking you when you changed diapers, biting, the "No!" yelled back at you, the child's fondling of his or her genitals, the boy's urinating as high as he can reach against the back fence, the girl's urinating standing up just to see what it feels like, and so on. Having been allowed these expressions of aggressiveness and self-initiated enterprise, the child has experienced no discouragement of experimentation and therefore continues to inquire and explore all the time.

Education in the early years is easy. If your child's idealized view of you is based on love, a large part of learning is too. Your child identifies with you, admires you, wants to do as you do. As a parent all you need do is allow learning to happen, with an occasional bit of promotion. Not putting obstacles in the child's path by discouraging curiosity is one way of promoting learning. Another way is to anticipate the child's next level of development by bringing to the child's attention interests that belong to that level. To do this in a systematic, tutorial way would be boring. The best way to do it is spontaneously, as you yourself occasionally feel like it.

For example, if you have been reading stories aloud, you might point out that these stories are printed on the page and the words can be read by anyone. Your child may not have realized that those bits of black ink arranged in lines are words, the same words you are speaking. As a next step the child might become interested in what individual words look like, and from that moment on the ability to read is not far off.

A child learns also by listening to you, through overhearing odd bits of information, or by asking you questions spurred by a wide-ranging curiosity. Why do we die? Is that worse than being dirty or very sick? Why do we eat? Why can't we eat soil? Why are animals different from us? Did they do anything to become animals? Can we speak animal language? Why not? What holds the clouds up in the sky? Why can't people fly? Why is sugar sweet?

It is not an exaggeration to say that a child learns every minute of the day. For example, there might be an occasion when you take five minutes out to relax, and your child, seeing you with an absent expression on your face, asks what you are looking at. You *could* say, "Nothing," just to be let alone. But your child would feel that this is not exactly a truthful reply. The fact is that you were not "looking at nothing." More accurately, you did not want to be bothered by anyone even to the extent of answering a question. Your child hears your answer as nonresponsive and therefore a rejection, even though only a temporary rejection and only out of a need to get away from it all. (A young child would not understand that last part.) You might feel that the five minutes are yours and the questioning is intrusive. But unless a child hasn't been getting enough attention, the question is not deliberately intrusive. It indicates curiosity. A reply that would answer the question, not discourage learning, be truthful, yet cost no great effort might be this: "I'm not looking at anything in particular, I'm just resting a moment." Or: "I'm just thinking." You surmount your irritation by reminding yourself that your child is not doing something *to* you but merely wants to learn.

Learning begins at the breast.

Why make so much of so small an event? Because learning and growth are promoted in precisely these subtle interchanges. If you honestly say to a child, "I'm frazzled right now. Could you just play quietly for a while by yourself?" that teaches. It teaches the child an important truth about living in the world: parents and adults get tired, and sometimes irritated, they too have needs, and they require moments of quiet and rest. It is obviously better to do this at the first sign of your fatigue than to wait until you explode.

In addition, this approach to education offers a reward. Children always give back to you whatever you give them. For example, one little boy's father picked him up on request, seldom pleading fatigue. Occasionally, in a mood of horsing around, the father said in response to a request to be picked up, "*Sure*, I'll be *glad* to!" All this happened when the boy was two and three years old. One day when the boy was five the father asked him to get something from another room. Even though the boy was busily playing he dropped his toy and out of a clear blue sky said, "*Sure*, I'll be *glad* to!" and did.

Eventually the child's enlarging sense of self becomes greatly aided by school, whether nursery school, kindergarten, or grammar school. The last especially will require an acceptance of a more structured life — school is to a child what work is to an adult: it is everyone's first job — and these increased bounds will foster real growth in a real world.

SEX EDUCATION

As Ogden Nash said, "Oh, what a tangled web do parents weave / When they think that their children are naive." Children may be ignorant but when it comes to sex they are *not* naive. They sense the basics on their own, however cloudily. They have an understanding of sex that is built in and that emerges according to the inner timetable. But their understanding leaves many gaps to be filled. A child's questions about sex and reproduction are merely attempts to fill those gaps and are a sign that *comprehension is already near*. If you sweep matters under the rug, brush questions aside, or give evasive answers, a child knows you are lying.

By the age of three, children have already experienced all the psychological manifestations of sexual love: devotion, tenderness, jealousy. All that remains is for the genital apparatus to mature and assert its sexual primacy over all other body parts for physical consummation. When the pleasures of full genitality supersede the less satisfying oral and anal ones, the emotional side of love finally joins with the physical side, and intercourse and reproduction become possible.

A child doesn't compartmentalize subject matter. Early questions about sex, if not discouraged or avoided in embarrassment, stimulate later curiosity about other subjects. Straightforward and truthful responses to questions of sex increase trust in you, especially retrospectively, when your responses are later verified by other sources. To say "You'll find out when you grow up" is both a rebuff and a damper on education. The increased openness about sex today can be understood in part as a healthy reaction to the old damaging hush-hush attitude of parents, when answers to questions on sex had the implied message that sex was something dirty, secretive, and in a special class rather than a natural expression of feeling.

One day you hear the question "Where do babies come from?" *First ask what the question means.* At different ages the question has different meanings. At three it may mean "Do you buy them in a store?" If you were to try explaining human reproduction at a time like that your answer would be confusing or boring. If the question is "How are babies born?" you might reply that they grow in a special part of a mother's body — *not* the stomach. (The analysis of adults shows that children are too prone, unconsciously, to develop erroneous theories, all on their own, of oral insemination, just as they often believe that if they swallow a watermelon seed a watermelon will grow in their stomach.) The question may mean "Where did *I* come from?"

Questions on reproduction are more than likely to pop up in the living room of someone you're visiting or in a supermarket, so it is good to be prepared for your unpreparedness. The temptation will be to postpone answering, out of social embarrassment, but if you are caught in an off moment you might say, "My mind is on something else right now. Give me a moment to think about your question" — or in the store, "Wait till we're outside and I'm all through shopping."

If someone in the store (or on the bus or in the street) should snicker at your child's question, make it a part of your explanation, in private, to say that the question is an intelligent one. Unfortunately, however, there are people in the world with emotional problems and they find the subject of sex and reproduction laughable, even though there's nothing funny about it.

Answer forthrightly and truthfully. The facts of sex sound natural and interesting to a child. Your manner and voice are an important part of your answer. If you smile in embarrassment or hem and haw you will convey the message that sex is dirty and lascivious or taboo. If you react atypically to questions about sex and reproduction — if you sound different from the way you do about other subjects — your child will sense this immediately and tend to avoid the subject with you, feeling that it is a forbidden one because it is embarrassing to you. If after that you never mention the subject again, you confirm the message that the child is not to speak of sex with you, and sex becomes "bad."

After you've answered the question, wait. See if there are requests for more information. "How does the baby get there?" "The father puts a seed there and the seed grows." Very often that's quite enough to satisfy curiosity at this age. The answer is quite plausible to a child. *Let the questions come from the child. Don't get ahead of the child's curiosity or need for knowledge.* A child needs time to assimilate each small amount of explanation before coming back for more. You might even be asked to go over the same ground several times, extending your answer a bit more each time.

Even highly intelligent parents, who pride themselves on their enlightened attitude, make the mistake of treating the subject with great seriousness. They teach their child the "facts of life" (why not "facts about sex"?) in the form of a lecture on one formal occasion heavily prepared for in advance. It would be far more healthy and natural for the facts of sex and reproduction to be an ongoing part of education, beginning with the child's first question, with answers suited to his or her advancing ability to understand. To wait until some "right" age to explain it all is invariably doomed. Parents too often wait until the child is eleven or twelve. But however shaky their knowledge, most children know all there is to know by the age of nine or ten.

The facts of sex sound natural
and interesting to a child.

This education should not be restricted to the privacy of the home either. Human reproduction should be taught in grammar schools starting in the fourth or fifth year, when children are approximately nine years old. By the sixth or seventh year they should be taking a course in sexual behavior and mating. Psychologically speaking, these are not radical proposals but common sense. And until such proposals are implemented we well continue to live in a society of sexual problems and pornography.

The whole aim of sex education is to foster an attitude of liking the human body and developing positive feelings about sex. And as sex entwines itself with love, love becomes doubly pleasurable. This fostering does not occur at any given moment but comes more from the intellectual climate of the family and the environment. Early masturbation, sex games with other children, a period of exhibitionism, erotic feelings toward mother and father — all these typical, universal events take place in an atmosphere that is either benign and accepting or guilt-ridden and condemning, depending on parents. The *facts* of life, so called, are the least important part of sex education.

This is why to attempt to stop sex play can do damage. The prohibition creates guilt and promotes clandestine behavior. If you observe closely you will see that sex play arises spontaneously among children, a part of ordinary play, and if allowed to happen undisturbed subsides just as quickly, in a natural way. After a period of such occurrences, interest in sex exhausts itself until its recurrence in adolescence.

Perhaps the most important part of sex education is for a child to see a loving relationship between husband and wife. The parents' feeling of closeness and love for each other, erotically tinged as those feelings are even in their ordinary daily expression, serve as a model. Nothing could help more to promote positive feelings about sex.

To thwart curiosity in so vital an area as sex is to put a damper on *all* learning.

The satisfaction of curiosity is at the bottom of most learning. Therefore, to thwart curiosity in so vital and pleasurable an area as sex is to discourage a child's eagerness to learn. Even to a child sex is a source of keen pleasure, exactly as it is with adults. This pleasure encourages still more curiosity and exploration on succeedingly higher levels of inquiry.

16 The Development of Conscience

It is... good... to sing praises.

Psalm 92

A conscience does not develop in a child until the age of six or seven: the newborn does not have one. Much of the child's conscience gets built in by you—your attitudes, feelings, behavior, value judgments. Schopenhauer was cynical but accurate: "There is no absurdity so palpable but that it may be firmly planted in the human head if you only begin to inculcate it before the age of five, by constantly repeating it with an air of great solemnity." But of course it is equally accurate that honesty, consideration of others, a good self-evaluation, and a pleasure-promoting system of values can also be inculcated or taught.

The full development of conscience, so critical to normal human functioning, still lies far ahead. But it doesn't spring to life all at once at the age of six or seven. The events of early childrearing contribute to it.

Most of us tend to think of conscience as something negative—prohibiting, criticizing, and punishing. Analysts, however, take a different view and call conscience by the more comprehensive term "superego."

Although prohibitions and obedience are an important part of it, the conscience or superego also regulates self-esteem, with all its fluctuations. Esteem of the self may be negative or it may be approving. But generally a benign and healthy superego is an "inner smile" that bestows good feelings on the self and makes life pleasurable.

Originally a child's self-evaluation comes largely from the outside. Your child's sense of worth depends on feeling loved by you. A child who feels loved and approved of by parents feels worthy of being loved and therefore, in a quite healthy way, loves him- or herself. The superego is an internal guidance system. A child who attains good superego development has less need of external praise and punishment.

The formation of the superego has many preliminary phases. Discipline, an important part of self-evaluation and obedience, begins at the breast. Obedience comes from a contented infancy in which needs were met. The contentment leads to love, and love engenders obedience. If you give your child love, aside from getting much love back, you also get acceptance of your rules: an unproblematic, spontaneous obedience.

A child loves you because he or she feels loved by you. You may not often be aware of it, but the child looks up to you and admires you. You are what the child wants to become. If you act as if you expect obedience your child will unresistingly go along with your friendly expectations. Why not? And there will be no need for threats, justifications, or even lengthy explanations.

Although the roots of the superego trace back to the first weeks of life, a fully developed superego cannot be formed in the earliest years. For the first four or five years a child understands the world only in concrete images, but to understand adult behavior and parental ideals requires an ability for abstract thought. It is usually around the age of six that the child begins to adopt selectively the parents' standards of behavior.

One of the forerunners of the superego is the word "no," which impressed the child so much. Originally directed at you with great pleasure, the "no" begins to be directed inward, at the child's own thoughts and impulses, as a preliminary phase of superego development. That is why you might sometimes overhear a child playing peacefully alone shout, "No *no!*" at him- or herself in response to a passing hostile thought. At that moment the child suddenly becomes both child and mother.

The reason children feel uncomfortable with their hostile thoughts is that they have not yet clearly distinguished be-

THE IMPORTANCE OF GUILT—IN *TINY* DOSES

In its prohibiting and punishing aspect, the superego works through guilt. "Guilt" as a jargon word means "self-punishment." It is the suffering caused by the withholding of love from oneself. Originally love is withheld from the outside, by the parents. But by the age of six or seven, when there is a conscience, the withdrawal of love happens inside the person.

But apart from this internalization of the parental withholding of love, there seems to be an innate sense of guilt. In healthy development this small innate guilt does not cause suffering but contributes to our benign impulses toward others: to be concerned and to give of ourselves.

It is because of this innate guilt that parents, in disciplining, need *withhold only a small amount of love.* A stern word to a little child sometimes feels as though all warmth and affection have gone out of the world. Too much withholding of love would be unbearable.

CONSISTENCY AND FIRMNESS

The development of conscience requires consistency and firmness. In an atmosphere of kindness, firmness is welcome to a child because the guidelines and rules that you lay down convey to the child that you care. They provide limits of behavior within which your approval is ensured.

Consistency is not rigidity. To be inflexible or unyielding imposes a strain not just on children but on parents as well. Guidelines are like the Constitution of the United States. The Constitution does not deal with every possible aspect of behavior. On the contrary, it is often admired for wisely limiting itself to the broadest rules. It offers reasonable limits within which everyone may function freely. And as with all good guidelines, the Constitution's strength is in its responsiveness not to abstract precepts but to life in that it can be interpreted in relation to evolving needs.

What would happen in the absence of guidelines or appropriate praise? What, for example, might happen in toilet education if parents were to use force in a too-early training? One common outcome is that the child might easily develop an overly strict conscience in response to massive anxiety over bodily impulses — and over the angry wishes about the parents that are sure to arise as a result of the suppression of those natural impulses. An overstrict conscience can come about in other ways as well. In an atmosphere of absolute permissiveness, the child could very well develop, in compensation, a rigid system of what is right and wrong, just as the children of some alcoholics become sworn teetotalers. An overstrict and a lax conscience are equally harmful.

One sign of an overstrict conscience among adults is the tendency toward perfectionism: such persons inevitably fall short of their unrealistic self-expectations and reproach themselves for not being as good as others, who appear to them "just naturally" good.

Sometimes the indications are subtle: they may always dress in the same kind of conservative clothing. (The Puritans dressed in black, brown, and white. Red was the color of sin.) Some not so subtle indications: if you praise them, they respond with instant demurrers or self-criticism. They are incapable of accepting merited praise. To them, in fact, it is not merited, because their self-evaluation is perpetually low. They seldom act spontaneously but quite often plan everything so as not to be surprised. They are filled with self-reproaches about minor "faults" that no one else either notices or would think twice about. They strive continuously—and hopelessly—for infinite improvement. And in extreme cases, if you're having fun and act a little silly in front of them at times, they are quite apt to respond with the silent treatment or, in the manner of Queen Victoria, with a look on their face that says, "We are not amused." Theirs is a clenched personality. They are difficult persons to like for long because they are usually cold, tense, and unwelcoming.

OVERPERMISSIVENESS OR DISCIPLINE?

Thirty or forty years ago, in the heyday of "progressive schools," some educators believed that a much relaxed discipline led to sound psychological development. The passage of time revealed the consequences of this view: the results were deplorable. The rudeness of bratty children, raised according to "advanced" views of the day, was excused on the grounds that they were only "expressing themselves," that smashing the host's ashtray was a child's way of demonstrating aesthetic judgment and not "holding things in." Anyone who found their unsocial behavior distasteful was dismissed as backward.

The trouble is that theorists with inadequate grounding in

infant and child psychology often overcompensate for the errors of the generation preceding theirs — even though overcompensation is *never* a reasonable course — and with the best of intentions they attempt to undo earlier errors by making the opposite, and new, errors. Preceding the "progressive" mistake, there was the behaviorist error of treating children not as children but as organisms to be conditioned into adulthood. J. B. Watson, the founder and most famous proponent of this school, said about the love and care of babies: "Treat them as though they were young adults. . . . If you must, kiss them once on the forehead. . . . Never hug and kiss them. Never let them sit on your lap." Fortunately most parents were and are too sensible to listen to such unnatural advice.

WHAT'S WRONG WITH BEING OVERPERMISSIVE?

To be overpermissive is to be indifferent. And indifference is disastrous.

If you say to your child, "You can do anything you want," the child unconsciously hears this as, "I don't really care what happens to you." On the other hand, "Don't do that!" (depending, of course, on the circumstances) can come across as "I *care* what happens to you." You must sometimes have the kindness to *withhold* gratification from your child.

Parental prohibitions that are reasonable and not excessive communicate love. *A child who feels that there are no limits feels unloved.* Overpermissiveness is frightening. All children need limits so much that without them they feel threatened and insecure. In fact, a child who does something wrong and is not reprimanded for it tends to punish him- or herself more, unconsciously. As Thoreau said, "Public opinion is a weak tyrant compared with our own private opinion." Excessive severity and excessive leniency — both lead to the development of a harsh superego.

The absence of parental guidelines can lead to delinquent behavior. The delinquent child provokes, attacks, and misbehaves in order to gain attention and to be told limits and controlled, *which is reassuring.* (Obviously it would be more reassuring if the delinquent were given guidelines before getting into trouble.) A significant portion of prison recidivism stems from the delinquent's need for the structure and limits provided by a penal institution. Guidelines and discipline, even the discipline of prison, are actually experienced unconsciously as expressions of love.

WHAT CAUSES PARENTAL INDULGENCE?

One cause of parents' indulgence is the attempt to make up for their own unfulfilled wishes by allowing a child to do all the things they were not permitted to do when they were children. That of course never works. What parents missed getting would be totally irrelevant to their child's needs. Other parents become indulgent because they are afraid of losing their child's love — or merely because they are afraid to be firm. These fears point to a problem in the parent's childhood.

> "You can do anything you want"
> means "I don't really care
> what happens to you."

A child likes you and respects you more when you are firm. Your firmness conveys the message that you are in charge, which alone reduces anxiety by keeping relationships and responsibilities clear. A child doesn't want to be asked *if* he or she wants to go to bed. The answer would be no: a child hates the idea of going to bed and needs to be told to. Your firmness, which can be expressed quite gently, lets the child know exactly where he or she stands. To be authoritative is not the same as being authoritarian. And in the long run, the child enjoys identifying with a parent who is strong and firm (without being overbearing) more than one who is weak and manipulable.

Basically if you feel at ease with your child you will not have great doubts about fairness or justice. Real love for a child is a counterbalance for occasional mistakes, for a few rare instances of unfairness, and even for a flareup of anger once in a while. As we have emphasized throughout, parents are human. If they have sure feelings of love toward their child, that love tempers any passing guilt that even an unusually good parent would sometimes feel. The trouble begins when love is unsure and guilt strong. Obedience then becomes a problem and indulgence creeps in: a guilty parent's self-doubts are all too easily transformed into indulgence, treating the child almost as an equal. The child then does become an equal, but only ironically, not the way the parent thinks or would like: they are equal in that emotionally they are both children.

This kind of parent does not question his or her own childhood emotional needs or fears. Even though in the older families the father was traditionally the disciplinarian, we sometimes now see fathers who are quite indulgent. They sidestep discipline and leave it to the mother, often with the secret hope of being the preferred parent. Obviously they are not concerned for their child but for themselves.

DISCIPLINE IS GOOD

The words "discipline" and "obedience" have unfortunate connotations. It would be wise to bear in mind that the child does not dread the attitudes these words refer to. We have already said that a child needs guidelines and well-defined limits. A child accepts rational discipline if it is not harshly administered. Rules of guidance must be based on the real world of social interaction and social responsibility that the child will grow into, the world of real people and real feelings. Such rules protect rather than restrict or regiment. To raise a child in the belief that *any* behavior is acceptable would be to make the child vulnerable to the pain of disapproval and rejection by the world later on.

If your child experienced an unbroken flow of love from you, it would be more difficult for him or her to separate psychologically when the appropriate time came. Punishment and discipline, even when the child feels they are justified, always create some ambivalence toward you, and this ambivalence emphasizes healthy feelings of separateness. Where the child's behavior calls for discipline that is not offered, an unnatural atmosphere, as of a hothouse, develops. Aside from fixating the child on the need for continuous love and support and nurturing an inability to tolerate frustrations, such closeness makes it difficult for the child to show the parents anger, which is so beneficial in fostering feelings of independence.

THE FAULTY DEVELOPMENT OF CONSCIENCE

Obedience rendered out of love needs no enforcing watchman. But there is another kind of obedience, an obedience rendered out of anxiety or fear. A child who obeys out of fear obeys only while the parent is there to observe behavior. It is pseudo obedience, expressive of faulty development of conscience. True obedience is an internalized code and eventually needs no outside policing.

Perhaps the most noticeable thing about political life today is the amount of psychopathy – dishonesty, bribery, fraud, and theft at all levels of society, from local crimes on up to the corruption of the heads of government. We would not be challenged if we said that a poorly developed conscience is a regrettably common phenomenon.

What makes for a defect in conscience is inconsistency – the double standard. The double standard is sometimes offered by parents as something acceptable, in fact as sound advice: "Do as I *say,* not as I *do.*" The intent is to be uplifting. But actions speak louder than words, and the child soon learns to adopt parental *behavior* as the norm and, like parents, learns to do things one way and pay lip service to the opposite. It is because of this split in conscience that a surprising number of people do not think it unusual or shocking to hear a politician pontificate on "decency and honor" a week before he is indicted for fraud and income-tax evasion. They think it's "sad" but it's "only life." The inconsistency is so common and familiar, so ingrained in our society, that dishonesty and deceit no longer shock and are often overlooked. Only most adolescents and a few adults protest, those in whom ideals still have value and continue to be worth striving for.

Some parents teach their child to be scrupulously honest in theory, yet instruct the child to lie about his or her age when the conductor asks, because of a cheaper train or bus rate. Or they lie on the phone to friends or employers and the child overhears them. Sometimes "conscience" is based on bribes: "If you are a good boy I will give you candy." But the point about conscience, as with all development, is that it is achieved for its *own* sake, not for payment or tangible reward.

At times the conscience develops irrationally, as when a parent tries to get compliance without explanations – demands, in fact, absolute submission. "Why do I have to brush my teeth?" "Because I *said* so. *Do* it!" If the parent persists in this treatment, the child reaching adulthood tends to seek relationships with other authoritarian personalities and to look for situations in which responsibility can be easily relinquished.

Nor does it help matters if parents say, "If you don't come along with me to the dentist I'll tell the policeman and he'll *make* you come" or "If you don't eat dinner I'll call up Doctor Jacobs and tell her you won't eat." There are two problems inherent in this approach. First, it shifts authority to someone else, away from the parent, and hence does not foster real superego growth in the child. The child does not internalize the parents' authority because they *have* no authority. The child merely develops a "policeman conscience," a pseudoconscience, while continuing to do *anything* he or she pleases as long as it can be gotten away with. Second, this approach makes police and doctors appear to be hostile, threatening figures rather than persons who are helpful and necessary. (And from this feeling to paranoia is barely a step.) A child should never be threatened with a visit to the doctor. A medical visit is not a punishment, and the threat distorts reality.

What makes for a defect
in conscience is inconsistency—
the double standard.

A common source of inconsistency is this: the father says one thing, the mother says another, and the child, torn between the two, feels compelled to satisfy the contradictory requirements of both. Also, when they disagree — on the matter of a punishment, for example — the child might try to manipulate one against the other. A united front avoids this danger.

WHAT IS A GOOD CONSCIENCE?

Spelling out examples of faulty development of conscience may make it clear what a good conscience is. A healthy, well-developed conscience is an internalized system of values — the *parents'* system of values, for the most part, taken over by the child. These values are consistent and rational and need no outside pressure in order to govern behavior. If the child's upbringing is experienced as benign and loving, the child's conscience will have a benign and loving character. A healthy conscience is that reassuring "inner smile," capable of being appropriately self-critical when necessary, never harshly or punitively so. And when it is well internalized it doesn't draw attention to itself: it is so integral a part of the person that it becomes an effortless control that is spontaneously exercised.

An adult once said to a three-year-old girl, "Melina, I love you." Melina said, "Me too!" She had no unhealthy, negative self-feelings, and if her development continued along similar lines, she would not end with an overbearing, punitive superego.

RESPECT

As with any other form of love, you can't demand respect and expect to get it. You can only earn it and allow it to come to you.

If you respect your child's feelings, he or she will respect you and your feelings.

To scold children in front of others hurts their feelings. If your child has done something that irritates you, you should wait to discuss it until you are alone with the child. This has the additional benefit of setting an example of behavior. There will be times when you will spontaneously admonish the child for bad behavior in the presence of others—as when the child hits another child—but that is not the same as a dressing down, and the child understands the difference.

If you should ever be in the wrong with your child and feel guilty about it, don't hide it by acting even worse or by letting it slip by. Admit you are wrong. If you never admit you are wrong, how will your child learn to do so? This not only teaches honesty by example and demonstrates that it is a sign of strength to acknowledge being in error, it also increases the child's respect for you. You are not pretending to be a model of virtue when you are only in fact a human being. You show that you are as objective about your own mistakes as you are about the child's. You don't have a double standard that protects you and leaves your child vulnerable.

If you were to force your child to say "Thank you" for something he or she doesn't feel thankful for, as when grand-parents give a child a practical gift of clothing rather than a longed-for toy, you would teach the child to express feelings insincerely. That would violate the child's sense of true and real feelings. The time for politeness and manners is in late childhood, when other people and their feelings become more real to the child. To teach children to say what they feel to be false is to damage emerging feelings of morality. The parents' intention is to teach respect, but what the child learns is that dissembling and pretending are valued. Respect has value only as a spontaneous expression of true feelings. Imposed morality promotes dishonesty — immorality. Also, as Dr. Winnicott says, it bores.

Don't expect a child to express respect for you in words. That seldom happens in childhood. For you to demand an outward show of respect might hide a narcissistic need for obeisance. It is especially true of children that actions speak louder than words.

Children don't need to be told that they have rights. They feel it. But they do need to be told that others have rights too. The easiest way for them to learn this is through having *their* rights respected. Their built-in empathy will help them in developing respect for the rights of others.

PUNISHMENT

Imagine a child's pain at being severely deprived — being left behind while everyone else goes off to a special event the whole family has been looking forward to (a harsh punishment), or being put to bed without supper (a cruel punishment), or being left behind in the care of others when the parents go off on vacation (an unbearable punishment). Drastic punishments teach nothing — except *never* to get caught again. They breed hatred and the desire for revenge. Extreme punishment does not change undesirable behavior but forces it underground. And the feelings of hatred and revenge become, in a young child, a developmental burden. A child is too fragile an organism to cope with such powerful, turbulent emotions. They upset a delicate inner equilibrium. As for "Mommy and Daddy don't love you any more!" that would break a child's heart. Such words should never be spoken.

In contrast, if you occasionally tell your child how pleased you are by his or her good behavior and do not just take it for granted, the child will feel encouraged to seek your further approval by building on the good behavior. Rewards are always more effective than punishment.

The younger the age, the lighter the punishment should be. And beyond a stern word or two, *there should be no punishment at all before the age of three.* By three a child can begin to understand your wishes more clearly and is able to begin to adopt your standards of behavior. Until psychological separation is accomplished, the child experiences even the mildest punishment as abandonment by you. "Abandonment" is an inner experience. A child who gets angry at *you* and thus gets rid of you in his or her feelings experiences that as *your* abandoning *the child.*

A mild scolding, even an unintentional scowl, is enough to make a little child fear that he or she has lost your love. It's suprisingly easy to be overbearing to a creature you tower over and who needs at all times to feel loved by you. Harsh treatment never accomplishes its purpose. Washing out a child's mouth with soap and water is not just cruel but a good way to make the child hate soap and you.

To teach children to say what
they feel to be false is to
damage emerging feelings of morality.

When you must punish because discipline has broken down, it is best to suit the punishment to the child's developmental level. If your child hits another child in spite of your having explained that hitting is forbidden, you might suspend all further play for a *short while.* (There would be far less hitting if your child never once saw you hit.) A child who smashes or breaks things on purpose might be confined to his or her room — again, *for a short while.* Ten minutes of detention is forever to a child. Perhaps five minutes might be enough. Or just having a talk might be what is needed. It would be cruelty to exact punishments that are out of proportion to the crime for the child's age, such as to deprive the child of a favorite toy for an entire week. The future doesn't exist for a child, and a week of being deprived of a toy is meaningless and therefore not even an effective deterrent. All a child does is suffer and resent you.

THREATS VERSUS PRAISE

Threats don't work. A very young child never stops misbehaving because of what might happen. *The idea of consequences is not yet real.* To think that way is adultomorphic. A very young child does not yet have an adult's understanding of cause and effect. To let the child suffer the consequences of an act is useless — or cruel. Adults who behave this way and authors who recommend this behavior are engaging in a power struggle without being aware of their need for this. There is another side to this issue too. If you tell a child you will punish some misconduct, he or she might nevertheless misbehave deliberately and philosophically accept the punishment as a part of the bargain, feeling it's worth it.

Punishment substitutes fear for the wish to please. A child who fears you hates you, and because the child also loves you, the young personality is split in half by ambivalence. It is extremely distressing for a child to hate the person he or she needs. It makes the child feel an unmanageable amount of guilt and creates many conflicting feelings about you.

Threats are a sign of weakness. To threaten a child is to admit that you lack real authority, that you are afraid you will not be obeyed. A threat indicates that there is an alternative to obedience. It challenges the child to disobey. True, disobedience will lead to punishment, as the slightly older child will understand, but it might be worth *choosing* punishment just to defy your authority.

SPANKING

The Talmud says, "If you must hit a child, use a string." A surprising number of parents still believe that spanking is good for a child's development. Parents who yell and hit were themselves yelled at and hit as children. They are repeating the pattern, although they consciously feel that they are exercising discipline for the good of their child. But spanking breeds unconscious hostility and resentment. Whatever is accomplished by spanking could be accomplished *much* more effectively in other ways and with far less damage.

Adults may not realize how powerful and booming their voice is to a child. One rebuke and a child feels much anxiety. If your child is used to your shouting, however, the only technique that can work would be a still greater show of strength, and some parents in this position resort to spanking. Although they do not recognize it, hitting is thus an admission of their failure at discipline: technique has broken down.

Some parents feel that to act reasonably with a child and not lash out requires either superhuman self-control or sainthood.

Those who feel this way might have a problem with their anger and more than likely were themselves hit as children.

A spanking feels to a very young child exactly the same as a slap would feel to you. You would be hurt not so much physically as emotionally. You would also feel, "How dare anyone hit me, as though I were a thing?" In fact the only difference between your reactions and your child's might be that the child's would be more intense. A child is new to living and takes much harder what he or she thinks is a personal rejection, an expression of "hatred" by you. The child feels painfully unloved, hates you in return — and feels anxious both ways.

As for the respect you may desire, a child will fear you instead. Can fear be equated with respect?

To threaten a child is to
admit you lack real authority.

Further, if you spank your child, you offer a model of behavior. The child learns from you that whenever he or she is angry, the child too has the right to hit someone. Aside from encouraging a callousness toward others and their feelings, a child's hitting out would work against something valuable that he or she has been learning, namely to put feelings into words rather than simply resort to action.

Another unfavorable result of spanking is that with spanking the "crime" is paid for and the child feels free to misbehave again. Conscience does not get internalized. A child may even provoke a spanking to make atonement for "criminal" feelings or for feelings of hatred or a desire for revenge — or just to get needed attention. This unconscious strategy becomes the behavior of delinquents. Hostile attention is better than no attention. Punishment is better than indifference.

A child might sometimes deliberately annoy you to make you react, but that does not mean that you should allow yourself to be provoked. The child may only be cranky out of fatigue or hunger, a possibility that should always be considered first. If the child is tired and pushing your limits, obviously he or she needs to be put to bed, not as a punishment but because rest is needed. (Like food, sleep is something a child needs, and to make it into a punishment would only create sleeping problems.) You let the child cry crossly for a few moments until sleep comes.

If you should ever get carried away and hit, that could become the new established limit, and from then on the child might push matters to that limit. Some parents spank not even out of a pretense of "teaching" a lesson but merely out of anger because they themselves never learned as children to express emotions verbally rather than through actions. And they are incapable of the self-control that, ironically, they might be trying to inculcate in their child.

There is also a danger in spanking: a child could conceivably grow to like it — an especially real possibility if after you have spanked you offer comfort and love. The thought "They spank me, then love me" can easily be misunderstood as "They spank me, *therefore* they love me," which is the origin of one form of masochism.

Therefore, if you *do* spank (because you are unable to control your impulses), don't shower the child with love immediately afterward in a rush of remorse. But do show your love sometime later, after the spanking has receded in the child's feelings. Best of all, however, never spank.

Let us suppose your child has been misbehaving for a while and you have been getting more and more exasperated until, without thinking, you impulsively deliver a clout to the bottom. If this is an isolated event it will merely take the child by surprise, and if you haven't hit hard, there is no harm done. But of course, that wasn't really a spanking either. And if it happens only once, it will be forgotten, leaving behind no harmful effects.

Better than spanking is a verbal reproach for any wrongdoing. If wrong really *has* been done, to explain what is wrong and that you are displeased finds a response in the child, who will accept your criticism as legitimate. When that is the case, the child modifies subsequent behavior to maintain your love, and that makes for true learning, not the fear and conditioning of spanking.

Never beat a child. If you are afraid you might lose self-control, leave the room — hit an object — do anything you want — *but do not give a child a beating.* You might do great and irreparable physical damage, and you most certainly will do incalculable psychological harm, engendering great hatred in the child that will later be turned against others as well as you.

BEDTIME

Once there is language to communicate with, bedtime becomes relatively easy, provided that you take charge. You might begin by announcing that it is approaching – "Bedtime in fifteen minutes" or "Bedtime soon" – to prepare the child for the inevitable. To end the enjoyment of play abruptly would understandably make bedtime a problem. And if the child has been playing with you, it would be selfish to spring bedtime without warning because you have suddenly grown tired of the play. That would give the message that you care little for the child's feelings.

It is wise to taper off the play just before bedtime because that makes it less difficult for the child to accept the inactivity of lying in bed. Fathers especially should avoid rough play before bedtime: pretending to be a monster or a lion might be fun for a while but could generate anxiety dreams.

Don't rush bedtime, but after ten or even twenty minutes have gone by (you don't always literally mean "fifteen" minutes, even assuming your child already knows how long fifteen minutes are), and the time has come for bed, it is best to be firm about it. "Time now for bed" or similar words might be the cue that the child gets used to, followed by an expression of affection and love. Saying goodnight is easier if you first spend a few moments together while tucking the child in. In this way a bedtime pattern is established and, if you handle it cheerfully, never becomes a dreaded event. "You don't have to sleep but you do have to stay in bed."

Bedtime generally does not become a problem if there has been no sudden, upsetting change in routine, such as being placed in the charge of a sitter or a day-care person. Children are creatures of absolute habit and, as we repeatedly discover, need reliability, consistency, and continuity. (Adults do too but less acutely.)

Bedtime is a rule imposed by parents and obeyed by the child – imposed firmly and with love, not hesitantly or inconsistently. If you weaken, even if only inwardly, the child will swiftly take advantage of your indecisiveness or "sympathy" and turn bedtime into a ritual chore and a bother.

It's best to be regular about bedtime too. Your child may not look tired, but you can be sure that the fatigue is there – it just hasn't set in yet. And if you have started your child off with a room of his or her own, one of the ways your efforts are rewarded is that now the child is used to going to bed alone.

What about the repertory of tricks that suddenly appear around bedtime, all those universal attempts to stall for time? It doesn't take you long to discover all the possible "reasonable" requests: a drink of water, a kiss, just one *more* kiss, the location of a favorite toy the child always sleeps with, one more trip to the bathroom, "I want to tell you something—no, come here, I want to *whisper* it in your ear." These ruses can tax your patience, and once you have caught on that you are dealing wih a con artist who so recently was only a helpless infant, you realize that you must learn to outwit the child by seeing to it in advance that the favorite toy is already in the bed, you have asked twice if there is any further need to go to the bathroom, you have offered water and whatever else. All avenues are now closed off. If the child tries the "one more kiss" routine, that might be a nice way to conclude matters. "Okay, one more kiss and then I'll say goodnight and you go to sleep." If there is still another delaying tactic and you feel that the demand is not outrageous just this one time and don't mind going along with it, judge for yourself. Being consistent does not mean being inflexible. But *then* it might be good to end up with: "Goodnight—and this time I'm not coming back in again." And don't go back in again.

Bedtime is a rule imposed by parents and obeyed by the child.

Once you have said goodnight, it would be a mistake to do interesting things within earshot, like laugh and talk with your spouse or guests, or go back into the bedroom before you are sure the child is asleep. Sometimes a child will play quietly and contentedly in bed after you have said goodnight, and if he or she hears the fun you're having or if you make the mistake of going into the bedroom before the child is asleep, you will reactivate the desire to be with you. This is particularly true of alert, intelligent children, who are always looking for more and more stimulation. (Inevitably you will misjudge once in a while. Hearing quiet, you will cautiously, stealthily, peer around the door, only to see a small figure sitting up in bed and a face in the semidark peering back at you intently, then in sudden delight as the child springs up—and your heart sinks.) Different ages require different treatment. Contrast this treatment with what happened earlier, in the baby's first year. Then it was possible to stay in the bedroom, or go in and out of it, while the baby fell asleep. At that age sounds were reassuring. No commotion could keep the baby awake: sleep came anyway.

SHARING MOMMY'S AND DADDY'S BED

What about those mornings when your child wakes up early and – old enough now to climb out of bed – comes to join you in your bed? If it happens once in a *long* while (perhaps twice in an entire childhood) there is no harm provided that it's the briefest of visits and, ironically, that you don't make it very pleasurable. We said earlier that as a giving parent you must sometimes have the courage to *withhold* pleasures: what you "give" sometimes is sounder development, always worth more than passing pleasures.

Sometimes a child wakes up from an anxiety dream and you pick him or her up and offer comfort. You hold the child closely to you and speak quietly for a while, perhaps sitting in a comfortable chair, and soothe away the tears. But then you put the child back in *his or her* bed, saying that there is no reason to worry, that everything will be all right now.

Sharing Mommy's and Daddy's bed is one of those homey domestic scenes that are so much fun for everyone that they don't seem at all harmful, but they can be. The harm comes from the child's unconscious fantasies (Mother "really" loves her little boy, Father "really" loves his little girl – not the mate) as well as from the establishment of patterns of gratification. But if the child knows definitely which is his or her bed and which is yours, it keeps relationships clear, which helps the child's growing sense of identity to become stronger and stronger.

An equally important point is that bedsharing undermines the ongoing work of psychological separation. Sometimes a well-chosen omission of gratification impels a child to move forward. It is frustrations of this kind that we had in mind when we said earlier that mild frustrations applied in easy doses promote growth.

It is quite another matter to play with a child who is just waking up in *his or her* bed. Talking and laughing together as the child clambers delightedly around is obviously good family fun.

17

More than One Child

When a younger brother comes, the elder weeps.

CONFUCIUS

Until now we have been talking about one child alone. But what about a second or third child? Can what we have said about the first apply to subsequent children, or does having more than one child introduce different psychological problems? And what about adoptive children and twins? Do they have special needs and involve special problems?

It is well known that the first child offers parents a unique opportunity in life, a glimpse into *their* infancy with all its long-forgotten delights and frustrations. It's like a second opportunity to see what growing up was all about. Parents tend to identify more with the firstborn precisely because it is their first experience of parenthood, and usually they try to see that he or she has a better time of it than they did. Typically, therefore, the first child gets greater closeness and concern, partly out of love but partly also to compensate for parental inexperience. First-time parents often feel they don't know what to do, and their insecurity makes them anxious to do especially well, to the extent that they sometimes feel guilt even though they have done the best that could have been done.

From the second child on, parents become more casual about childrearing. The experience is no longer novel, and they have had enough practice to know that things generally do work out whether or not they worry. When they discover that their new attitude hasn't the slightest adverse effect on their children's growth, they become even more relaxed. Many second children are more easygoing than first ones (depending on constitutional givens), no doubt reflecting the parents' attitude. Childrearing feels easier to do. For example, the second child learns language more quickly by both emulating and competing with the older brother or sister. Even toilet education proceeds more smoothly for this reason. "You peed in your pants," the older child might taunt the younger, thus spurring the younger to learn toileting as quickly as his or her body can.

The cause of psychological separation is helped by having another child. Having a sibling or two makes it easier for children to separate from parents because their ties are not exclusive. This natural outcome could be subverted, however, if parents, tiring of the childrearing experience, try to accelerate development in the second baby by rushing through toilet education or forcing independence prematurely, as if the second child were not an entirely new being with individual needs.

SPACING CHILDREN

How close together should you have your children, and does it make any difference?

A new baby is an even happier event if the baby is wanted and the parents are ready for him or her. If you are among those who believe in planning your children, you would be giving yourself and your children a decided advantage. Children should be spaced three years apart—better more than less.

From the parents' point of view it is easier to deal with a newborn when the older child has learned to use the toilet, is gaining independence, and communicates fairly well. A child who can speak understands things better and can be managed with less trouble. If the gap in age between the two children is wide enough, the baby is put to sleep earlier than the older one, which means that there are periods during the day when you have only one child to contend with at a time rather than two together. Aside from making things easier for you, this arrangement benefits the older child by providing a block of time with you entirely to him- or herself.

Spacing babies has a beneficial effect on mothers. "The longer the space between babies, the more likely the mothers were to report pleasure at the idea of a new baby. Those with the traditional two-year gap were still not as likely to be delighted as those with a three- or four-year gap."*

From the older child's point of view also, spacing children three years apart makes for sounder and smoother development. Psychological birth having been achieved, the older child feels less need for sole possession of you. The newborn's arrival means far less of a threat of losing you or your affection. Emotional growth continues relatively more smoothly, and everyone is better off for that. And incidentally, having a second child is an excellent opportunity to instruct the first one about human reproduction.

Some parents believe that children who are close in age become playmates for each other, but experience shows that this is largely a vain parental hope. The smaller the difference in age between siblings, the greater the rivalry. Children who are three or four years apart have a better chance of getting along with each other.

Children should be spaced
three years apart—
better more than less.

SIBLING RIVALRY AND THE FIRST OR OLDER CHILD

Rivalry is inevitable. It is difficult for any child to accept a baby brother or sister. As far as the child is concerned, there are the two parents and the child, and that is a family. What more is needed? *Every* first child reasons this way. It would be the mistake of adultomorphism to expect a child to understand the parents' wish to have more children.

Children understand events egocentrically. They tend to believe that almost every event has reference to them. Unless they are carefully told otherwise, therefore, the birth of a rival is taken to be a hostile act directed against them by the parents.

But a child is afraid to be angry at the parents for their "hostility" and takes it out on the baby instead—or hits the pets—or develops an "eating problem." Or the older child tries

*The Boston Children's Medical Center, *Pregnancy, Birth and the Newborn Baby,* New York, Delacorte Press/Seymour Lawrence, 1973, p. 8.

to yank the baby away from the mother's breast, earnestly suggests that the baby be put to sleep in the garbage, and reminds the parents pointedly that "the baby's poopoo stinks! And he can't even *talk*." (What an outrage!) The older child is often tempted to hit the baby for being "no good" because "too little." One three-year-old girl in whom the hostility had considerably subsided, but only after one long year of living with a new sister, said with heartfelt finality about her rival: "*Okay!* she can play with my blanket, my books, and my toys. *But*—she has to leave them here when she goes *home*." That took care of *her*. Once, hearing a game played on "Sesame Street" called "One of These Things Doesn't Belong Here," she innocently singsonged, "One of these people doesn't belong here," and in case the reference was obscure, she hinted that the person she had in mind might be a certain little sister, quite possibly the one she was pointing at.

THE SECOND CHILD

In one respect, the second child has it easier than the first: the environment he or she is born into already includes a child, and so the new baby does not face the necessity of slowly getting used to an unwelcome newcomer (unless, of course, you have a third child).

Precisely on this same account, however, the second child very often suffers. Born into a family of a mother, father, and child, he or she is naturally accepting of *all* the members. There they are: a given situation. The older child, however, regards the younger as an intruder—worse, as the cause of the older one's suddenly no longer being the sole recipient of love. The older, therefore, treats the younger with the cordiality accorded an enemy, and the younger, looking to the brother or sister with innocent love and even admiration, is saddened and hurt by being incomprehensibly subjected to repeated rejections. In the view of the younger child, there is never any catching up, never any moving to a position of equality. When the older child learns to read, it is an occasion for pleasure in the parents. When the second one starts to read, this does not register as a particularly large step forward because it has been done before. Besides, the parents are now *very* excited about the older one's going to school. Therefore, as the younger child moves into the period of development vacated by the older one, he or she might begin to feel like a perennial runner-up rather than an individual. No matter how much harder Number Two tries, events seem to conspire to make the child feel inadequate and underappreciated. If the second child is two years younger than the older one, he or she has an earlier bedtime in some families, which feels highly unjust to the child. It is not surprising that some second children get the feeling of not being loved as much as the first.

And as we noted, some mothers rush the second child through a drastic toilet training either because they feel they now have the experience to do it more expeditiously (as if the maturing of the anal sphincters of the second child happened more swiftly) or because they've lived with diapers for four or five years and are fed up.

Critical moments come when the baby moves forward in development, as in learning to stand and walk. The older child might push the baby down or become caustically critical of the baby's accomplishment at such times. There begin to be times when extra supervision is necessary.

It is incomprehensible to the older child that an adult should blindly persist in retaining the younger child despite all reason — and with *affection* at that. Parents should secretly welcome the older child's open hatred because they know that eventually it will turn into love. After hate gets expressed, love has a chance. Gradually the older one reaches a begrudging acceptance of what simply must be lived with, although disparagement of the younger one goes on for years. The younger one, by sheer hanging in there, slowly becomes a part of the environment, and as the months pass, the lion finally lies down with the lamb. The two work out a *modus vivendi* and learn to coexist. Of course it makes matters easier that there simply is no alternative. And as laughable as the notion might have seemed earlier, after the two have learned to live together, if the younger should leave or be absent for any time, the older will be surprised at the unexpected feeling of loss he or she experiences.

It is nearly universal that there are times when the older one will regress and talk like a baby, crawl, ask to be fed from the bottle, or have a bowel movement in his or her underpants even though control has been achieved. As most parents understand, these are unconscious bids for attention and love. The older child might be feeling that it is infantile *behavior* that makes the baby the recipient of so much of parental time and therefore that the way to win attention "back to where it belongs" is to emulate the baby. This behavior is transient and not cause for concern if you help the older child to adapt to the new family circumstances.

THE MIDDLE CHILD

The children who face the most difficulty in adapting seem to be the second of three, especially if all three are of the same sex. They suffer by being neither the first nor the last. The first child has the advantage of being more able and more experienced, thus continually having a clear competitive edge. The third and last child of three has the advantage of being born into a stabilized family structure of older brothers or sisters, with no one to come along and "replace" him or her.

The middle child never feels quite so well loved as the other two, though parents might in fact love the middle one just as much, sometimes bending over backward to show even *more* concern. Although these are generalizations, middle children have been known to steal, lie, or fabricate tales a bit more than other children, to become moody and resentful more frequently, to demonstrate insecurity or introversion, and to hold grudges. All of these behaviors could stem from their feeling of not getting enough love and attention.

The second child might feel
like a perennial runner-up
rather than an individual.

Since parents sometimes fail to respond to this emotional need, at a loss to know what to do, the middle child's behavior sometimes shows a permanently regressive character. For example, he or she may develop a need to eat even when not hungry, and we have already understood that food and love are unconscious equivalents. A middle child might as an adult unconsciously arrange to lead an unfulfilling life, settling for little in an attempt to preserve the unhappy status quo. This reflects the unconscious need to hold a grudge and be moody or resentful and thus "prove" that those feelings are justified. People tend to be comfortable in the roles they have grown up with, even when they consciously feel unhappy or unproductive.

The way to avoid this outcome is to see to it that the middle child feels loved from the outset and on through all the months and years of growth, *especially* when the third child is born. At that time care and attention should be lavished on the second child, to reduce the feelings of rivalry. Since the firstborn is always in a superior position, the oldest child can tolerate this campaign, provided that he or she too feels loved and secure. We are on familiar ground again: each child should feel deeply loved and cared for, and each child's current emotional needs should be met. Though they may be brothers and sisters, each is an individual.

People tend to be comfortable in the roles they have grown up with, even when they consciously feel unhappy or unproductive.

REDUCING SIBLING RIVALRY

Sibling rivalry can never be altogether eliminated, but it can be substantially reduced. The first helpful step is to anticipate the arrival of the baby so that the older child can grow accustomed in advance to the new member of the family. As a part of this preparation parents reassure the older child that they will continue to love him or her every bit as much as before, that the new baby will in no way replace the older child in their feelings. It helps to appeal to the growing sense of self by pointing out how advanced in development the older child is compared with a baby. This makes sense to the older child and is gratifying to the vanity, and it tends to encourage even further development.

The time to tell a child about the expected baby is before the mother's pregnancy shows. To do so conveys the feeling that the child is a full-fledged member of the family from whom matters of importance are not arbitrarily withheld. If parents wait until the pregnancy is quite obvious before discussing it, the child will have guessed long before that something unusual is going on and will feel that the parents are being secretive. This suspicion does not help to foster trust. It will also not help after the baby is born: the baby will be blamed all the more for the changes in the family structure. The baby will always be blamed, in any case, not the parents, because it is safer to hate the baby. The child needs love too much to risk losing it by allowing anger at the parents to show.

To tell a child that Mother is pregnant allows the child to "permit" Mother to have the baby and thus to "welcome" the new arrival. While expecting, it is best to call the sibling a brother or sister rather than "a nice playmate for you" or any equivalent phrase. The child would love to have a playmate and from then on looks forward longingly to the second child, whom he or she imagines as an agemate, all ready to share fun and games. This can only lead to disappointment when the "playmate" finally arrives and turns out to be a tiny, helpless, crying bundle. ("Why did you get *that* thing?") The months and years go by, and the older child waits with thinning patience for the younger one to catch up in age and become the promised playmate.

After the baby is born, it is important to give much attention to the older child, perhaps when the newborn is asleep, which is most of the time. When parents show interest in the older one's activities the child feels certain that the parents' love is as strong as before and that therefore the baby is not so much of a threat. That would tend to reduce the hatred and resentment toward the baby. The feelings of reassurance become reinforced if parents are careful not to take anything away from the older child or, in the ensuing months, to compel the older to share with the younger what he or she feels are personal possessions. When friends visit, parents might mention to them some recent accomplishment of the older child. All adults understand the need for the maneuver and respond with a favorable comment.

It also helps not to play up the baby. On the contrary, for as long as the baby does not understand language, to play up the older child helps the child's feelings to mellow toward the baby. As the older child begins to show any liking at all for the baby without a campaign of persuasion, the affection will be more genuine and lasting because more truly felt. Letting the older child feel included in the parents' life encourages identification with them and their love for the baby. Love always engenders love.

There is an easy principle involved in reducing sibling rivalry. In the beginning, the helpless infant, not knowing that there are others in the world, cares only that his or her needs be met. And this, of course, is all the older child cares about too: each has needs, and each wants those needs to be met.

"Good enough" parenting in this situation means not making some well-intentioned but meaningless attempt to give each child "equal time" or identical or equal gifts in order to reduce rivalry but meeting the different specific needs of each. It helps if parents think of the two as individuals, not as "the children," even though the latter is certainly the convenient way to refer to them with adult friends. From all we have seen, we know that the psychological development of a two- or three-year-old is far ahead of a newborn's, and their different needs cannot be lumped together.

The difference in developmental level points up another advantage in spacing children. Children who have different needs tend to compete less. In fact, the best way to reduce rivalry is to have the second child only after the first has received all the attention, closeness, and love needed in the first three years to effect good psychological separation.

It does not help the cause of reducing rivalry to make statements in front of the children that foment competitiveness. "The little one is usually easygoing but the big one now and again gives us a little trouble." This is a highly injurious statement. The "little one" might resent it as a slight: it is bad enough *being* the little one without being reminded of it, and also there is a cumulative erosion of self-image. And the older child could only hate the younger as being the person against whom he or she is unfavorably compared. Besides, all children naturally feel that they exist in their own right, and each wants to be appreciated for the sheer fact of existing. That is the birthright of each. A child does not need to be a certain way to be loved. Parental love is by nature unconditional.

As the children grow older your preference for one over the other (which you will inevitably feel at times) should remain unexpressed and guarded against in your dealings with each. Favoritism, even if revealed only inadvertently, engenders rivalry. And later too, when brothers and sisters fight, you might cool things off if you refrain from exploring who started what (unless there has been obvious unfairness) and see to it only that they stop. Without playing the role of a court of appeals, you distract them and love them both: hugs all around and changing the subject are easy ways to end a dispute, no matter how it started. In the case of true injustice, however, the issue should be discussed and resolved fairly. Children readily understand fair play — if there are no problems in your relations with them.

Another way to reduce the rivalrous feelings of the older child while the younger is still a baby is to enlist his or her relative maturity in your care of the infant. You have about a year and a half before the baby understands speech, before you have to be careful what you say, and that gives you a fair amount of time to speak freely to the older child and consolidate your already good relationship. "You're so *big* now, you're a great help to me. Would you get me the baby powder over on the table?" The older child feels almost adult by helping you and being on your side and therefore doesn't feel so keenly competitive.

It would be wise not to trust the older child to help you by watching the baby while *you* go to get the baby powder. For some time to come the older child's unconscious rivalry still will be intense and potentially dangerous to the baby. Keeping an eye on the older child to see that no harm comes to the younger is to protect both. The protection of the younger is obvious, but the older is protected from the inevitable guilt that would follow from inflicting harm.

A child does not need to be a certain way to be loved. Parental love is by nature unconditional.

If you suspect that your older child has hostile feelings that are causing guilt, you might explain that older children sometimes hate a little baby brother or sister because they are afraid they will not be loved as much as they were before the baby came along. You stress that this is *not* true, that you love both children very much. You explain that it is perfectly understandable to have two different feelings about a baby brother or sister: "Most of the time you love the baby very much, but there are moments when you must wish we never had him." Your verbalizing of these feelings lets the older child know that they are acceptable and normal to have. This reduces guilt about the baby, and that in turn reduces hostility and rivalry. Of course the foregoing presupposes that the children are far enough apart in age for verbalization to be possible with the older one.

As we discover with so many of the psychological events of

life, rivalry too has its positive uses. The sibling who arouses rivalry (and envy, anger, and resentment) in a child is clearly a different person from the older child. Awareness of this difference contributes to the ever continuing work of differentiating the self from others and bolsters identity.

Sharing the formerly undivided parental care and concern awakens new emotions in the older child, and it spurs thinking in the attempt to understand these different relations. Having other children in the family also develops, however painfully and slowly, a sense of sharing and a feeling of community. Most children with brothers or sisters find it somewhat easier later on to move out from family life to living in the world.

When the needs of each child are not met, the rivalry tends to intensify. One mother had a happy boy who was developing well until a baby sister was born when he was two years old, and she diverted most of her attention to her daughter. Having a rival in the house would have been bad enough from his point of view. But his mother decided that taking care of a baby and a child would be too much for her and that therefore it was time for the boy to "learn independence because it would be good for his character." He was "too dependent" on her. At the time of the birth of her daughter, therefore, she turned her back on her son.

His world went to pieces. Not only was there a rival on the scene but he "lost" his mother. He hated her for abandoning him abruptly and prematurely, and he hated his baby sister all the more for being the apparent cause of this unhappy change. He became furious for long periods until he was rebuked for his rage, after which he became sullen and depressed. The change did not strengthen him or make him self-reliant, nor did he move toward greater independence. On the contrary, he began now to cling to his mother *in his feelings,* something she had no control over. She might be able to force him to suppress any expression of his feelings, but there was no way she could alter the feelings themselves. She concluded that he was already spoiled and that she had acted too late. She intensified her frustration of the child in an attempt "to get him over it." As the years went by he directed his hatred against his sister too, who was truly an innocent bystander and who couldn't understand why her older brother should hate her so much. In the end, deeply hurt, she lost any shred of love for him, and they grew up with extremely hostile feelings toward each other and frequent bitter fights. Both brother and sister, as adults, endured bouts of depression.

Neither child could understand, of course, that there had been a failure of parenting for which they were paying in a brother-sister hatred. Their mother's attempt to force the boy to maturity and independence, being based on her own (unacknowledged) needs and not his ability, very badly arrested his emotional growth and permanently damaged his feelings of love — and his sister's feelings of love too.

THE ADOPTIVE CHILD

What about adoptive children? Should parents tell their child that he or she is adopted?

Yes, and at the earliest possible time. It is easier for the child to grow up with the knowledge and become accustomed to it. And if *you* do the telling, rather than have the child hear rumors about the adoption from other children, you can explain matters in their best possible light. A three-year-old would suffer little if any impact on being told the truth. But the older the child, the more he or she tends to brood about who the *real* parents might be, especially when the child is unhappy or frustrated or disappointed by the parents. By adolescence, all children have the fantasy that the parents they've grown up with are not their real ones, that the children were switched in the nursery or given out for adoption at birth. Freud called this universal fantasy "the family romance."

Interestingly enough, the imagined "real" parents are invariably of noble birth, wealthy, or in some other respect quite out of the ordinary. The more unhappy the children are with their true parents, the more they are prone to such fantasies. *The Prince and the Pauper* gives literary expression to this universal fantasy, and there are dozens of myths from all parts of the world on the same theme. When adoptive children are told as late as early adolescence about their being adopted, this fantasy suddenly becomes reality for them. It is extremely common for such children to undertake an immediate search for their real parents.

But that is something most adopted children do in any case. This attempt to learn who their real parents were or are, even if they find out nothing, is a move toward independence. (They almost never are told by the hospital or others for the protection of everyone involved. The laws in almost all states require that the original birth records be sealed.*) Some adoptive parents feel hurt by this effort, as if the child were disloyal or ungrateful to them. But most understand the strong curiosity of their adoptive children and answer questions as forthrightly as they can to avoid causing psychological injury. "Who was my mother?" "We don't know" (almost always the case). "What happened to her?" "She died while giving birth."

In those rare cases where the adoptive parents happen to know that the mother was a prostitute or that the baby was left on a doorstep it would be better never to reveal this. A prostitute would become someone to identify with, and being left on a doorstep would mean to the child that mother didn't love the baby or care what happened to him or her. If that is the case, or is even felt by the child to be possible, it can be psychologically devastating. Far better to say, "She was all alone and so poor that she couldn't take care of you as she wanted to, so she asked the adoption agency to let *us* adopt you and try to be good parents to you."

All children have the fantasy
that the parents they've grown
up with are not their real ones.

As the subject comes up from time to time in the course of childhood, the best way to deal with it is to tell the adoptive child that you *chose* him or her at the hospital. You loved the way the baby looked at you in a cute and friendly way, and all three of you seemed to get along with each other right from the start. You were not *given* the baby: your adoptive child would like to feel wanted, as someone special you picked out.

It sometimes happens that a couple adopts a baby because the wife has been unable to conceive, but a year or two later she becomes pregnant and gives birth. Does this create any special problems between the siblings? If the emotional needs of each child are met, there is little likelihood that any problem will arise. The biological child might develop special

---

*A group called the Adoptive Liberty Movement Association is currently attempting to get legislation enacted that will give adoptive children the right to know who their parents are.

feelings toward the adoptive child (principally that the adoptive child is different), but these feelings will be revealed in the child's questions and can be dealt with.

WHEN SHOULD YOU ADOPT?

If you adopt a child, it is easiest for everyone to adopt a newborn, if possible. That way the baby has been subjected to a hospital's scheduled feeding for no more than a few days at most and has not yet begun to get accustomed to one mothering person only to be taken away by someone else. Thus the child is not confused about who his or her psychological parents are.*

However, if you feel you can handle it, it may be a challenge to adopt an older baby or a child who would otherwise be reared in an orphanage. There might be some developmental problems to deal with later on, but if you have the patience and much love to offer, you may be able to surmount these obstacles without too much stress. And it would give one more child in the world better development than most foundling homes or orphanages are equipped to provide.

WHEN NOT TO ADOPT

It is generally not a good idea to adopt a baby to "replace" one who died or was stillborn. Some negative feelings seem almost bound to creep into the relationship. The adopted child reminds parents of the death of their baby, and the child runs the risk of eventually becoming relegated to stepchild status.

However, if parents are aware of the possibility of these problems they may be able to guard against them, taking extra care to provide a warm and loving environment at all times.

TWINS

Caring for twins is difficult for just one person and the birth of twins is an especially good occasion for both Mother and Father to be involved in parenting. The inherent problem in being a twin is that the needs of each child can't always be met immediately and with optimal gratification. Sometimes the twins clamor for food at the same time, and although they can

*For an excellent book on adoption and the matter of psychological parents as opposed to biological parents, see Joseph Goldstein, Anna Freud, and Albert J. Solnit, *Beyond the Best Interests of the Child,* New York, The Free Press, 1973.

be fed, even breastfed, together, all too often one begins to fret or needs burping while the other is still contentedly feeding. Or as you change one's diaper the other crawls swiftly away and needs to be chased before disappearing from view, so that the first one's needs are momentarily unattended to. (It might be helpful to have them sleep in widely separated beds so that if one cries, the other won't always wake up and join in.)

The one unalterable fact about twins is that neither child is *ever* alone. This compounds some problems. For example, a parent can give only a part of herself or himself to each twin: from the outset, parents must be shared. Twins often grow up with the feeling that they never got quite enough of Mother or Father. They were never alone with them, never were their sole or primary concern for a while. As Winnicott says, a baby likes to dominate a scene, and it is maddening to "have a rival in early infancy, at the stage of natural dictatorship." This *could* make for difficulties in psychologically separating from Mother if either or both feel that there was not enough satisfaction of emotional needs to give the impetus to move forward to greater independence.

When twins look at each other they see a mirror image. This makes development of a sense of being separate more problematic. This is truer of identical twins than fraternal twins, who may in fact look quite dissimilar.

The compensation for the fact peculiar to twinship of never being alone is that each twin is a ready playmate for the other. Twins have a quite special feeling for each other. They like the other but they also like themselves in the other. This is true, however, only where rivalry is kept low, a situation requiring even greater care if one twin is a boy and the other a girl and the feelings of penis envy might be strong. Even ordinarily a sister and brother feel much rivalry with each other. When they are twins, the rivalry can become intense. Where this is the case, twinship is experienced as a protracted state of war.

Twins are caught in a perpetual struggle. They simultaneously feel great sibling rivalry and great mutual dependence. Rivalry in twins, in fact, hides an intense struggle for individuality and independence. On the one hand, differences of opinion are passionately fought over: the twins' continuing need for dependence requires absolute agreement on opinions. On the other hand, *anything* that could be fought over or argued about is seized on in an unconscious attempt to assert individuality and clear-cut autonomy. It is as if twins are constantly attempting to be free of each other while at the same time maintaining the familiar security of closeness and sameness.

Some twins learn speech somewhat later than other children, probably because they are never altogether alone while growing up and therefore do not have the same need that others have for verbal communication as a way of achieving closeness.

But the matter of identity is complex. To ensure the healthy growth of the identity of each of the twins, their differences must always be stressed (but not by comparing them competitively). The simplest and most important way is never to refer to them as "the twins" but always to address them by their individual names. (And don't name them "Rick" and "Dick.") Anything that emphasizes their differences emphasizes their separateness and their unique identity: different clothing (unless they prefer to look alike on occasion), different possessions, different toys according to the wishes of each (unless they both want the same toy), and, as they grow older, different decor in their separate rooms. (If you can't afford another bedroom, the room might be partitioned.) In other words, twins should be treated as individuals, not as a pair.* Parents should examine their feelings in this respect to make sure they do not regard each twin as only *half* a person. (Even twins, especially identical ones, tend unconsciously to think of themselves in this way.)

Rivalry in twins hides
an intense struggle for
individuality and independence.

Members of the family easily see physical differences even between identical twins, and it is all to the good if they distinguish between them constantly. This is gratifying and quite pleasurable to each twin: each feels, "My mother and father know me. I'm *me*."

*Twins usually differ in their birth weights. They differ even earlier, in fact, in their access to nutriment while still in the uterus (which may in part account for their different birth weights), and in this sense their environments differ even though they share the womb. Identical twins therefore can have distinctly different experiences even before birth. See The Boston Children's Medical Center, *Pregnancy, Birth and the Newborn Baby,* New York, Delacorte Press/Seymour Lawrence, 1972, p. 244.

18

What Lies Ahead?

The man who says, "My children are a burden to me"—there are no flowers for him.

BASHO

THE CHILD'S INCREASING AWARENESS OF FATHER

In the ordinary course of events, a baby slowly distinguishes between self and Mother, then recognizes that other delightful person, Father, and then others in the environment — family, friends, and strangers. All of these persons assume importance in the order of their discovery and to the extent of their constancy. As childrearing is done now in our society, the father is usually secondary and begins to come into focus in the second half of the first year. A father's importance increases in later development, sharing, for example, the work of identification and the striving toward ideals. From the second year on, the child gradually becomes aware of Father as another kind of person, interesting because he is so different from Mother, smells different, feels different. He seems in a certain way somewhat more active even when he is being gentle and tender. He swings the baby around until they are both dizzy or throws the baby high up into the air, a thrilling stunt and one that the baby's mother seldom if ever does. Father also has the immensely delightful habit of carrying the baby on the shoulders much more often and with much more gusto than anyone else. Father has his special qualities.

THE EVER WIDENING WORLD OF THE CHILD

As father and child move ahead over the months and years, one of the important functions of the father becomes to help widen the child's world, not in any conscious or planned way but merely by having fun together, making faces at each other, and playing games while mother takes a break. These happy times, like comparable times with the mother, build happy feelings about life.

As the father does things around the house, some of them with the child, the child learns what a father is and how he moves and acts. He's different from the mother and her way of behaving and talking and moving. When the father goes out to work, the child wonders what is there outside the home that occupies him, and this awakened curiosity begins to open further and further the sense of a larger world by broadening the child's perspective. (This happens too if Mother goes out to work.) Why does Father disappear through the door in the morning and just as suddenly, after a long absence, reappear at night, like some figure of mystery? What *does* Father do? What is "work"? Why can't it be done at home? He goes to "the office" or "the plant" or "the store." But what are they?

MOTHER AND FATHER ARE DIFFERENT

The child begins to compare father and mother. There are exceptions, but usually mother is higher-voiced. She is stimulating but can be quite stern at times. Father is deeper-voiced, and more vigorous in his play. There are two kinds of beings in the world, different in appearance, movement, and manner. Therefore, the child feels there is more than one way to grow up to be, and that means the child too can be *different.*

Of course the picture is not always so simple. Many fathers are passive and many mothers are active. Some mothers are physically or emotionally stronger than their husbands.* These variations can sometimes complicate a child's development. They can create problems of identification, for example, in that children of both sexes tend to identify with strength, with the more powerful or dominant parent. To cite, in greatly

---

*Usually, however, Father is the powerful, dominant figure to a baby and young child. Even a weak father, as seen realistically in maturity, was once perceived as strong, muscular, and commanding in the early years. Moreover, a weak father sometimes *seems* strong to a young child if he behaves in a manner that is domineering and even violent in compensation.

oversimplified form, two possible outcomes where there is a problem, if later on a girl should identify with a powerful mother and require a passive husband, this could make for marital difficulties. A boy unconsciously identifying with a powerful mother might turn to homosexuality if his masculine identifications are weak.

But even with the contemporary concern over equality between the sexes, there are biological differences that take psychological expression. Equality is not sameness. Take the father's voice as an example. For physiological reasons, it is usually deeper than the mother's and has a different resonance. If it has a deep quality, it inevitably has an effect on the child that the mother's voice does not have. It sounds strong, and the person to whom it belongs is therefore strong. And whoever is strongest in the child's environment is the one to look to for protection and is the one to fear the most. So although at an earlier age it is the mother who is the protector, at a later age there seems to be a biological basis, not just a cultural bias, causing a child to think of the father as the protecting parent — in the same way that there is a clear basis for thinking of the mother more as the nurturing parent, even when the father shares in holding, feeding, and diapering the baby.

But it is important that the differences between men and women not be *over*stressed, distorted by value judgments. As Dr. Lee Salk says, "a good father is a little bit like a mother." A child identifies with both parents. A boy patterns himself after his father, but if he were to identify only with his father (a purely hypothetical possibility) he would grow up to be a male with not much regard for women, devoid of empathy for them, sorely lacking in feelings of tenderness for them, as well as toward himself and all of life — in short, severely disturbed. It is the boy's identification with his mother, as well as his love for her, that makes it possible for him to empathize with women and feel tenderness and love for them (and therefore for himself too) and thus get along with them quite well. Women are not some different species, nor are they to be devalued — an extremely common feeling, regrettably, and not restricted to some male homosexuals.

All this applies to the girl too. She is an amalgam of mother and father, combining their traits and selectively identifying with their characters and styles. This helps to make her relations with men more pleasurable and satisfying. She needs to see how father moves and talks and reacts. She doesn't pattern herself predominantly on him but enjoys interacting with him and feeling approved of by this loving male, who tells her how well she does things and how intelligent she is. She forms a relationship with him that soon will take on a definitely romantic tinge and become a full-blown (but unconsummated) love affair. For this reason it is especially important how a father behaves with his daughter. Everything a father does or says will later contribute to her feelings about men. The love, if spurned, can grow into coldness and anger, and that could, of course, lead her into unhappy relations with men. The equivalent can be said about boys and their mothers.

It is the boy's identification with his mother that makes it possible for him to empathize with women and feel tenderness and love for them.

And the other way around: men's feelings toward men and women's feelings toward women are affected by their earlier relations with the parent of the same sex. But it is not necessarily restricted to that. Sometimes a woman will treat her husband the way her *mother* treated her, demanding that her husband supply the infantile emotional satisfactions that her mother deprived her of. Sometimes a husband will mistreat his wife because of a hatred he feels toward his *father,* who was so authoritarian that even a casual statement by the man's wife sounds authoritarian to him and triggers a rage reaction.

Patterning after the parent of the same sex is important, but it cannot happen unless the child feels that the parent loves him or her. A girl who feels unloved by her mother will pattern herself after her father. If the identification is extreme, it could lead to problems of gender identity. If a father is always demanding and dissatisfied, the boy, feeling his disapproval and absence of love, would tend to pull away and pattern himself after his mother. Sometimes there is a terrible irony in this, as when a father disapproves of his son for being a "sissy," only to drive him toward greater identification with his mother as the reassuring, uncritical parent.

THE OEDIPUS COMPLEX

After the age of four, when psychological separation has been fully achieved and consolidated, the child has become an individual and has begun to understand that there are other individuals in the world. The child can now relate to these others in a new way. No longer are people merely means to gratify needs. They exist independently of the child's needs — have a life of their own. In fact, the child will move from this time to a position where he or she can sometimes supply *their* needs, or at least for the time being acknowledge that they have needs. You can say to a three- or four-year-old child who has asked to be read to, "Could we read together in a little while? I'm tired right now and need a rest" and have the child accept that with comprehension. The child is beginning to understand what it is to give to others and allow for their requests.

A child's relations with others receive their greatest impetus from his or her feelings for you. The child's deep affection for you, appreciation of you, and pleasure in being with you all intensify into a deep love: the oedipus complex. The oedipus complex is not a psychological illness, as some seem to think, but a phase of normal development that all human beings experience.

"Oedipus complex" is the name Freud used to describe the feelings of a child who, beginning in the fourth year, falls in love with the parent of the opposite sex and as a result feels rivalrous toward the parent of the same sex.* A boy forms a deep attachment to his mother and yearns to have her all to himself. Until this point he has had a loving relationship with his father as well, but now there are moments when he feels that he and Father are in competition for Mother. He feels an antagonism for his father in this new development and is afraid that his father feels the same way toward him.

The boy's subsequent feelings of love for girls and women will be to a great extent determined by the oedipal experience and its outcome. If the mother is warm and requites the love, the growing boy will feel that women are delightful creatures and pleasurable to form ties with. (This could, incidentally, reduce somewhat the boy's devaluation of girls during the

---

*In Sophocles' play *Oedipus Rex,* Oedipus, king of Thebes, comes to realize through an accumulation of evidence that he unwittingly murdered his father and took his own mother as wife. The word "complex" means a group of repressed feelings and thoughts.

latency years, between six and twelve.) Similarly, fathers and daughters enjoy a special closeness at this time, which gives girls the feeling that relations with men are pleasurable and exciting.

This turn of events — the love of the son for the mother and of the daughter for the father — although erotically tinged, is more subtle than those early flirtations that were so obvious in their expression, like the boy's pressing his erect penis against his mother's leg at the age of three or four or the girl's wanting so often to sit in Daddy's lap and snuggle her body against his chest. Because parents have become more real as persons, children now feel concern about their parents' feelings — especially the parents' feelings toward the children. It is a touching love affair, the first and most direct, and so tender that the feelings may easily be damaged by parental callousness or indifference.

The erotic feelings of both boys and girls originally fasten onto mother. Therefore girls have an extra step to take in emotional development. Boys simply continue in their love for mother for a longer period, since their choice is a heterosexual one. Girls, however, need to make a shift: some of their love transfers to father, and thus they attain heterosexuality. What motivates girls to shift from mother to father is the realization that they are built differently from boys. Lacking a penis, they can't win mother. (Some women turn lesbian in an unconscious attempt to deny this truth.)

But boys have an extra step to take too. Boys and girls first identify chiefly with mother. Girls can simply continue to do so, but boys must shift toward identifying more with father if their sexual development is to reach its most advanced expression. This is why attaining "masculinity" seems to be more difficult for boys than attaining "femininity" is for girls.

A girl identifies with her father up to a point and then yields to the reality that she and he are not of the same sex. However, her erotic feelings fasten with great durability onto her father. Every girl dreams of being in her mother's place: being the adult woman of the house, having her father as a mate, and being the mother of his children. She would like to have a baby by him: to please him, to identify with her mother, and to have a "penis." (To the unconscious, a baby and a penis are equivalent. Both grow out of the genital area of the body.)

These fantasies are normal. A girl's wishing to take Mother's place does not preclude her loving her mother. But there is also now a rivalry between them. The mother, being adult, sympathizes with her daughter's predicament, which is nothing less than a passionate affair with her father that cannot be consummated. The affair is foredoomed because it admits of no practical solution: her father belongs to her mother. The mother can afford to be generous in her feelings and thus reduce the rivalry between herself and her daughter, all the more so as she, through empathy, is touched by this perennial human drama.

The child soon renounces oedipal strivings. The girl becomes a woman by identifying principally with her mother and the boy a man by identifying principally with his father. Once they have grown up they will start dating and eventually find mates of their own — and watch the same drama unfold in their children.

Every girl dreams of being in her mother's place: being the adult woman of the house, having her father as a mate, and being the mother of his children.

The father is in too secure a position to be seriously threatened by his son's libidinal wishes, and he usually reduces the rivalry, as a victor would, by playing down his strength. But not playing it down too much: the mother *is* his wife, and it's helpful to the boy to know what his parents' relationship is and that it is permanent. Thus the child's identity is more easily kept intact and strengthened. The same applies to mother and daughter.

In any case, a boy can't have his mother, and something in him knows this. In the rivalry between himself and his father, he knows that he cannot be the victor. This recognition of his father's relative superiority has pathos in it, but he accepts it and goes on from there. His anxiety over the unfair rivalry makes his oedipal attachment too problematic for it to be pleasurable for long. He knows he is loved and cherished by both parents but cannot enter their adult, private relationship. Nor can he expect to get the exclusive love of a parent — he can only fantasize getting it. With time and development the fantasy is given up, as so many fantasies are, yielding eventually to reality.

What induces the boy to renounce his wishes toward his mother is an intervening experience that seemed innocent at the time but now makes its power felt: when he saw girls nude while playing hospital or doctor and nurse, the boy remarked on the difference in genitals and unconsciously fantasized that girls originally had a penis and then lost it. If a penis can be lost, it means that his too could be lost. This arouses in him castration anxiety, no less powerful for being completely unconscious. He puts it together this way: "If I persist in my rivalry with my father, with his strength he will win and as punishment take my penis away, the way that girls have had theirs taken away. Rather than risk having my body violated, I would prefer to renounce my mother as mate and let my father have her. When I grow up I'll have a wife of my own."

What also induces both boys and girls to renounce their incestuous wish is love for the parent of the same sex.

The developmental paths of boys and girls diverge when they discover the sex difference. The boy is not so shocked by the discovery as is the girl, who devalues her mother for not having given her a penis and also for not having one herself. This devaluation of mother turns the girl to father — the one with the penis — and heterosexuality.*

OEDIPAL FEELINGS AND IDENTIFICATION

Psychology might be described on one level as the emotional expression of biology. Having come this far in our study of early childhood we see how important it is for a child to have a mother *and* a father to grow up with. The presence of mother protects the little girl from overly coveting her father, and the presence of father safeguards a boy from a too great possessiveness toward mother. Excessive possessiveness would cause anxiety because of built-in feelings against incest. But if mother is there for the girl and father is there for the boy, the child can give in to deep feelings of love for the parent of the opposite sex without the danger of any symbolic consummation. This is important because adult erotic feelings, in their intensity and character, will derive their quality and depth of

*Edith Jacobson, *The Self and Object World,* New York, International Universities Press, 1964, p. 113.

expression partly from this stage. The mere presence of mother and father, therefore, which seems like such an ordinary circumstance, is quite essential to a child's emotional growth.

His father's presence also gives a boy's feelings of hostility free play within safe confines (he sees that his father *does* continue to love him despite the rivalry), and it activates more fully his competitiveness and ambition. The same is true of daughter and mother. Each child admires the parent of the same sex and identifies with him or her. At the same time each wants to outdo the parent, even though painfully aware of being at a disadvantage in size, experience, and some mysterious knowledge about life that parents seem to reveal when they smile indulgently at their strivings.

What induces boys and girls
to renounce their incestuous wish
is love for the parent of the same sex.

In the matter of identification there is the other side of oedipal feelings too. The little boy identifies with his *mother* and wishes for his father's love. The little girl identifies with *father* and falls in love with mother. Identifying selectively with both parents irrespective of sexual difference is extremely important for psychological growth and the growth of love.

Therefore, the oedipus complex is a psychologically advanced development. If a child were emotionally arrested back when he or she was striving to separate psychologically from mother, the full oedipal position would not be reached, because other people would not yet be real, not separate individuals for the child to fall in love with. The oedipus complex is a sign that all is going well and full emotional development will encounter few obstacles.

LATENCY

With the flowering of oedipal love we come to the end of the first four or five years of development, the most important years of growth in human life. Anything that happens after this will have far less impact in shaping personality and character. Although development continues in one way or another till death, few periods of growth will be so formative as these first fifty to sixty months. What lies ahead now is the lengthy period of latency — before puberty.

"Latency" refers to the state of dormancy in the erotic side of the child's development, which persists for five or six years, from six till about twelve. All other areas of functioning will continue in their course during this period. Latency is as much a time of consolidation as of growth. The ongoing inner growth prepares for the great surge forward that will come in adolescence, whose momentum will carry the person through adult development. Possibly the most important side of a child's personality to be consolidated in latency is the conscience (superego), the forerunners of which we discussed in an earlier chapter. Outwardly in these years the child will suddenly become enthusiastic about tidying up his or her room (once in a *long* while), more aware of clothing and appearance, more concerned about how things are done in the adult world. And you will feel quite pleased at these signs of a developing sense of responsibility.

As the child gradually detaches erotic and romantic feelings from the parents, his or her interests turn away from the home and more toward the world. Encouraged by school, curiosity attains a new keenness, and the child begins to ask questions — about art, mathematics, astronomy — even what the earth was like millions of years ago. Instead of wanting to know where he or she came from or how the uterus works to produce babies, the child now becomes interested in how various mechanical things work or in the origin of the human race or the sun and the earth. The questions are still about origins and creation or the inner workings of things, but they are at more sophisticated levels of inquiry and are concerned with the outside world — not the child's private world but the world common to everyone.

The child has come a long way from infantile omnipotence to the acceptance of smallness and dependence. This is still a concern, though, as can be seen by questions about size: interest in the tallest building in the world or the largest number in the universe or the magnitude of space or how many dinosaurs there were and how high they stood. It is revealed more directly in the delight the child takes at knowing that there are tiny insects and in telling you how much like a giant he or she is compared to these little creatures.

What begins to happen now — largely below the surface — is a transformation from being just your child to becoming a member of the world. The child begins to look at the larger outside world for certain guidelines and regulations. At this age, for a while, if a parent and an admired schoolteacher disagree, the teacher's opinion will carry some weight. The child, seeing that there are other authorities, now might at times challenge yours. But what the child is fighting and challenging is not you but dependency on you. A child yearns to be the equal of an adult. Childhood is a prolonged yearning to be a child no longer.

A FINAL WORD

Knowing what we do, there is a temptation to ask again if it is *possible* for a parent to do a good job. It is worth repeating what we said at the beginning: a parent who does a "good enough" job is in fact doing *well*. Each child's innate endowment, which is the true core of psychology, has within it all of development. Parents who allow the unfolding of what is innate, taking care to provide behavorial guidelines and models, do a great deal. Dr. Winnicott's appreciation of mothers might also be worth repeating: it is truly impressive how *little* psychosis there is on earth, and credit for this must be given to the common sense and emotional wellbeing of billions of parents who came before us, of whom up until our times, and probably in the future too, it is the mothers who deserve the larger share of the praise.

In latency, the child goes
from being just your child to
becoming a member of the world.

Concern over doing what is best for their child is often linked in parents' minds with the idea of normality. Every parent wants the child to be normal, even though there are many who say that there is no such thing as normality. Perhaps many shy away from the concept because they are afraid that it connotes conformity or disrespects individual differences.

Nothing could be farther from the truth.

WHAT IS NORMALITY?

It is pathology that has a monotonous sameness, not normality. It is pathology that makes for a colorless existence, not normality. Pathology is predictable. Normality is too varied even to be described. Normality cannot be fully understood by making comparisons. There is no "normal person." There are only normal persons. Since everyone is unique, everyone is normal in a different way.

Normality is benign emotional development. It is a state of great stability, yet has within it the possibility for change and adaptability. It means being capable of the broadest spectrum and greatest depth of emotions, from sorrow to joy, from depression to elation, from calm to exuberance. The normal human being is not free of problems or conflicts: normality is the ability to work through problems and conflicts without avoiding them or being stopped by them. Normality is not bland mediocrity or humdrum functioning. To have a normal child is not to have a "model" child. Who would want that?

Without drawing any particular attention to it, throughout the book we have been saying what normality is in its different expressions at different levels of development. Normality is a clear sense of an independent self, so natural a sense that we are seldom conscious of it. Normality is the capacity for the continuing love of another person despite our own state of need. Normality is a good blend of the two instinctual drives, with love predominating over aggressive feelings. Normality is full adult genitality in its ultimate expression, the enjoyment of heterosexual intercourse, which is preferred over the earlier forms of sexual expression. Normality is the superego's "inner smile" at the self. Normality is the capacity to continue to grow to wherever development might lead. Normality is the ability to throw oneself into the struggle of living in a world of change, without suffering undue anxiety, and to come out enriched by the experience. *Normality is spontaneity itself*—spontaneity, the only real freedom—the act or word that leaps without premeditation from inner conviction. As Dr. Winnicott says, "The spontaneous gesture is the true self in action."

Sometimes normality is confused with "mental health." But health is only a relative state.* Besides, normality is a highly *individual* thing. Some babies are born intensely active, with more physical drive than others. Some are born placid and easygoing. Some are persistent in their efforts to get what they want, and others don't insist at all. What is normal for one is not normal for the other. We might conclude by going back to those early months of infancy, as Dr. Winnicott does when *he* describes normality: "The normal child has a personal view of life from the beginning. Healthy babies often have strong feeding difficulties; they may be defiant and willful in regard to their excretions; they protest often and vehemently with screaming, they kick their mothers and pull their mother's hair, and they try to gouge their eyes out; in fact, they are a nuisance. But they display spontaneous and absolutely genuine affectionate impulses, a hug here and a little bit of generosity there; through these things the mothers of such infants find reward."

There is no "normal person."
There are only normal persons.

A "personal view of life from the beginning": no conformity. Unfortunately, all too many lose that personal view — or are made to lose it. But where physical maturing, psychological development, and the environment fit together in an easy, natural way, and where "good enough" parents meet the child's evolving emotional needs in an atmosphere of constancy and reliability, the child stands the greatest chance of maintaining that unique, personal view of life and attaining the happiness and fulfillment that all human beings are born to enjoy.

Normality is spontaneity itself.

---

*"Healthiness is a purely conventional practical concept and has no real scientific meaning. It simply means that a person gets on well: it doesn't mean that the person is particularly worthy." (Sigmund Freud in Joseph Wortis, *Fragments of an Analysis with Freud*, New York, Simon and Schuster, 1954, pp. 79–80.)

Selected Bibliography

Paperback editions are cited where available.

GENERAL BOOKS

ABRAHAMSEN, DAVID. *The Emotional Care of Your Child.* New York: Pocket Books, 1970.

BECK, HELEN L. *Don't Push Me — I'm No Computer.* New York: McGraw-Hill Book Company, 1973.

The Boston Children's Medical Center. *Pregnancy, Birth and the Newborn Baby.* New York: Delacorte Press/Seymour Lawrence, 1972.

The Boston Women's Health Book Collective. *Our Bodies, Ourselves.* New York: Simon and Schuster, 1971.

BRAZELTON, T. BERRY. *Infants and Mothers: Differences in Development.* New York: Dell Publishing Company, 1973.

——. *Toddlers and Parents: A Declaration of Independence.* New York: Delacorte Press/Seymour Lawrence, 1974.

BRENNER, ERMA. *A New Baby! A New Life!* New York: McGraw-Hill Book Company, 1973.

COFFIN, PATRICIA. *1, 2, 3, 4, 5, 6: How To Understand and Enjoy the Years That Count.* New York: Macmillan, 1972.

DEUTSCH, HELENE. *The Psychology of Women.* Volume II: *Motherhood.* New York: Bantam Books, 1973.

ERIKSON, ERIK H. *Childhood and Society,* 2d ed. New York: W. W. Norton, 1963.

FLANAGAN, GERALDINE LUX. *The First Nine Months of Life.* New York: Pocket Books, 1965.

FRAIBERG, SELMA. *The Magic Years.* New York: Charles Scribner's Sons, 1959.

GESELL, ARNOLD, and FRANCES L. ILG, *Infant and Child in the Culture of Today.* New York: Harper and Row, 1943.

GESELL, ARNOLD, et al. *The First Five Years of Life.* New York: Harper and Row, 1940.

HAIRE, DORIS, and JOHN HAIRE. *Implementing Family-Centered Maternity Care with a Central Nursery,* 3d ed. Hillside, N.J.: International Childbirth Education Association, 1971.

ILG, FRANCES L., and LOUISE BATES AMES. *Child Behavior.* New York: Harper and Row, Perennial Library, 1966.

MILINAIRE, CATERINE. *Birth.* New York: Harmony Books, 1974.

MONTAGU, ASHLEY. *Life Before Birth.* New York: New American Library, 1964.

NEWTON, NILES ANNE. *The Family Book of Child Care.* New York: Harper and Row, 1957.

The Princeton Center for Infancy and Early Childhood. *The First Twelve Months of Life.* FRANK CAPLAN, General Editor. New York: Grosset and Dunlap, 1973.

RIBBLE, MARGARET A. *The Personality of the Young Child.* New York: Columbia University Press, 1955.

———.*The Rights of Infants,* 2d ed. New York: New American Library, 1973.

SALK, LEE. *What Every Child Would Like His Parents To Know.* New York: Warner Paperback Library, 1973.

SALK, LEE, and RITA KRAMER. *How To Raise a Human Being.* New York: Warner Paperback Library, 1973.

SPOCK, BENJAMIN. *Baby and Child Care,* rev. ed. New York: Pocket Books, 1968.

———.*Dr. Spock Talks with Mothers.* New York: Fawcett World Library, 1961.

WINNICOTT, D. W. *Mother and Child.* New York: Basic Books, 1957.

Your Child from One to Six. New York: Award Books, 1968.

TECHNICAL BOOKS

ERIKSON, ERIK H. *Identity and the Life Cycle.* New York: International Universities Press, 1959. In *Psychological Issues 1* (1959).

FREUD, ANNA. *The Ego and the Mechanisms of Defense,* in *The Writings of Anna Freud,* Vol. II, 1936. New York: International Universities Press, 1966.

——. *Normality and Pathology in Childhood,* in *The Writings of Anna Freud,* Vol. VI, 1965. New York: International Universities Press, 1965.

——. *Psychoanalytic Knowledge Applied to the Rearing of Children,* in *The Writings of Anna Freud,* Vol. V, 1956–1965, New York: International Universities Press, 1969, Ch. 16, pp. 265–80.

——. *The Psychoanalytical Treatment of Children.* New York: Schocken Books, 1964.

FREUD, ANNA, and DOROTHY BURLINGHAM. *Infants Without Families: The Case For and Against Residential Nurseries,* in *The Writings of Anna Freud,* Vol. III, 1939–1945. New York: International Universities Press, 1973, pp. 541–664.

GREENACRE, PHYLLIS. "Considerations Regarding the Parent-Infant Relationship," *International Journal of Psychoanalysis,* Vol. 41, 1960, pp. 571–84.

HARTMANN, HEINZ. *Ego Psychology and the Problem of Adaptation.* New York: International Universities Press, 1958.

SPITZ, RENÉ A. *The First Year of Life.* New York: International Universities Press, 1965.

——. *A Genetic Field Theory of Ego Formation.* New York: International Universities Press, 1959.

WINNICOTT, D. W. *The Maturational Processes and the Facilitating Environment.* New York: International Universities Press, 1965.

PREPARED CHILDBIRTH

BEAN, CONSTANCE A. *Methods of Childbirth: A Complete Guide to Childbirth Classes and Maternity Care.* New York: Dolphin Books, 1974.

BING, ELISABETH. *Six Practical Lessons for an Easier Childbirth.* New York: Bantam Books, 1967.

BING, ELISABETH, and GERALD S. BARAD. *A Birth in the Family.* New York: Bantam Books, 1973.

BURYN, ED, JANET BROWN, EUGENE LESSER, and STEPHANIE MINES. *Two Births.* New York: Random House Bookworks, 1972.

CHABON, IRVING. *Awake and Aware.* New York: Dell Publishing Company, 1966.

DICK-READ, GRANTLY. *Childbirth Without Fear.* 2d ed. New York: Harper and Row, 1973.

KARMEL, MARJORIE. *Thank You, Dr. Lamaze.* New York: Doubleday, 1970.

KITZINGER, SHEILA. *The Experience of Childbirth,* 3d ed. Baltimore: Penguin Books, 1972.

LAMAZE, FERNAND. *Painless Childbirth.* Chicago: Henry Regnery, 1970.

WRIGHT, ERNA. *The New Childbirth.* New York: Hart Publishing Company, 1968.

NURSING

EIGER, MARVIN S., and SALLY WENDKOS OLDS. *The Complete Book of Breastfeeding.* New York: Bantam Books, 1973.

GERARD, ALICE. *Please Breast-Feed Your Baby.* New York: New American Library, 1970.

La Leche League. *The Womanly Art of Breast Feeding.* Franklin Park, Ill.: La Leche League International, 1963.

PEARLMAN, RUTH. *Feeding Your Baby: The Safe and Healthy Way.* New York: Random House, 1971.

PRYOR, KAREN. *Nursing Your Baby.* New York: Pocket Books, 1973.

SPOCK, BENJAMIN, and MIRIAM E. LOWENBERG. *Feeding Your Baby and Child.* New York: Pocket Books, 1956.

ADOPTION

GOLDSTEIN, JOSEPH, ANNA FREUD, and ALBERT J. SOLNIT. *Beyond the Best Interests of the Child.* New York: Free Press, 1973.

INDEX